State and Peasant in Contemporary China

This volume is sponsored by the
Center for Chinese Studies,
University of California, Berkeley

State and Peasant in Contemporary China

The Political Economy of Village Government

Jean C. Oi

UNIVERSITY OF CALIFORNIA PRESS
Berkeley · Los Angeles · Oxford

Chapters 1, 7, 8, and 9 contain material previously published in the
following publications and revised for this book:

"From Cadres to Middlemen: The Commercialization of Rural
Government." *Problems of Communism,* September–
October 1986.

"Peasant Grain Marketing and State Procurements: China's Grain
Contracting System." *China Quarterly,* no. 106 (June 1986).
Reprinted by permission of the Contemporary China Institute of
the School of Oriental and African Studies.

"Peasant Households Between Plan and Market: Cadre Control
over Agricultural Inputs." *Modern China* 12, no. 2 (April 1986).
Reprinted by permission of Sage Publications, Inc.

"Communism and Clientelism: Rural Politics in China." *World
Politics* 32, no. 2 (January 1985). Reprinted by permission of The
Trustees of Princeton University.

University of California Press
Berkeley and Los Angeles, California

University of California Press, Ltd.
Oxford, England

©1989 by
The Regents of the University of California

Library of Congress Cataloging-in-Publication Data

Oi, Jean Chun.
    State and peasant in contemporary China: the political economy of
village government / Jean C. Oi.
        p.   cm.
    Bibliography: p.
    Includes index.
    ISBN 0–520–06105–5 (alk. paper)
    1. Communes (China)   2. Peasantry—Government policy—
China.   3. Elite (Social sciences)—China.   4. Local government—
China.   5. Collective farms—China.   6. Grain trade—
Government policy—China.   7. Communism—China.   I. Title.
JS7352.034   1989   88–20767
352.051—dc19

Printed in the United States of America

1   2   3   4   5   6   7   8   9
The paper used in this publication meets the minimum requirements of
American National Standard for Information Sciences—Permanence
of Paper for Printed Library Materials, ANSI Z39.48-1984. ∞™

To the memory of
my father Hong Lem Oi
and to my mother
Moy Fung How Oi

Contents

Illustrations

Figures

Map

Tables

Acknowledgments

A great many people and institutions deserve thanks for their help and service during the researching and writing of this book, but I can only mention a few in this formal acknowledgment. Because the first part of this book, which covers the pre-1979 period, began as a doctoral dissertation at the University of Michigan, let me begin with my dissertation committee: Samuel Barnes, Robert Dernberger, Albert Feuerwerker, Michel Oksenberg, Allen Whiting, and Martin Whyte. Each was generous with his time and provided helpful comments on the various drafts. To Allen Whiting, my cochairman, I offer a very special thanks for his wise counsel and support in the best and worst of times. To Michel Oksenberg, my major adviser and teacher, I owe the largest debt. His astute comments along with his seemingly unceasing demands for more detail provided me with a head start in writing this book. The work of Barrington Moore and James Scott inspired me to formulate my topic and approach it as I have.

Many people have provided useful comments on parts or the whole of this manuscript. James Scott carefully read and provided perceptive comments on the dissertation. Thomas Bernstein read and commented on both the dissertation and the initial version of the book manuscript. Andrew Nathan challenged me with his penetrating questions on an earlier draft of Chapter 7. Others include Dorothy Solinger, Carl Riskin, Donald Barry, Gail Henderson, and Daniel Kelliher.

The people to whom I owe the largest debt must remain anonymous. They are the former residents of China's countryside whom I interviewed in Hong Kong and the peasants and cadres I interviewed in China. They have shared their experiences and taught me about rural China.

A number of institutions have provided assistance. The one that stands out is the Universities Service Centre (USC) in Hong Kong. Over the years John Dolfin and the staff of the USC have provided office space, a wonderful research library, and support facilities for me to conduct my interviews and learn about Chinese rural politics. Equally important, it provided a home away from home where warm and lasting friendships developed, not only with other scholars, but with some interviewees as well. One special person from that setting is Jean Xiong. She was undoubtedly the best research assistant that I will ever have; but also, through her experiences and insights, she taught me how to "read" the Chinese press. To my other research assistants in Hong Kong, Mr. Y. S. Wang and Mr. Yang, I also owe much thanks. I would like to recognize Yeung Saichueng for his help in the early stages of my research at the University of Michigan. Steven Li at Harvard University deserves much thanks for intelligently, diligently, and cheerfully chasing down incomplete citations, helping with translations, and doing other tedious bits of work essential in the final stages of manuscript preparation. Nancy Hearst of Harvard's Fairbank Center Library similarly deserves much thanks for her meticulous attention to the smallest detail during the proofreading stage.

Over the years I have been fortunate to receive substantial financial support for this project. An International Doctoral Dissertation Research Award given by the Social Science Research Council and financial assistance from the University of Michigan funded my dissertation research. The Center for Chinese Studies at the University of California, Berkeley, provided a fellowship for the 1981–1982 academic year and a stimulating and enjoyable environment where this book had its beginnings. Lehigh University, where I taught until 1987, funded my interviews in Hong Kong in 1984 and part of my initial research in China. Funding for my later research in China was provided by the Committee on Scholarly Communication with the People's Republic of China. The American Council of Learned Societies Mellon Fellowship for Chinese Studies provided one year's support that allowed me to write the first full draft of this manuscript.

Finally, an immeasurable degree of thanks goes to Andrew Walder, who is my harshest critic and greatest supporter. He has faithfully read the various drafts of this manuscript and provided me with excellent comments throughout. Our discussions have been a constant source of stimulation and insight. Perhaps more important, his encouragement and support have contributed enormously to my completing this book as we have tried to juggle our personal and professional lives.

Abbreviations of Newspapers and Journals Cited

BJRB	*Beijing ribao*
DGB	*Dagong bao* (Beijing and Tianjin)
DZJYB	*Dazhong jingying bao*
DZRB	*Dazhong ribao*
FBIS	*Foreign Broadcast Information Service*
FJRB	*Fujian ribao*
GDNMB	*Guangdong nongmin bao*
GMRB	*Guangming ribao*
GRB	*Guangzhou ribao*
GXRB	*Guangxi ribao*
GZRB	*Guizhou ribao*
HBJJB	*Hebei jingji bao*
HLB	*Huili bao*
JFRB	*Jiefang ribao*
JJCK	*Jingji cankao*
JJRB	*Jingji ribao*
JNB	*Jiangsu nongmin bao*

JPRS-CEA	*Joint Publications Research Service—China Report: Economic Affairs*
JPRS-CPS	*Joint Publications Research Service—China Report: Political, Sociological, and Military Affairs*
JPRS-CRA	*Joint Publications Research Service—China Report: Agriculture*
JPRS-CRF	*Joint Publications Research Service—China: Red Flag*
MBRMB	*Minbei renmin bao*
NBRMB	*Nanbei renmin bao*
NCGZTX	*Nongcun gongzuo tongxun*
NFRB	*Nanfang ribao*
NMRB	*Nongmin ribao*
NYJJWT	*Nongye jingji wenti*
RMHYB	*Renmin hangyun bao*
RMRB	*Renmin ribao*
SCMM	*Survey of China Mainland Magazines*
SCMP	*Survey of China Mainland Press*
SPRCM	*Survey of the People's Republic of China Magazines*
STJP	*Singtao Jihpao* (Hong Kong)
SXNM	*Shanxi nongmin*
TKP	*Ta Kung Pao* (Hong Kong)
XGSB	*Xianggang shibao*
XHNB	*Xin Hunan bao*
XHSDX	*Xinhuashe dianxun*
YRB	*Yunnan ribao*
ZGJJJB	*Zhongguo jingji jibao*
ZGNMB	*Zhongguo nongmin bao*
ZGQNB	*Zhongguo qingnian bao*
ZJRB	*Zhejiang ribao*

Note on Measures and Transliteration

1 *mu* = 1/15 hectares = 1/6 acre

1 *jin* = 0.5 kilogram = 1.1 pounds

100 *jin* = 1 *shidan* (*dan*)

10 *fen* = 1 *mao*

10 *mao* = 1 *yuan*

1 *yuan* = from approximately U.S. $0.40 to $0.279 (value
has decreased since the late 1970s)

All transliteration of Chinese terms is in the *pinyin* system of romaniza-
tion of Mandarin (*putonghua*).

CHAPTER I

Peasant Politics in a Communist Economy

An Introduction

Communist revolutions eradicate traditional power structures, but they do not alter the basic issue of peasant politics: how the harvest shall be divided. Although the revolution removes landlords from the historical stage, the state and its agents appear as newly powerful claimants on the harvest. To a historically unprecedented degree, the state directs the division of the harvest, and this brings it into direct conflict with the peasantry. Before the revolution the harvest was divided in the context of a class relationship, but after the revolution it is divided in the context of an increasingly direct state-society relationship.

In most agrarian regimes, the state levies taxes but does not otherwise intervene in the local grain distribution. Grain surpluses are commodities bought and sold through the medium of money. In many socialist, centrally planned economies rationing replaces markets and limits the value of money. The state becomes a grain monopoly that purchases and distributes the food supply, regulates grain prices, dictates cropping patterns, imposes output targets, and directly extracts grain to feed the cities and finance industrial growth. The need for grain, made more urgent by ambitious industrialization policies and a strong commitment to the welfare of the urban population, brings the state into a protracted, though muted, conflict with its peasantry and even its local leaders.

Procuring sufficient grain is doubly difficult for those communist states that achieve power through peasant support. Their revolutionary mantle constrains them to extract grain without resorting to heavy taxation. In China, the Communist party has devised an elaborate set of regulations designed to maintain the fiction that the state only procures the agricultural "surplus," while in fact it exploits rural areas to fund industrial growth. This process, the crux of peasant-state relations and village politics, is the subject of this study.

THE STATE-SOCIETY RELATIONSHIP

The prevailing models for understanding state and society in communist states have focused on the autonomy of either the state or society, or the relative strength of each. The totalitarian model discounts the ability of civil society to influence state actions. It stresses the absolute power of the communist party and its efforts to mobilize and control, but it obscures citizen efforts to influence elites, affect policy implementation, and pursue interests. Citizens are depicted as atomized, passive, and politically ineffectual.[1]

In contrast, the interest group model provides a more complex picture of communist politics,[2] claiming that various identifiable groups have influenced policy formulation, particularly since Stalin's death.[3] According to this later model, the state is an arena where different groups pursue their interests, an image akin to that of the pluralist state.[4] Some scholars have employed such terms as "institutional pluralism" to describe a system where, in their view, interest groups, especially elite bureaucratic actors, influence the policy-making process.[5] Students of Chinese politics have adopted this model to study how mass groups—such as workers, students, and peasants—participate in politics.[6]

1. The "totalitarian" model encompasses a number of variations. The major elements presented here are based on Friedrich and Brzezinski's classic formulation in Carl J. Friedrich and Zbigniew Brzezinski, *Totalitarian Dictatorship and Autocracy*. The idea of an "administered society" is a modified version that deemphasizes the reliance on terror but basically accepts the major premises of the classic totalitarian model. See Allen Kassof, "The Administered Society."

2. For an early critique of the totalitarian model for the Chinese case, see the preliminary but useful article by Michel Oksenberg, "Local Government."

3. See, for example, H. Gordon Skilling and Franklin Griffiths, *Interest Groups in Soviet Politics;* H. Gordon Skilling, "Interest Groups and Communist Politics Revisited."

4. For a useful discussion of the difference between the statist and the pluralist views of the state, see Stephen D. Krasner, "Approaches to the State Alternative: Conceptions and Historical Dynamics."

5. Jerry F. Hough, "The Soviet System."

6. Michel Oksenberg, "Occupational Groups in Chinese Society"; Marc Blecher, "Leader-Mass Relations"; John Burns, "Elections of Production Team Cadres"; John Burns, "Chinese Peasant"; Hong Yung Lee, *The Politics of the Chinese Cultural Revolution;* Victor Falkenheim, ed., *Citizens and Groups;* David S. G. Goodman, ed., *Groups and Politics.*

This study departs from both models and shifts the focus of inquiry from the relative power of either the state or society to the way that state and society interact. I begin with the premises that in a communist system a distinction exists between the interests of the state and society and that each has the means to pursue its own interests. I do not assume, however, that individuals will necessarily act as groups or use formal channels of interest articulation to pursue their interests as they do in pluralist systems. The word "society" is but a shorthand for a whole spectrum of organized and unorganized interests.[7]

In collectivized agriculture, if people act together, they are more likely to do so in a local corporate group created by the process of collectivization itself than in one based on occupation or class. In China, this corporate group is the village, where peasants work and live. It lies at the intersection of state and society; it can be reduced to neither. As a political actor, its interests are distinct from those of both the state and the individual members who constitute it. Local personalities, local interests, and demands on village resources define it as a community.[8] Here state meets society; here politics takes place. Here one can observe how state regulations shape political strategies and action as well as how state directives are circumvented, twisted, or ignored. Here is where I focus my research on the state-society relationship.

In this study I distinguish between the power of the state to formulate policy and the ability of the state to implement it. Relatively speaking, communist states are still among the most powerful and autonomous political actors,[9] but their implemented policies are not necessarily the same ones that they formulated or intended. The term "state" usually refers to the central government and its directives, and this is how I use the term in this study. However, the state as represented at the local levels by its *agents*—the local level cadres who are also responsible for representing their collective's and their own interests—is a distinct entity whose interests cannot be assumed to be the same as or even compatible with those of the central government.

7. For a fuller discussion of this point, see Andrew Walder, *Communist Neo-Traditionalism*, introduction.

8. The importance of taking an inclusive view of peasant villages is increasingly being recognized by political anthropologists. See Judith Strauch, *Chinese Village Politics*.

9. Among the most prominent works of political scientists and sociologists who view states as autonomous political actors is Theda Skocpol's *States and Social Revolutions;* but the literature has become extensive. Although useful, for those who work on communist states this approach is all too familiar. Under the influence of the totalitarian model, we have overemphasized the state's autonomy and insufficiently considered the constraints on state action, almost to the point of denying the "autonomy" of society.

The central state dictates policies and creates the political and economic context in which local political actors must operate but, because of the nature of the state control system, in practice these policies may exert no more than a restraining influence by delineating the boundaries of legal action. In the village, the state-society relationship is played out by people who have assumed the role of cadres, who interpret the will of the state to the peasants. Rural politics is composed of the interactions of the different political actors within state and society as they pursue their interests.

The major reorganizations that have taken place since 1949 require that I further clarify the term "village." What anthropologists call the "natural village" was submerged in the process of collectivization. By the late 1950s the natural village became part of a much larger commune (*gongshe*), into which peasants were incorporated until the early 1980s.[10] The natural village, in most cases, became a "production brigade" (*shengchan dadui*), the second tier of commune administration.[11] Each brigade was divided, in turn, into several "production teams" (*shengchan xiaodui*), the lowest tier.[12] With the return of household farming, the natural village reemerged as an administrative unit and was renamed the "village" (*cun*), now the lowest level of administration. The production teams were abolished, although in some places they were renamed "village small groups" (*cun xiaozu*) and in others they simply disappeared. The commune became, in most instances, the "township" (*xiang* or *zhen*; see Table 1).[13]

Regardless of these administrative changes, the village that I see as the intersection of state and society is the unit of organization where peasants live and work, where the harvest is collected and divided, where peasant incomes are earned and distributed, and where the state procures its grain. Because I am concerned about the functions rather

10. Communes were formed during the ill-fated Great Leap Forward beginning in 1958 but were reorganized by the early 1960s. Prior to that, peasants were organized into collectives, but these were known as agricultural producers' cooperatives. For details of these earlier forms see Vivienne Shue, *Peasant China*. For a technical description of the commune system see Frederick W. Crook, "The Commune System."

11. In some areas, between commune and brigade was an administrative office known as the management office (*guanlichu*). After the reforms this was changed to the business office (*banshichu*).

12. Numerous studies have described at length the administration and organization of production teams. See, for example, William Parish and Martin Whyte, *Village and Family;* Steven Butler, "Conflict and Decision Making"; Benedict Stavis, *People's Communes;* and A. Doak Barnett and Ezra Vogel, *Cadres, Bureaucracy.*

13. The townships with larger urban households are designated *zhen*. For details of the reorganization of local rural government after 1978, see Frederick Crook, "The Reform of the Commune System."

TABLE I.   RURAL ADMINISTRATIVE UNITS AND
AVERAGE CHARACTERISTICS, 1974 AND 1986

Collectivized Agriculture, 1974	Household Agriculture, 1986
Commune (*gongshe*) (70,000) 2,033 hectares 15 production brigades 3,346 households 14,720 persons 100 production teams	Township (*xiang/zhen*) (71,521) 1,317 hectares[a] 12 villages 2,737 households 11,886 persons
Brigade (*shengchan dadui*) (750,000) 133 hectares 220 households 980 persons 7 production teams	Village (*cun*) (847,894) 111 hectares[a] 231 households 1,002 persons
Team (*shengchan xiaodui*) (5 million) 33 households 145 persons 20 hectares	⟨Village Small Group (*cun xiaozu*)⟩ irregularly organized

SOURCES: Statistics on the number of units at each collective level are from Frederick W. Crook, "The Commune System," pp. 366–410. Statistics on the average number of villages and population in the postreform system are calculated from *Zhongguo tongji nianjian 1987*, p. 137; on average land holdings, from ibid. and *Zhongguo nongye nianjian 1987*, p. 316.

[a] These figures do not include the 20.63 million hectares of land under cultivation by state farmers.

than the designation of an administrative unit I shift the unit of analysis from the production team in the commune period to the natural village in the post-Mao period.

One might argue that for the collectivized village, the proper unit of analysis should be either the commune or the brigade. The commune was formally the lowest level of state administration. Only commune-level leaders were considered "state cadres" (*guojia ganbu*), receiving salaries from the state payroll and ration coupons for their grain. Brigade and team leaders were considered "local cadres" (*difang ganbu*), whose wages and grain rations came from village coffers; they were still officially required to participate in collective labor. However, these are less useful units of analysis because they represent only units of administration, not units of production or accounting; peasants did not directly participate in politics at this level.[14]

14. The brigade was the unit of accounting and production in those few areas where the Learn from Dazhai Campaign was successfully implemented. In such cases, the proper unit of analysis would be the brigade. On the attempts to raise the level of accounting, see David Zweig, "Strategies of Policy Implementation," and his *Agrarian Radicalism*.

The struggle over the harvest took place in the team, not in the brigade or the commune. Although the production team owned the harvest, the state decided how and how much the team had to pay in taxes and sell in grain. If the state took too much grain, the team and its members suffered. Consequently, the team also tried to hide grain from the state and keep more for its own needs. The brigade and the commune only oversaw the procurement process; they inspected the fields to make sure that the teams were not trying to hide grain and cheat the state and that sufficient amounts of the harvest would be left as the surplus. It was their duty to call all the team leaders together and act out the fiction that peasants wanted to sell large amounts of grain to the state. They chaired the meetings where the team leaders pledged the amounts their teams would sell to the state and ensured that those amounts would sufficiently meet the state's quotas.

The brigade and commune were higher administrative units that peasants saw as the "upper levels": officials with whom they had infrequent contact. Daily activity centered on the production team. In fact, peasant interaction with the state was filtered through the intermediary of the team, primarily the team leader. Collectivization coupled with rationing and closing free grain markets made teams into closed corporate villages and allowed team leaders to act as gatekeepers. For these reasons, in the period of collectivization I focus on the peasants' relationship with team, rather than brigade or commune, leaders. Brigade officials were unquestionably more powerful than team leaders in the larger scheme of commune politics. Yet, the political actor most directly engaged in a day-to-day relationship with the peasants, routinely interpreting state law for them, was the team leader. The team leader was not a "state cadre," but he was a state agent. To the peasant he represented the state; he implemented state policy and controlled the upward flow of information.

The state's decision to abolish communes and return to household farming in the 1980s eliminated the production team as a claimant on the harvest and turned over direct administration of peasants to the former brigade, now village, cadres.[15] The household is once again both the producer and the owner of its harvest. The state is still a claimant but less rapacious. Instead of administrative means to force peasants to sell all the grain they have at unfairly low prices, the government allows them

15. Note that in some cases, as I will describe in detail in Chapter 9, former team leaders (i.e., the newly established group leaders) still perform certain functions and have some power, such as distributing agricultural inputs.

to keep what they want and uses economic incentives to get the rest. Village officials no longer direct the production of the harvest; they only administer the contracts that individual households sign with the state for the purchase of their crop. Now village cadres assume responsibility for enforcing state policies, ensure prompt payment of taxes and sales to the state, and issue authorizations and licenses allowing peasants economic opportunities. For the peasant, political power now rests in the village rather than the team.

COMMUNISM AND CLIENTELISM

Village politics in China is best described as clientelist. Yet, despite its widespread currency in political science, the concept of clientelism has rarely been used to analyze communist systems. Students and journalistic observers of communist politics regularly note the importance of personal ties, and many recognize the significance of informal bonds in economic and political spheres at *all* levels of society.[16] Some even apply the term "clientelism" to the political behavior they describe. But the use of the term clientelism is generally limited to elite-level politics, factionalism, career mobility, recruitment patterns, and attainment of office at the top- to middle-level echelons of the bureaucracy.[17] Few have considered clientelism as a type of elite-mass linkage through which both the state and the party exercise control at the local level and individuals participate in the political system. Students of communist states see their subjects as rather unique systems where mobilization is achieved through coercion or commitment to either an ideology or a leader, but rarely is mobilization achieved through using patron-client networks—a well-accepted fact in the study of political systems.[18]

I adopt the clientelist perspective to look beyond the formal structures and official channels of participation and to explore the less obvious but perhaps more important methods by which citizens pursue their interests in a communist system. It makes me question whether the

16. Franz Borkenau, "Getting Behind the Facts"; Hedrick Smith, *The Russians;* Zygmunt Bauman, "Comment on Eastern Europe"; Fox Butterfield, *China.*

17. T. H. Rigby, "The Soviet Leadership"; T. H. Rigby, "The Need for Comparative Research on Clientelism"; Andrew J. Nathan, "A Factionalism Model of CCP Politics"; Lucian Pye, *The Dynamics of Chinese Politics;* John Willerton, Jr., "Clientelism in the Soviet Union"; Jacek Tarkowski, "Poland"; R. H. Baker, "Clientelism in the Post-Revolutionary State"; and T. H. Rigby and Bohdan Harasymiu, eds., *Leadership Selection.*

18. On the importance of patron-client ties in achieving mobilized participation see, for example, Samuel Huntington and Joan Nelson, *No Easy Choice.*

"group" is the basis of politics.[19] In fact, it challenges the notion that citizens in communist systems, such as China, routinely articulate their interests through either the formal prescribed channels familiar in pluralist societies or the distinctively communist modes developed out of the so-called mass line style of leadership.[20] Instead, the clientelist view has led me to look at how personal relationships, which have so enmeshed China's control system, affect the state's policy goals and outcomes.

Studies of political participation and elite-mass linkages have shown that in developing countries, where the formal channels for meaningful participation and interest articulation are weak, individuals regularly pursue their interests using informal networks built upon personal ties. Peasants are integrated into national politics primarily through clientelist political structures.[21] I shall argue in this study that in China, and most likely in other communist states, local politics tends to be structured along similar clientelist lines because formal channels for meaningful political participation by groups or individuals are weak.

Unlike the totalitarian and the interest group models, the clientelist model focuses on the political behavior of *individuals* in dyads. Participation is viewed not merely as formal input into the policy-formulation process. Instead, the line of inquiry focuses on the myriad ways in which nonelites try to affect the policy *implementation* process and to further their particular interests. Rather than end with the finding that formal channels of participation are usually ineffective, I begin at that point to search out the strategies nonelites have used to supplement or circumvent official channels. The deviant behavior of local cadres keeping grain from the state is not simply a case of personal greed or the desire of peasants to consume more grain. On the contrary, I shall argue that such "corrupt" behavior at the local levels had a rational basis, tied to the state's own actions regarding the allocation of the harvest. Instead of viewing such behavior as simply corruption, it may be more usefully understood as a form of peasant participation and strategy for survival.[22] Unlike the totalitarian model, which assumes an atomized so-

19. For a parallel critique of this aspect of the group politics perspective, see Carl Landé, "Group Politics and Dyadic Politics, and his "Introduction."
20. The classic study of mass line is by Mark Selden, *The Yenan Way in Revolutionary China;* also see Blecher, "Leader-Mass Relations."
21. John Duncan Powell, "Peasant Society"; James C. Scott, "Patron-Client Politics"; Rene Lemarchand and Keith Legg, "Political Clientelism."
22. A particularly useful study of the functions of "corruption" is James Scott's work on Southeast Asia, "Corruption." For a study of how illegal practices allow the Soviet system to work, see Jerry F. Hough, *The Soviet Prefects.* The role and usefulness of illegal

ciety and politically neutralized nonelites, the clientelist model hypothesizes a rich field of patron-client ties through which individuals pursue their interests.

In contrast to the totalitarian model, which views control in communist systems as formal, impersonal, and effective, the clientelist model assumes considerably more flexibility, subjectivity, and personal sentiment in the exercise of control that may or may not result in effective policy implementation. From the clientelist perspective, authority is routinely exercised through allocating opportunities, goods, and resources over which the elite have monopolistic control and on which the nonelite depend. China's communist setting, with its centrally planned economy and rationing, by definition provides a fertile breeding ground for such exercise of power.

Previous studies make clear that different types of clientelism exist.[23] My task is to describe both the form clientelism takes in a centralized planned economy that holds a strict egalitarian communist ideology and the way it changes as the political economy changes. Previous analysts of rural China have dismissed clientelism as neither a "helpful tool for the analysis of contemporary rural Chinese politics" nor "a useful way to characterize elite-mass relations at local levels in China." The "argument that patron-client relations characterize subsistence peasant society no longer applies to China (if it ever did), simply because *most* peasants in contemporary China do not live at subsistence levels."[24] Regardless of whether peasants did or did not live at subsistence level, concern for subsistence is not the only rationale for clientelism; nor will guarantees of subsistence be sufficient to eliminate clientelism. I will show that under socialism a different type of dependence gives rise to a form of clientelism characterized by *interest-maximizing* rather than risk-minimizing strategies.

My point is not that clientelism as a model is useful, but that at the village level a communist system is clientelist.[25] I will show that clien-

---

practices has emerged in the "second economy" literature, mostly concerning the Soviet Union. See Anita Chan and Jonathan Unger for one of the few articles on the need for and use of this illegal activity in the Chinese countryside: "Grey and Black: The Hidden Economy of Rural China." Most literature on China tends to stress personal gain rather than focusing on the systemic factors that give rise to such illegal behavior. See, for example, John Burns, "Rural Guangdong's Second Economy."

23. See n. 21 and James C. Scott, "Political Clientelism"; Anthony Hall, "Patron-Client Relations"; Carl Landé, "Introduction."

24. John Burns, "Comment on China," p. 193.

25. Walder makes a similar case for the urban factory setting; see his *Communist Neo-Traditionalism.*

telism is not an aberration from, but an outgrowth of, the communist system. As long as China or any other communist system is characterized by a scarcity of goods, a centralized distribution system, and unequal access to and personalized control over allocation of goods and opportunities, there will be clientelist politics.

Moreover, partial change of that economic structure is inadequate to eradicate that characteristic of the system. In the period under study, 1955 to 1986, the economic environment of the village has changed radically.[26] China created and then dissolved a highly centralized system of commune agriculture in favor of household production. The government replaced mandatory sales of key items such as grain and cotton with a contract purchase system meant to allow individual peasants to decide how much to sell to the state. The once highly centralized command economy is now, again, a mixed economy.

At the risk of overstatement, these changes are both comparable to the spread of world markets into traditional agrarian economies[27] and analogous to Karl Polanyi's "great transformation."[28] Yet clientelism remains the key to rural politics. The distribution of goods, resources, and opportunities is still the basis of political authority and clientelist politics.[29] The terms of exchange and the identity and the style of patrons have changed, but local society and politics continue to be organized in a clientelist fashion.

PRÉCIS OF THE STUDY

This is a study of peasant-state relations and village politics as they have evolved in response to the state's attempts to control the division of the harvest and extract the state-defined surplus. To provide the reader with a clearer sense of the evolution of peasant-state relations over almost a forty-year period and to highlight the dramatic changes that have taken place since 1978, I have divided my analysis into two parts: Chapters 2 through 7 are on Maoist China, and chapters 8 and 9 are on

26. The bulk of my research for this book includes materials published before 1987; however, there are scattered references to events and materials from 1987 and 1988.

27. This is the focus of much literature on peasant societies. See, for example, James C. Scott, *The Moral Economy;* Samuel Popkin, *The Rational Peasant;* Joel S. Migdal, *Peasants, Politics, and Revolution;* and Eric Wolf, *Peasant Wars.*

28. Karl Polanyi, *The Great Transformation.*

29. This aspect of clientelism has most usefully been explicated in S. N. Eisenstadt and Louis Roniger, "Patron-Client Relations." For an interesting case study of the changing basis of power as societies modernize, see Judith Chubb, *Patronage, Power, and Poverty.*

post-Mao China. The first part examines the state's grain policies and patterns of local politics that emerged during the highly collectivized Maoist period, when the state closed free grain markets and established the system of unified purchase and sales (*tonggou tongxiao*). The second part describes the new methods for the production and division of the harvest after 1978, when the government decollectivized agriculture and abolished its unified procurement program; I analyze the resulting changes in the relationship between the state and village and between the peasants and their village leaders.

Chapters 2 through 5 examine the state's strategies for controlling the distribution of the harvest in production teams and extracting the surplus. Chapter 2 describes the state's limiting the distribution of the harvest to both the team and the household in order to create a maximum surplus. Chapter 3 analyzes the procurement process; describing the state strategies to induce production team leaders to pledge large sales of the so-called surplus, as well as team leader strategies to resist such pledges. Chapter 4 studies the state's back-up plan for controlling the grain it failed to extract. This chapter reveals the hidden agenda of policies. I argue that a close relationship existed between a nominal welfare policy, the putting aside of reserve grain for emergency use, and the state's relentless concern with production and procurements. These chapters are highly detailed, but the details are not irrelevant, for these state-imposed regulations shape local politics.[30] To use Merilee Grindle's terms, these chapters will provide the reader with the "content" of the policies, but these policies also created the structural "context" that shaped the political behavior of village cadres and peasants and fostered the development of clientelist politics.[31]

Chapter 5 examines the mechanisms the state used to ensure that its policies were correctly implemented. I stress the degree to which the state depended on the cooperation of local cadres, especially production team leaders. How the resulting personalization of authority affected the implementation of state policies is explored in Chapter 6. Here I detail the ways village cadres circumvented the constraints created by the state's regulations. I provide a structural explanation of why evasion, illegality, and a "facade of compliance" became necessary strategies of survival for team leaders who needed to function as both agents of the

30. For an early statement of a similar perspective, see Oksenberg, "Local Government."

31. See Merilee S. Grindle, ed., *Politics and Policy Implementation;* see especially her "Policy Content."

state and representatives of their localities. Chapter 7 discusses politics within the village. I examine leader-peasant relations under collective agriculture and explain why this relationship took a clientelist form. I describe the basis of clientelist power held by team leaders and strategies for getting ahead in this system.

Chapter 8 concerns the state's new strategy for grain procurement, which emerged after 1978. I analyze the new approach to procurement: the state price increases of 1979 and the decision to replace the system of unified procurement with a system of contract sales. I study how this new structural context affects the state's relationship with the peasantry, specifically what has happened to the struggle over the harvest. Chapter 9 looks at the effects of markets and production contracts on politics within the village. The analytical question is how the clientelist system of village politics has changed; here I examine the new roles for cadres and the new contours of local power.

As in any study, this one raises new questions that cannot be fully answered. The reader should view my descriptions and generalizations as tentative findings that require further testing and elaboration by future field research in different parts of China. It is well known that the implementation of state policies and the local response vary considerably by time and place. Ideally, I would have been able to describe precisely how behavior varied when the team was grain-rich or grain-poor, near larger cities with good transportation or in remote areas, during radical and liberal periods. However, I feel confident that I have identified the general patterns around which the search for variation should be organized.

CHAPTER 2

Dividing the Harvest

Legitimacy is a difficult political concept to define. As much seems to rest on form as on substance; the way a government handles a situation is often as important as its resolution.[1] Nowhere is this more true than with regard to conflict over food. Charles Tilly argues:

> The initial choice of methods of extraction, . . . the type of response to conflicts over food supply adopted all independently affected the path and pace of state making, as well as the structure of power which emerged around the nineteenth- and twentieth-century state.[2]

James Scott, who studies the normative roots of peasant politics, states that peasant political behavior is closely tied to perceptions of elite legitimacy and the fairness of elite claims on the harvest. For both Scott and Tilly the peasant economy is a moral economy. Subjective criteria such as the quality of elite-mass relations, the health of clientelist bonds, past precedent and recent memory of earlier conditions as well as tangible criteria such as the amount of the harvest left in the village are essential to that perception. Scott states:

> The crucial question in rural class relations is whether the relationship of dependence is seen by clients as primarily collaborative and legitimate or as pri-

1. See Charles Tilly, "Food Supply."
2. Tilly, "Food Supply," p. 393; on page 392 he writes that "the life of the state depended on the success of the battle for food." Quoting Jean Meyer, he continues: "Under the old economic regime, . . . the grain problem dominated all the worries of the government, took precedence among all questions of welfare."

marily exploitative. Here the issues of compliance and legitimacy are ana-
lytically distinct.[3]

The amount of the harvest left is likely to be more important than the
amount taken out of the village in prompting peasants who live on the
edge of subsistence to political action.[4] Tilly echoes this view: "Serious
conflicts over the food supply occurred not so much where men were
hungry as where they believed others were unjustly depriving them of
food to which they had a moral and political right."[5]

The question this chapter addresses is how the struggle over the harvest was resolved *after* a communist revolution: the "exploiting classes"
of landlords, grain merchants, and markets have been eliminated; peasants no longer farm as individuals but are organized into collectives that
jointly work and own the harvest. The Soviet experience, especially
Stalin's forced collectivization of Russian peasants in the late 1920s and
early 1930s,[6] certainly reveals that the struggle over the harvest does not
end with a communist revolution; only some actors in the cast change.

The brutality of the Soviet experience further suggests that concern
for legitimacy by a communist state is minimal at best. The use of fear
and coercion seems to have replaced concern for legitimacy. Whether
this is true for the Soviet Union cannot be ascertained in this study. But
the history of the Chinese communist state's relations with its peasantry
over the issue of the harvest indicates that at least one communist regime is sensitive to the issues described by Scott and Tilly. The process
by which the Chinese state under Mao tried to control the disposition of
the harvest and extract needed grain from the countryside provides a
vivid example of the interplay of form and substance and the state's concern for legitimacy. Without recognizing this aspect of Chinese communist rule, it is difficult to make sense of the various retreats in grain procurement policy, shifts in strategies, but most important the complex
and time-consuming method adopted to determine the amounts to be
sold by each team.

The reader should not conclude, however, that the Chinese state was
any less intent on procurements or any less capable of leaving peasants
grain-short. As examples will show, state interests had priority, regardless of the peasantry's expense.[7] Nonetheless, while the results may be

3. Scott, *Moral Economy*, p. 170.
4. Scott, *Moral Economy*; also see his *Weapons of the Weak*.
5. Tilly, "Food Supply," p. 389.
6. See Moshe Lewin, *Russian Peasants*.
7. Lardy also questions the long-term difference between the Chinese and Soviet poli-

similar, there clearly is a qualitative difference in the style of leadership, the nature of rule, the flexibility of tactics, and the lengths to which the state is willing to go to control the harvest that distinguishes the Chinese political system and the dynamics of Chinese politics from those characteristics suggested by the totalitarian model and the Soviet experience.

DEFINING THE SURPLUS

China, like other communist systems, relies on government *procurements* instead of direct taxation to secure sufficient supplies of grain to fuel industrialization. In so doing it creates for itself the difficult task of extracting sufficient amounts of grain at minimum cost while trying to maintain legitimacy in the eyes of the peasantry. To achieve this the state claimed that it was procuring only surplus grain.[8] This notion of surplus became the centerpiece of the Chinese state's attempts to legitimate its extraction of grain from the peasants from the mid-1950s to the late 1970s.

A surplus in the pure economic sense is that amount left after basic needs are satisfied. But how are the basic needs defined, and who decides? In China's centrally planned economy, the state did. It divided a team's collective harvest into two categories. One portion, allotted to meet a team's essential expenses, was limited to amounts sufficient for the state agricultural tax and the "three retained funds"—for seed, fodder, and team members' grain rations. For purposes of analysis, I will call this the "basic share" of the harvest claimed by the state, the production team, and the peasant households. The state considered the remaining portion of the team harvest "surplus grain" (*yuliang*). The size of the surplus was thus inversely proportional to the size of the state's taxes and the team's basic share (see Table 2).

As this chapter and the next chapter will show, the surplus was nothing more than an artifact of state regulations that manipulated the harvest's apportionment to legitimate the notion that the state was procuring only excess grain. Neither the state, the collective, nor the peasants were satisfied by their basic shares of the harvest.

---

cies toward peasant interests with regard to the amount of grain peasants ultimately had. Nicholas Lardy, "State Intervention."

8. No comparable study exists on the Soviet Union's procurement system. However, in conversations with Soviet scholars, it appears there is a Soviet term that refers to the "surplus." In the last few years under the *glasnost* policy, this term has begun to come under increasing debate with regard to the burden of the peasantry.

TABLE 2.   THE DIVISION OF THE HARVEST

State Share	Collective Share: "Three Retained Funds"	"Surplus"
Agricultural tax	Seed Fodder Grain rations (peasants' share)[a]	State grain procurement Local grain reserve Team utility fund

[a] Grain rations are distributed to the peasants by the collective.

The arbitrary definition of surplus lies at the root of why peasants were unwilling to sell more of their output to the state. The absolute size of the harvest provides few answers; the size of the harvest increased almost annually from the early 1960s. Grain shortage is important, but resistance to grain sales was not limited to grain-short areas.[9] Neither the failure of the state's grain procurement system nor the reported food shortages can be understood from grain statistics alone. The problems must be traced to the *political* process that apportioned the harvest and defined the surplus. The formal institutions of political power and the policy process directly affect political behavior.[10] The illicit behavior of local-level cadres is linked to the rigidity of the state's grain policies.[11]

What follows is a description of how the state controlled the allocation of grain to maximize the surplus.[12] It will become clear that the peasant was the producer and the collective the legal owner, but the

9. "Jinyibu fazhan yijing kaichuangde nongye xin jumian" (Move Forward the New Aspect of Agriculture That Has Already Begun), *RMRB* 23 December 1982: 1. "A Document of the Central Committee of the Chinese Communist Party *Chung-fa* (1979) No. 4: Decision of the Central Committee of the Communist Party of China on Some Questions Concerning the Acceleration of Agricultural Development (Draft)" (hereafter cited as "Decision"), pp. 105–106, stated that 100 million people were still grain-short in 1977.

10. A number of descriptions of commune administration exist, but few make the link between behavior and structure. See, for example, Byung-Joon Ahn, "The Political Economy"; Stavis, *People's Communes;* Butler, "Conflict and Decision Making"; and Barnett and Vogel, *Cadres, Bureaucracy.*

11. Thomas Bernstein is one of the few researchers to pursue the effects of the state's overzealous procurement of grain on peasant behavior. See his insightful article "Cadre and Peasant Behavior"; also see his "Stalinism, Famine."

12. Earlier studies have addressed various aspects of China's grain policy, but none has focused on the issue of "surplus." David Ladd Denny, "Rural Policies," details the history of the system of unified purchase and sales. The most detailed statistical study of grain procurements and consumption through the early 1960s, with some information on the late 1970s, is Kenneth Walker, *Food Grain.* On the history of grain policy for the 1950s and early 1960s, see Audrey Donnithorne, *China's Economic System,* and T. J. Hughes and D. E. T. Luard, *Economic Development.* Nicholas R. Lardy, *Agriculture,*

state dictated the use and division of the harvest. I will discuss the actual process of grain procurement in the next chapter.

THE STATE SHARE

The state's basic share of the harvest is surprisingly small. Since the state instituted its grain monopoly in 1954, the agricultural tax has decreased as a percentage of the total grain harvest.[13] The agricultural tax in the 1950s averaged about 10.5 percent of the total grain output and constituted a little more than one-fourth of state-procured grain.[14] By the late 1970s taxes represented only 4.5 percent of the total grain output and decreased in actual amounts from an average of 19.1 million tons for the period 1953–1957 to only 13.8 million tons.[15]

Statistics from one county illustrate more precisely the fall in tax rates.[16] From 1952 to 1983 they fell from 14 to 4 percent (see Table 3).

The decreasing importance of the agricultural tax is further reflected in total county revenues. In 1957 it accounted for 31.8 percent of Minhou county revenues; by 1983 it was only 9.4 percent. Per capita tax burdens also fell as a result of population increases relative to land under cultivation. In 1952 it was 102.6 jin per person; by 1983 it was 22.7 jin, a 78-percent decrease.[17]

---

provides one of the best economic studies of the costs of the state's grain self-sufficiency policy. For a political account of the state's policies on taxes and quotas during collectivization, see Shue, Peasant China, pp. 214–245. On elite-level policy debates on China's grain policies in the mid-1950s see Roderick MacFarquhar, Origins of the Cultural Revolution, pp. 293–297. For an interesting treatment of the "Three Fixes Policy," which sets the debate as a "three-line" struggle, see Dorothy Solinger, Chinese Business, chap. 2.

13. It has become, however, a larger percentage of the grain procured because of the smaller size of procurements. By the mid-1970s, the agricultural tax was equal to one-third of the state's procured grain; Lardy, Agriculture, p. 52. Parish and Whyte, Village and Family, p. 49, on the basis of interview data mostly from south China, found that in the late 1960s and the mid-1970s the tax was between 3 and 8 percent of a team's gross income.

14. Walker, Food Grain, p. 48, shows that there was great provincial variation in rates of taxation from 1953 to 1957. He found that seven provinces paid over half (55 percent) of the total amount of grain taxes received by the government. For example, Heilongjiang as a province paid 18 percent of its grain output in taxes. Nicholas Lardy, in Economic Growth, p. 126, reports that provincial rates for the period after 1958 ranged from a high of 19 percent in Heilongjiang to a low of 13 percent in Xinjiang.

15. Walker, Food Grain, p. 179.

16. Department of Agricultural Economics, Fujian Agricultural Institute, "Dui gaige nongye shuide shexiang" (Tentative Plans on Reforming the Agricultural Tax), NYJJWT 1985, no. 4, pp. 36–38.

17. The population increased by 83.8 percent during this same period while reported land under cultivation decreased 47,011 mu.

TABLE 3.   AGRICULTURAL TAXES, MINHOU COUNTY,
FUJIAN, SELECTED YEARS, 1952–1983

	1952	1957	1965	1979	1983
Total grain output (million *dan*)	1.9	2.2	2.8	3.6	3.8
Tax as % of total grain output	14.4	8.3	5.5	4.3	4.1
Tax as % of agric. income	9.0	4.5	2.8	2.2	1.4
Tax as % of county revenues	n.a.	31.8	n.a.	n.a.	9.4

SOURCE: "Dui gaige nongye shuide shexiang" (Tentative Plans on Reforming the Agricultural Tax), *NYJJWT* 1985, no. 4, pp. 36–38.

The small size of the agricultural tax starkly contradicts the state's urgent need for grain and its overall strategy for controlling grain supplies. Why is the amount that the state collects in taxes so small? The answer reflects, on the one hand, the state's decision to keep taxes low, and on the other, the peculiarities and weaknesses of the tax assessment system.

The current Chinese government, like that of the Soviet Union (not to mention imperial China), has avoided using direct taxation as its main source of grain. The regime has kept taxes low to smooth the socialist transformation of agriculture and spur production.[18] The structure has been such that if a team's population grew but its land area and yield stayed the same, the agricultural tax would decrease as a proportion of the harvest. Taxes have been fixed, usually for three or five years, regardless of productivity increases within that period.[19] Increases occur only when new land is brought into cultivation. Even then, a tax-free period of three to five years is allowed after a field has been put into production.

The agricultural tax is based on the amount of cultivated land, estimated output, and population. Yields, actual or normal, play a relatively minor role in the way the tax is calculated. As Minhou county's statistics show, official tax rates are also relatively meaningless. In 1962, when the statistics were still somewhat accurate, the nominal tax rate was 10 percent, but only 8.7 percent of production was taxed. By 1983

18. Shue, *Peasant China.*
19. From 1953 to 1970 it was set for three years; in 1971 it was changed to five years. The change applied also to the basic quota sales that I discuss in Chapter 3. I 5/3680.

the nominal rate had increased to 10.8 percent, but, because of inaccurate statistics and various deductions and exemptions, the actual rate of taxation was only 3 percent.[20] Tax rates given as provincial rates are similarly misleading; variation within provinces was large, and actual tax levies vary by as much as 100 percent.[21]

The amount of land in production and the general evaluation of that land are key in determining the tax. Instead of relying on a percentage that varies with output, the tax is based on a limited amount per *mu* of land. Interviews with former provincial officials indicate that the tax could not exceed more than forty-five to fifty *jin* of grain per *mu* of land, regardless of output.[22] Within that limit the amount of tax was determined according to whether the land was graded as good, average, or poor, each of which had a different tax rate based on output.[23] For average to good areas forty-five *jin* was the standard assessment, thirty to forty *jin* for poorer areas, and twenty-seven *jin* for the worst areas.[24] The commune standing committee set the figure, and the county government, which made the final decision about tax cuts or remittances, approved it. Counties assessed communes, communes assessed brigades, and brigades assessed teams. In theory, because the unit taxed (*bao*) was the brigade, the official county tax notice was sent only as far as the brigades, not to teams. In practice, the production teams, as the basic accounting and production units, paid the tax and were responsible for the grain's quality and timely delivery. The brigade's responsibility was seeing that its teams delivered their tax grain.[25]

The decreasing size of the agricultural tax is not entirely intentional but certainly understandable given the problems of state assessors. Spe-

20. "Dui gaige," *NYJJWT* 1985, no. 4, p. 37.

21. See Lardy, *Economic Growth*, p. 126. Donnithorne, in *China's Economic System*, p. 339, makes a similar point. She reports that Edgar Snow was told during a 1959 visit that the rate was 5.4 to 14 percent. In 1961 another visitor was told it was 7 to 19 percent. Yet a report from a commune in Guangdong said the rate was 4.4 percent.

22. Again, as with most regulations, this was not a hard-and-fast ruling. There are examples where the rate was fifty-four *jin* per *mu*. I 4/30180.

23. This description was given by a former cadre closely involved with taxation in north China. Rates varied, but similar accounts were provided by accountants and team leaders from other parts of China. No one ever gave the agricultural tax as a percentage of production; it was always expressed as fixed amount per *mu*. I 29/27680; I 29/22680.

24. During the Gang of Four period, some teams went for long periods without paying tax, in part because of the chaotic conditions but also because local cadres wanted to get mass support, to "*la nongmin xin*." These occurrences, however, were relatively rare. I 29/27680.

25. In most areas teams could go by themselves to pay the tax. However, there were areas in the north where brigade cadres personally lead the teams under their control to pay the tax. I 29/23680.

TABLE 4.   AGRICULTURAL TAXES, MINHOU COUNTY,
FUJIAN, 1962 AND 1983

	Normal Yield (*dan*)	Actual Production (*dan*)	Tax Base (% of Output Taxed)
1962	1,442,568	1,664,239	86.7
1983	1,438,222	3,769,025	38.2

SOURCE: "Dui gaige nongye shuide shexiang," *NYJJWT* 1985, no. 4, pp. 36–38.

cial work teams were sent to resurvey commune land and production, but the difficulty of accurately measuring increases in land under cultivation and yields often resulted in little change in the agricultural tax. According to a former team leader, one resurveying raised taxes only two hundred to three hundred *jin* for the entire commune—a minimal amount. This did not mean that no new land had been put into production; it was more a reflection of the work team's inefficiency and the difficulties of measuring each plot of land. Outside officials or work teams were largely dependent on the honesty of team leaders to guide them to all the fields.

In many cases the tax was calculated on the basis of outdated land information and production statistics. Minhou county records, for example, show that the normal yield figure used to calculate the tax in 1983 was virtually the same as in 1962, despite dramatic increases in production. As a result, the amount taxed in 1983 was only 38.2 percent of the actual yield (see Table 4). In other communes, as little as 25.3 percent of actual yields were subject to taxation.[26]

The assessment system also suffered from the general political turmoil and breakdown of government effectiveness accompanying the Cultural Revolution that began in 1966. The regular three-year reassessments were halted and did not resume until about 1978.[27] This laxity, commonly reported by former team leaders who have emigrated from China, has been confirmed by those in China who have called for the total revamping of the tax system, pointing out that most statistics are more than twenty years old.[28]

26. "Dui gaige," *NYJJWT* 1985, no. 4, p. 37.
27. I 3/15480; I 4/30180.
28. *Renmin shouce 1979*, pp. 666–667.

THE INEVITABILITY OF THE
AGRICULTURAL TAX

For most collectives and peasants the burden of the agricultural tax was not its size. For most teams in times of normal or bountiful harvests the amount of grain the state demanded in tax was a relatively minor expense. But the size of the agricultural tax masks the burden it created for peasants in times of shortage and poor economic conditions. Like the fixed rents applied by landlords, which Scott and others have described, the tax had to be paid at all costs.[29] It was difficult, if not impossible, for a team to get a remission and receive state relief.

Officially, taxes could be remitted in the case of major disasters. But tax remissions were usually limited to cases severe enough to warrant national attention. In those situations, relief and remission were quick to arrive. But in the more common, more marginal cases, where teams experienced a bad but not disastrous year, the chances for relief and tax remittance were small and slow in coming.[30] In those situations, guidelines for giving aid were extremely subjective. Poor teams in generally prosperous areas faced particular hardship because cadres involved with grain relief work tended to overlook isolated pockets of poverty.[31]

Securing a tax remittance, or any form of relief, was a long and complex process.[32] First, a team had to petition its brigade. If the brigade thought the request warranted consideration, it would forward it to the commune. It was then up to the commune to send it to the county's bureau of civil affairs (*minzhengbu*). The relief section of the bureau would send investigative work teams to assess the degree of damage and decide the disposition of the taxes.[33]

In theory, the issuance of relief and tax remittance was based on an official baseline of approximately twenty-six *jin* of grain rations per

29. See, for example, Scott, *Moral Economy.*
30. I 4/30180; I 30/1680; I 29/20680; I 7/19680.
31. This is suggested by the special warnings given in *Nongcun liangshi zhengce zhaibian* (Rural Grain Policy Handbook) (hereafter cited as *Nongcun liangshi*), p. 53.
32. The difficulty of getting relief has varied over time. According to a former relief worker, the situation was better in the 1950s, when the individual peasants could go to the *xiang* government to take out loans. The situation began to deteriorate after 1956 and worsened during the Cultural Revolution. I 5/121279.
33. There were various types of relief investigators and investigative work teams. The ones described here are those sent from the bureau of civil affairs from its regular staff. There were also ad hoc investigators deputized in the aftermath of major disasters. I 29/30680; I 30/1680; I 30/25480.

month per peasant.³⁴ If on average the team's rations fell below the minimum of twenty-six *jin* per month, the team did not have to pay taxes. Moreover, the state was supposed to sell these grain-short teams relief grain (*fanxiao liang*) to bring a team's average rations up to a minimum of twenty-five to thirty *jin* per month.³⁵ In practice, assessment of need was often based on subjective criteria. The twenty-six *jin* per month minimum was not a hard-and-fast rule; it varied from place to place even within the same province.³⁶ Each area had its own accepted minimum poverty line based on the normal harvest and past grain rations of the area.³⁷

The shortcomings of the relief system also stem from local cadres who for political reasons hesitated to apply for relief. From the time that grain self-sufficiency became a major goal of agricultural policy, political competence was measured by economic performance. Asking for relief, especially grain loans, had negative political connotations. Few cadres were willing to be labeled backward and risk their political reputation and position (see Chapter 6).

It is outside the scope of my study to discuss all the complexities of the relief system. My purpose is to highlight the difficulty of securing a tax remission and to show why the seemingly low agricultural tax was a substantial burden for poorer teams. The state's claim on the harvest had priority; the state was assured this part of the harvest in all but the most chaotic of situations.³⁸ Furthermore, once obtained, the state insti-

---

34. I 29/8680; I 30/1680; I 30/25480. A more complex 1950s tax relief schedule provided for proportional tax remission based on the percentage of crop failure. A 10-percent crop failure was set as the minimum amount of loss before relief would be granted. See "Guangdongsheng yijiuwuliunian nongye shui zhengshou shishi banfa" (1956 Measures for Collecting the Agricultural Tax in Guangdong Province), *NFRB* 22 June 1956.

35. I 29/30680. *Fanxiao liang* translates as resold grain, meaning grain sold at the state prices to teams that were either overtaxed or sold too much grain to the state and were therefore left grain-short.

36. I 30/1680; I 30/25480.

37. In deciding to give relief, a distinction was made based on whether a team had other crops such as sweet potatoes. The limit was actually closer to 18 *jin* of grain, rather than 26. Three *jin* of sweet potatoes were figured as equaling 1 *jin* of husked rice (*dami*) or about 1.3 *jin* of unhusked rice. If a team's distribution was under 18 *jin* but it had a crop of sweet potatoes, then it would not get relief. The details of this are not entirely clear. The criteria seemed extremely subjective, often based on such factors as previous conditions and limits. I 30/1680; I 30/25480. A 1979 reform has eliminated some difficulties by ruling that taxes are not to be assessed in those areas whose production does not meet the minimum standard of the basic grain ration set by individual provinces. See "Caizhengbu jueding bing guiding shishi banfa jinyibu jianqing nongcun shuishou fudan" (The Ministry of Finance Decided and Outlined Procedures for Implementation to Further Alleviate the Agricultural Tax Burden), *RMRB* 10 February 1979:1.

38. A limited number of areas during the Cultural Revolution did not pay their taxes. See footnote 24 of this chapter and Chapter 4. See, also, "Guangzhoushijiao Sanyuanli

tuted tight restrictions on the movement and use of the agricultural grain tax. County or commune authorities had no authority over tax grain, which was considered national property (*guojia suoyou*). Provincial authorities could use this grain only after permission from Beijing, even though some agricultural tax grain was stored in commune granaries throughout the province.[39] Wherever the tax grain was stored, it was always separated from the other grain stocks given its better quality. The state used the agricultural tax grain to build national reserves and sold it for export or as "commercial grain" (*shangpin liang*) to urban residents.[40] County grain bureaus (*liangshiju*) apportioned the tax grain, but they were required to send reports to both the prefecture (*diqu*) and the province. The counties themselves seldom kept large supplies, unless they had a well-developed granary system.[41]

THE HIDDEN COSTS OF THE AGRICULTURAL TAX

Poorer teams most heavily felt the direct burden of the agricultural tax, but the burden must also be measured in hidden costs that *all* teams paid. These stem from the state's requisite terms of payment. In theory, the agricultural tax could be paid in cash.[42] In practice, especially after the mid-1960s when all areas were urged to become self-sufficient in grain, the state demanded that the agricultural tax be paid in kind. A few teams in nongrain-producing areas did manage to pay in cash;[43] a few others paid in a combination of grain and money.[44] But such cases

---

fasheng nongmin kangjiao wenjian" (Peasant Riots Taking Place in Guangzhou Suburb, Sanyuanli), *STJP* 30 December 1970:4.

39. I 29/23680.

40. "Tan liangshi wenti" (Talking About the Grain Problem), *RMHYB* 21 August 1957. The best rice was used primarily for export, high-level cadres, first-class hotels, and hospitals. Only the lowest acceptable grade of grain used for payment of the agricultural tax was sold to the urban grain shops. I 5/10380. See footnote 47 of this chapter for details of the grain grading system.

41. In one grain-rich county in Guangdong, the county granary kept about 10 percent of the *zhenggou liang* (the agricultural tax plus the basic procurement). I 5/18380.

42. See Donnithorne, *China's Economic System*, pp. 336–346, on the forms of payment for the agricultural tax through the early 1960s.

43. I 4/6380. According to interviewees, the conversion rate used to pay the tax differentiated between early- and late-crop rice. It was usually somewhat higher (8.5 *yuan* for 100 *jin* versus 9 *yuan* in one example, 9.5 versus 10 to 12 in others) for the late crop. I 3/26380.

44. One interviewee's team paid a total of 800 *jin* of grain and 200 *yuan* in cash annually, beginning in 1959. In the late 1970s it owed three years' worth of back taxes, about 600 *yuan*, that it had failed to pay during the Cultural Revolution. The members

were the exception; most team leaders had no idea the agricultural tax
could be paid in anything but grain. Those from teams that paid in
money or in a combination of grain and money acted as if they had
managed to get away with something illegal. The general assumption
that taxes had to be paid in kind is further reflected in the colloquial
term for the agricultural tax, *gongliang* (public [state] grain).

Because the tax had to be paid in kind, grain-short teams had to either reduce their other allocations of grain, meaning smaller grain rations for the team members, or buy grain elsewhere at high prices to pay
the tax in kind. Moreover, teams could not just pay in any type of grain.
Tax grain had to be fine grain (*xiliang*), usually rice or wheat.[45] Unfortunately for the peasant, rice and wheat brought the highest prices on the
state and black markets. Lardy has pointed to the cost of buying grain at
high prices to meet the state tax and quotas as a primary cause of poverty in rural China.[46]

Furthermore, tax grain had to meet strict standards of grade, clean-
liness, and dryness.[47] Wet grain weighs more, and that weight can be
increased when mixed with small particles of sand or pebbles.[48] When
teams delivered the grain to the commune, granary managers used a
bamboo pole to scoop samples from the bottom of the bag or cart to
prevent teams from putting the best grain on the top to conceal inferior
grain and foreign matter underneath.[49] If the grain did not pass inspec-

---

were allowed to make this up in grain and in money. The team did not want to pay in
grain because it could have sold the grain on the black market for at least twice as much.
This area had many overseas ties and a shortage of labor power but considerable money
from overseas remittances, mostly from Hong Kong. I 3/26380; I 3/25380.

45. Some exceptions were made. For example, one area of north China, which grew a
lot of sweet potatoes and corn, was allowed to pay 50 percent of the tax in these crops, but
the amount of sweet potatoes could not exceed 30 percent. I 29/22680. A corroborating
press account is "Xianwei shuji ganji" (County Party Secretary Goes to Market Fair),
RMRB 20 December 1979:2.

46. Lardy, *Agriculture*, chap. 4.

47. Rice in China is divided into seven grades; the best is Special Grade No. 1 Rice,
and the most inferior is Grade No. 5 Rice. The grain used to pay the agricultural tax had
to be no lower than the fifth grade (Grade No. 3). I 5/10380. This was a burden for teams
because not only did these higher grades bring high prices on the black market but also
they had lower yields. Instead of the 1,200-*jin* yield of No. 3 rice, the Special Grade would
only produce 500 to 700 *jin*. According to one interviewee, teams had to plant a certain
amount of both Special Grade No. 1 and No. 2. *Nongcun liangshi*, p. 135, shows that 100
jin of Special Grade No. 1 Rice is figured as equal to 180 *jin* of No. 3 Rice; 100 *jin* of
Special No. 2 Rice is figured as 170 *jin* of No. 3 Rice.

48. The grain's moisture content (*shuifen*) had to be below 13.5 percent, the impurity
(*zazhi*) level below 0.5 percent, and the percentage of broken (*bushi li*) kernels below 1.5
percent.

49. I 5/10380.

tion, the granary manager could order further cleaning or drying of the grain, reducing the total amount of grain available for payment. As a precaution, teams often took more grain with them than was required to prevent making another trip to the granary, wasting more time and labor.[50]

The state, however, was not completely successful in preventing such cheating. Local-level granary cadres exercised considerable discretion in grain testing. In many places, despite the precise percentages given for such things as moisture content, the methods used to determine the quality of grain were based on subjective evaluations by granary cadres, not on precise tests. In both north and south China, the granary manager or inspector would bite on a kernel of grain to see if it made the proper sound. To test for the fullness of kernels, he would crack or press the grain with a stone. More scientific methods for testing dryness were available in China, but even in the late 1980s, cadres preferred traditional methods.[51]

Wise and experienced team leaders would try to actively cultivate friendly relationships with the granary cadres, who had the power to refuse a team's grain.[52] If the team cadres were on good terms with the granary manager, he might accept grain of slightly inferior quality and only give the team leader a warning that it should not happen again.[53] The state had tried to minimize collusion and patronage by appointing granary managers from outside the local area; however, such measures did not always work. As one cadre explained, the commune granary head (*zhanzhang*) was usually an outsider, a party member and a state cadre appointed by the county, not by the commune. But even so, the cadres often worked in the same granaries for as long as ten or twenty

50. The demand that the tax be paid in kind also meant that teams had to bear the physical costs of transporting the grain to the state granaries. The state reimbursed teams on a per mile basis for this labor, but it was seen as a time-consuming burden nonetheless. Teams had to deliver their tax grain to the commune granaries or, in a few areas, to the county granaries. Richer teams in south China, to save time and labor, hired trucks at their own expense to deliver the grain for them, rather than using carts or mobilizing the entire team to carry the grain on their backs. I 1/24680. In one such area, teams that used this service paid 0.9 *yuan* per kilometer per ton of grain transported. They called the county grain bureau or the commune grain station and made an appointment to have their grain picked up; the team leader was accompanied by only one or two team members, at most. In some areas the brigade paid for the cost of the transport of the grain. I 29/23680. The costs of delivery, however, were of minor concern compared to the other hidden costs of payment in kind.

51. I 29/23680; I 21/15180; I 5/10380. Personal visit to Shandong grain station, 1988.

52. I 1/24680; I 29/23680; I 21/15180.

53. I 21/15180.

years. Friendships naturally developed.[54] As I shall discuss at length in later chapters, the formation of stable personal ties with those in positions of authority was a key element in the pursuit of interests in the countryside.

Although the state did take precautions to get the best grain as its basic share of the harvest, the state's major concern was not with the agricultural tax. Underlying the state's slight attention to the size of the agricultural tax are its alternative strategies for monitoring the shares of the other claimants by either extracting or controlling that same amount as surplus.

THE TEAM SHARE

This chapter began by discussing peasant perceptions of legitimacy and the importance of "what was left in the village." The assumption of students of peasant societies who have developed the moral economy perspective is that the members of the peasant village have both autonomy and control over the use and distribution of what is left of the harvest. But this assumption does not hold in the context of the collectivized centrally planned economy of China.

The production team legally owned the harvest and received payment from its sale, but neither the team as a collective nor individual peasant households as members of the collective had autonomy over its disposition. The state determined how much grain would remain for collective use and regulated that use. Individual peasants had even less power over the harvest; they received their shares from the team's allotment.

The state granted production teams only three legitimate expenses: grain for the coming year's seed, the current year's fodder, and the team members' rations—the "three retained funds" (see Table 2).[55] To ensure that the team retained only the "appropriate amounts," a team leader had to submit a budget to his brigade for approval before any grain could legally be used from the harvest.[56] No other team expenses were provided for when apportioning the collective's basic share of the har-

---

54. I 21/15180.

55. The investment fund or accumulation fund, often referred to in the budgets of teams, was not figured in grain. It came from the cash that teams received from the sale of their grain to the state.

56. For a discussion in the press of the strict limits imposed on the "three retained funds," see "Jining diqu sheyuan yongyue jiaoshou xiaomai zhiyuan jianshe" (Jining Area Peasants Enthusiastically Sell Wheat to Support Construction), DGB 28 June 1964.

vest or taken into consideration when determining the surplus. I will discuss how teams dealt with this shortage in Chapter 6. In this section I address the question of how adequate these shares were.

The seed fund was based on a straightforward calculation of need per *mu* of land. Few complaints are heard about these allocations. Teams were allowed to retain a certain amount per *mu* depending on the variety of seed and the type of crop as well as the region.[57] Perhaps because the state recognized the importance of seed grain for a successful harvest, in practice it was quite lenient in regulating the amount teams retained for this purpose. An official granary handbook states that seed grain should get first consideration in the harvest allocation, even before the agricultural tax. Seed is the best and the first grain saved. Regulations further warn that the seed fund should not be encroached upon by the need for sales (*zhongzi diyi, buke qingfan*).[58] The state's view is very much in line with peasants' views of the seed fund. They have a saying: "Your mother may starve, but you cannot eat the seed grain."[59]

Consequently, the amounts retained per *mu* usually included extra as insurance against disease or crop failure or frost in the early stages of growth. However, Walker's dramatic finding that the average seed allotment per hectare increased 130 percent in the late 1970s, compared to the late 1950s, leads one to question whether this grain was used for other purposes. He estimates that in the 1950s the national average was 67 kilograms of seed per sown hectare; by 1980, he found that the amount had risen to 154 kilograms per sown hectare.[60]

Fodder was the second legitimate expense for which teams could retain a portion of the harvest. Teams always wanted to keep maximum amounts to support animal husbandry, a profitable sideline for both teams and individual households. Moreover, the sale of pigs yielded bonus grain rations. For every pound of pork sold to the state, a team or peasant household (if it were a private sale) was allowed to buy extra amounts of grain at the low state price as incentive for raising more

57. Some peasants said they kept twenty to twenty-five *jin;* others said their teams kept between forty and fifty *jin* per *mu* for rice and approximately forty-five *jin* per *mu* for wheat. Press reports cite forty-five *jin* of seed per *mu*. See "Lixiahe diqu chao'e wancheng zhenggou renwu" (Lixiahe Region Has Overfulfilled Its Grain Procurement Task), *DGB* 7 November 1964:3.

58. *Nongcun liangshi*, p. 105.

59. I 17/91180.

60. Walker, *Food Grain*, p. 177. Alan Piazza, in *Trends*, p. 94, estimates that in 1979 total seed requirements should have consumed 2.4 percent of rice production, 10 percent of wheat, 2.5 percent of corn, 2 percent of sorghum, 4.5 percent of millet, and 2 percent of tubers.

pigs.[61] Regulations, however, allowed teams to retain fodder sufficient only to feed the collective livestock.

Fodder for private livestock had to come from the by-products of a household's own grain rations, usually given in unhusked grain. Peasants could buy fodder, but, because it was a cereal by-product and rationed, supplies on the black market sold at high prices. The state grain stores sold the by-products of milled rice (*liangpi*) at 0.65 *mao* per *jin*; the price on the open market was 2.5 *mao* for the same amount.[62] As an incentive to sell more grain to the state, teams were sometimes offered the opportunity to buy extra bran or husks (*kang*) at the low state price.[63] The collective grain mills charged peasants different prices depending on whether a peasant wanted the husks or not.[64] Peasants in almost all instances preferred to get their rations in unhusked grain and keep the millings for fodder.

Teams were required to calculate fodder needs according to the number and type of livestock and poultry in the collective, although considerable variation exists among provinces in the amount allowed.[65] Interestingly, as in the case of seed, Walker found that the amount of grain kept for feed doubled between the 1950s and the late 1970s; for the 1950s it was only about 5 percent of the national output, but in the 1970s the amount went up to 10 percent.[66] As I have indicated, there is evidence that the state purposely allowed teams some slack in the seed fund, but it is less clear this was the case with grain kept for feed. As in the case of the seed fund, one must question what this grain was actually used for after it was retained for fodder. The grain kept as fodder included corn, barley, and *wandou* (a special variety of garden peas), all

61. I 14/201279. In some areas there was an overabundance of pigs, so much so that for a period in 1978–1979 the state refused to buy them from the peasants. It is unclear whether the grain bonus was given in those areas or not. Public lecture by Steven Butler at the Universities Service Centre, Hong Kong, spring 1980.

62. I 29/24680.

63. I 21/13180. If teams took advantage of this opportunity, they could buy *kang* at the state price.

64. I 29/24680.

65. Walker, *Food Grain*, pp. 110–111.

66. Ibid., p. 177. A team accountant reported that in the late 1970s his team set aside 400 *jin* of grain a year for each ox, which was equal to approximately 5 percent of the harvest. I 4/63080; I 4/30180. Piazza, *Trends*, pp. 96–97, estimates that feed grain consumption was fairly stable at 11 percent of total grain production, including millings, in 1957, 1977, and 1979. He assumes that 25 percent of the coarse grain crop, 1 percent of the rice crop, and 3 percent of the wheat crop were used as feed. His calculations assume that rice husks were not fed to animals because of their nominal nutritional value and abrasive texture. My interviews with former peasants and cadres question whether they had the luxury to worry about such problems.

of which are suitable for consumption,[67] but teams often only used the husks or chaff for feed. Chapter 6 will consider the question of whether both feed and seed grain were kept for other purposes.[68]

THE PEASANT SHARE

Only when one examines how the peasant share was determined do the state's true aims with regard to the harvest, which were masked by its rather ineffective and lax policy of agricultural taxation, become apparent. As the following sections will show, the peasants' share bore little correlation to work or the absolute size of the harvest. In large part it was determined by factors outside the peasants' control. They had no direct or legitimate claim on the harvest; their due came out of the share retained by the collective. The state placed the collective between the peasants and their harvest to check peasant claims on the harvest and create a larger surplus. Just as the state limited the amount that teams could retain for seed and fodder, it also limited, but much more strictly, the amount that collectives could retain and distribute as peasant grain rations.

The state cannot simply be charged with discriminating against the peasants in limiting their food consumption. A societywide rationing program was instituted to ensure a planned and equitable distribution of grain. One could view the limit on peasant grain consumption as simply one part of the larger policy of rationing, but to do so would miss the most important half of the picture. Rationing had a far more significant impact on the lives of rural rather than urban dwellers. Before examining this issue, it will be useful to step back and look at both the broader policy of rationing, as applied to both urban and rural areas, and the household registration system, a necessary correlate to rationing. In the context of a collective agricultural economy these two policies defined the position of peasants in China's countryside. These policies returned Chinese peasants to a state of dependency reminiscent of those in closed communal villages found in traditional agrarian societies, and peasant response to these same policies ultimately led the state to embark on the program of reform, which I will discuss in the last chapters of this book.

67. I 29/8680; I 29/22680.
68. In north China *kang* was also used for lining floors of granaries, making mud walls when mixed with cement, and making certain types of vinegar. I 29/21680.

HOUSEHOLD REGISTRATION AND
FOOD RATIONING

In China each person has a household registration (*hukou*). This registration signifies the legal residence of an individual, and, most important for the purposes of our analysis, it determines how that individual is to be supplied his or her grain ration. People who have legal urban status, regardless of their place of residence, have city household registration (*jumin hukou* or *fei nongye hukou*).[69] This status allows them access to a set amount of grain coupons (*liangpiao*) to purchase commercial grain (*shangpin liang*) at a low state-set price (*paijia*).

Most urban households are issued family grain books (*liangben*), which list family members, their age, work, or position, and their grain allotment. The ration book must be presented when purchasing grain at the state-run grain shops (*liangdian*), until the late 1970s the only legal places to buy grain after the last free grain markets were closed in 1957.[70] Urban residents also use the grain book to obtain coupons from the state-run grain shops to buy prepared cereal products and to eat out. Urban residents, such as university students or unmarried workers living in unit dorms who do not live with their families, are included in a collective household registration, and they are issued monthly grain coupons by their units.

One could not purchase more grain- or cereal-based food than one had coupons for during most of the period of institutionalized rationing.[71] Restaurants and bakeries collected grain coupons when selling any prepared cereal-based foods. Rice and noodles were ordered by the ounce and paid for in money *and* grain coupons. These coupons were place-specific; there were national, provincial, and municipal grain tickets. For example, if one wanted to eat in a restaurant outside of one's registered province, national grain coupons had to be procured.[72]

69. Also see Martin King Whyte and William L. Parish, *Urban Life*, particularly pp. 18–19 for details of the registration system.

70. Free markets for grain were permitted briefly in 1959. However, because of the severe grain shortage, little was available on the free market. After that one could buy grain in rural markets, but this was only surplus grain that individuals sold. Teams were not allowed to sell their collective grain to anyone but the state. Even in 1988 free grain markets were closed during the period of state procurement. China Interviews, 1988. For a brief synopsis of the changes in the grain marketing policies, see "Liangshi jingying qudaode baci bianqian" (Eight Changes in the Channels for Grain Management), *NCGZTX* 1983, no. 9, p. 46.

71. High-priced grain sales (*yijia*) existed in the early 1960s, officially from 1962 to 1966; see Chapter 4. I deal with post-1978 changes in policy in Chapter 8.

72. "Tantan shiyong liangpiao wenti" (Speaking of Problems of Experimenting with Grain Ration Tickets), *JNB* 10 December 1955. Prior to 1966 there were county grain

Peasants have what is called "peasant household registration" (*nong-min hukou* or *nongye hukou*); they are not issued grain tickets. They obtain their grain rations in kind directly from their production teams, either monthly to ensure planned consumption or, more commonly, semiannually after each harvest.[73] Like urban residents, peasants must pay for their grain. But unlike urban residents, peasants had to participate in collective agricultural labor and pay for their rations with work points earned for their collective labor. Only if a peasant's work points were not equal in value to the cost of the grain rations did he pay in cash. The price used to calculate the costs of peasant rations is the same as that paid by urban residents—the state-set ration price (*gongjia* or *paijia*). If a peasant had neither the money nor sufficient work points, then he had to go into debt to his production team. Like urban residents, peasants could buy no more than their rationed allotment of grain.

The combination of the household registration system and rationing made all persons with "peasant household registration" directly dependent on their production team for grain, the staple of the peasant diet. This was true even if they lived and worked temporarily in an urban area. The possible exceptions were those peasants who became long-term temporary workers and obtained temporary urban household registration. They could go to the urban grain stores to procure their rations, but the grain was allotted from an account set up for and charged to their production teams. Under certain circumstances peasants were given grain coupons to use in urban areas, but these were special tickets issued by their production brigade. In contrast, urban residents sent to the countryside, particularly cadres, had free access to their own grain coupons while exiled to the countryside.

This rationing system severely limited peasant movement outside the collective. Those who needed to travel had to either secure special grain coupons from their brigade leaders or carry a supply of grain with them.[74] The latter option was obviously inconvenient and not very feasible for trips of any duration, and regulations were strict for obtaining

---

tickets as well as special provincial tickets called "*liudong liangbu*" and "*liudong liang-piao*" for fishermen and professional drivers. I 5/4380.

73. I 19/13380. An article from 1955 indicates that in the early years peasants also could freely trade grain for grain coupons. "Tantan shiyong," *JNB* 10 December 1955. It is unclear exactly when this policy changed; however, it seems likely that restricting peasants' access to grain tickets began as the state started to curb migration to the cities in the late 1950s.

74. I 21/23180; Trip notes from Taishan county, Guangdong, spring 1980.

grain coupons. Only peasants on official business or with special approval of the brigade were issued grain coupons. Consequently, rationing, in conjunction with the household registration system, effectively controlled migration.

Peasants could only circumvent the rationing system by illegally buying grain rations tickets on the black market. One strategy was to sell their goods in the cities, not for money but for grain coupons.[75] Another strategy was to trade with the city residents who were sent to live in the countryside. Former city residents say that they were able to get many specialty food items and help from the peasants, simply by bartering with their ration coupons.[76]

HARVEST SIZE AND THE PEASANT SHARE

In assessing the adequacy of the peasant share of the harvest one should first know the size of that share. For China this is very difficult to calculate accurately. Economists using aggregate figures have made various estimates of changes in grain consumption. Lardy finds that rural grain consumption declined 5.9 percent from 1957 to 1978 (from 204.5 kilograms to 192.5 kilograms of commercial grain [*shangpin liang*] per person per year).[77] Walker argues that rural consumption did not decline but showed only a small increase and never surpassed that of 1956, when rationing was only loosely implemented. The average consumption increased from 245 kilograms for the period 1953–1957 to 252 kilograms (unhusked) in 1978–1979.[78] One Chinese publication has presented statistics showing the changes in the average amount of grain available per person (see Table 5). The official grain "consumption" fig-

---

75. I 7/14680. In order to stop this, the state began dating tickets so that they were valid for only one year. Urban residents who did not need all of their ration tickets were given the opportunity to put the grain on reserve at their local grain store. The grain books were used partly to control the black market in grain tickets. I 7/19680. The practice, nonetheless, continued. A number of articles in *BJRB* 14 January 1981:1, describe the various forms this illegal practice has taken: see "Chachu yiqi daomai daohuan piaozheng anjian" (Investigation and Punishment of a Case of Illegal Sales and Trading of Grain Ration Coupons), "Daomai daohuan liangpiao shi feifade" (Speculating in Grain Coupons Is Illegal), and "Liangge sheyuan daliang daomai liangpiao shou chengchu" (Two Peasants Who Bought Grain Coupons in Large Numbers Were Punished). Peasant construction teams that did not have official approval to leave the commune and therefore did not have access to legal coupons were some of the biggest customers of the speculators. The problem of illegal trading of grain tickets still existed in 1988.

76. I 2/181279; I 26/1229.
77. Lardy, *Agriculture*, p. 158.
78. Walker, *Food Grain*, pp. 190–191.

TABLE 5.   PER CAPITA GRAIN AVAILABILITY,
SELECTED YEARS, 1949−1978

	1949	1952	1957	1965	1978
jin/person	418	na.	612	544	637

SOURCE: "Xinzhongguo nongyede sanshiwunian" (Thirty-five Years of New China Agriculture), *NCGZTX* 1984, no. 9, p. 8.

ure for both urban and rural residents is 200 kilograms per person (400 *jin* per person—33.3 *jin* per month husked or 43.3 *jin* per month unhusked).[79]

Regardless of which set of statistics is most accurate, none tells us the amount of grain peasants actually received as their rations or the amount they consumed. The statistics simply reflect the amount available when the total harvest is divided by the population.

Another rough measure of the amount of grain peasants received would be the amount of grain left in the village after procurements. Changes over time are reflected in Table 6. But these figures include the amount that must be deducted for seed, fodder, and reserve and utility funds. As indicated previously, one cannot assume that peasants have access to the amount of grain left in the village.

Given the problems in calculating precise figures for the per capita grain left in the village, it is more useful to delineate the limits imposed by the state on the peasant's share of the harvest. Attempts to specify the change in the precise amount of grain available to peasants miss the point that peasant rations did not necessarily change with production size; larger harvests did not necessarily mean that peasants received more grain for their labor. A number of limitations prevented peasant rations from rising with production.

LIMITING THE PEASANT SHARE

A peasant's total grain ration (*kouliang*) consisted of grain distributed on a per capita basis, the basic grain ration (*jiben kouliang*), and grain distributed on a labor basis, the work-point grain (*gongfen liang*). The basic grain ration was allotted each peasant for being a member of the collective, without regard to contribution in collective labor. During

79. Cited in ibid., p. 190.

TABLE 6.   GRAIN LEFT IN THE VILLAGE AFTER PROCUREMENTS, SELECTED YEARS, 1952–1986

Year	Grain Left After Gross Procurements (million tons)	Percent of Harvest Left After Gross Procurements	Grain Left per Capita After Gross Procurements (tons/person)	Grain Left After Net Procurements (million tons)	Percent of Harvest Left After Net Procurements	Grain Left per Capita After Net Procurements (tons/person)
1952	130.7	79.7	.260	135.7	82.8	.270
1957	147.0	75.4	.269	161.2	82.6	.295
1962	121.9	76.2	.219	134.3	83.9	.241
1965	145.8	75.0	.245	160.9	82.7	.271
1970	185.5	77.3	.271	197.9	82.5	.289
1975	223.7	78.6	.293	240.6	84.6	.315
1976	228.1	79.7	.295	245.6	85.8	.317
1977	226.1	80.0	.289	245.2	86.7	.313
1978	243.0	79.7	.308	262.1	86.0	.332
1979	260.1	78.3	.329	280.4	84.4	.355
1980	247.6	77.2	.311	272.6	85.0	.343
1981	246.5	75.8	.309	276.2	85.0	.346
1982	262.6	74.1	.327	295.4	83.3	.367
1983	267.4	69.1	.341	302.0	78.0	.385
1984	265.6	65.2	.377	312.7	76.8	.444
1985	263.5	69.5	.397	320.8	84.6	.484
1986	256.9	65.6	.415	291.4	74.4	.470

SOURCES: *Zhongguo tongji nianjian 1985*, pp. 185, 482; *Zhongguo tongji nianjian 1987*, pp. 89, 570.

the initial stages of collectivization the State Council decided in favor of distribution according to age (*yiren dingliang*).[80] The assumption was that age would correlate with participation in collective labor. The difficulty was that the ruling did not ensure uniform standards; it lacked hard-and-fast rules on how much each age group should receive. Great variation existed in the distribution to those under fifteen and those over sixty—considered to possess less than full labor power.[81] Sixty was the age at which a peasant often retired or was downgraded to less than full labor power ranking.[82] In some teams, no distinctions were ever made according to age; all team members received the same amount.[83]

One should be careful not to confuse the basic grain ration with "free supply."[84] The basic grain ration was the minimal amount that the state supposedly guaranteed each peasant within the collective agricultural system.[85] Technically, each peasant, except for the "five guaranteed

80. State Council Directive from 1957, cited in "Yiren dingliang you wu da haochu" (Distribution According to (Individual) Age Has Five Big Advantages), *RMRB* 13 August 1957; also see "Nongcun liu kouliang yao fen daxiao kou" (Retention of Grain Rations Should Accord with the Distinction Between Adults and Children), *NBRMB* 28 May 1957. No distinction was made between men and women.

81. "Xianfengshe shiying kouliang fendeng dingliang fenpei banfa" (Xianfeng Cooperative Experiments with Distributing Grain Rations According to Age), *DZRB* 10 September 1957:2, suggested that the group under fifteen and over sixty years of age be divided into four categories: those from twelve to fifteen and those over sixty would be one class; those eight to eleven, four to seven, and one to three would be classified separately. "Pingjun jikou shouliang bibing henduo" (Distributing Grain According to Average Population in a Household Has Many Drawbacks), *RMRB* 28 May 1957, suggested that the distribution be divided into four different gradations, ranging from 10 *jin* per month for a newborn to between 35 and 40 *jin* per month for those over ten years old. Yet some places in Hunan gave basic grain rations of 150 *jin* per year for those from one to two *sui* (birth to one year) to 620 *jin* per year for an adult male. Other places within Hunan divided peasants into eight categories and provided grain rations ranging from 200 *jin* per year for a one-year-old to 550 *jin* per year to those older than nineteen. "Nanhu, qunjian nongshe shixing 'yiren dingliang' fenpei kouliang de banfa" (Qunjian Cooperative of Nanhu Sets Grain Ration "According to the Individual"), *Liangshi* 1957, no. 7, pp. 5–7.

82. Sixty is not always the age at which peasants retire. As with other matters, there is variation. Peasants who do retire sometimes continue working, but the minimal work attendance rules no longer apply. In parts of Guangdong, a peasant's work rating was reduced at the meeting to evaluate work performance following the peasant's sixtieth birthday. This reduction was often accompanied by a little ceremony commemorating the peasant's contribution and presenting the retirement (and reduced rating) as an earned rest. I 2/131279.

83. I 8/18680; I 18/28380; I 4/30180; I 4/12280.

84. See, for example, the reference to "free supply" by Donnithorne, *China's Economic System*, p. 77. This term applied only briefly during the Great Leap Forward. Only the "Five Guaranteed Households" receive free grain and other necessities of life—the teams pay for this as part of collective welfare. They are neither expected to work nor to pay for their food and other distributed goods in any way; everyone else must pay by one means or another.

85. I use the term "supposedly" because the state did not always maintain this minimum. Only a few peasants were even aware that such guidelines existed.

households," had to pay for his or her grain or go into debt. Only for a very brief period during the height of the Great Leap Forward, when all ate in mess halls, was there free supply; peasants ate as much as they wanted without worry about payment. Even then it was assumed that the peasants were participating in collective labor and therefore paying for their food. In practice, however, as the following section will show, for most of the Maoist period peasants received this amount regardless of how much they went into debt.

The work-point grain is the amount a peasant received above the basic grain ration as payment for participating in collective labor, measured by the accumulation of work points. But one cannot equate the number of work points with the amount of grain a peasant received in a year. Payment for participation in the collectivized system of agriculture consisted of a grain ration and cash. The amount of money a peasant received depended not only on the total number of work points that a peasant family accumulated; it also depended on the collective's profits from the sale of its harvest and the total costs of such goods as oil and vegetables and the grain rations a family received from the collective.

Past studies of peasant income have assumed that different work-point systems allowed individual peasants to earn more work points and therefore more income. Work points and various work-point systems have been seen as the crux of the incentive problem.[86] Without question the work-point system was important; it determined a peasant's *claim* on the total income of the team. However, work points did not always determine how much payment a peasant actually received for his labor, and they certainly did not determine how much grain a peasant received. Because of grain rationing, work points differentiated incomes mostly in terms of cash. The degree to which work points provided an incentive for increased participation in collective labor therefore depended on the amount of cash income a team had to distribute; some had none. In teams that had no cash income to distribute, an abundance of work points was essentially meaningless, even though technically it entitled a peasant to a larger share of his team's cash income.

In practice, work points primarily determined whether a peasant had worked a sufficient number of days to cover the cost of his basic grain

86. See, for example, Stavis, *People's Communes*. Other works that deal with the work-point system and incentives include Andrew J. Nathan, "China's Work-Point System"; and Martin Whyte, "Ta Chai Brigade." Parish and Whyte, *Village and Family*, p. 66, note the importance of the distribution ratio, but they do not discuss the implications.

ration. An excess of work points would be noted in the accountants' records as cash due, if and when the team received some cash profit; they could not be used to buy unlimited amounts of extra grain. But a peasant who lacked sufficient work points to cover the cost of his grain rations at the end of the agricultural year simply owed his team the difference in cash.[87] If the peasant had no other source of income, from either his private plot or sideline activities or overseas remittances, and could not pay the balance on his account for the grain distributed that year, he merely became an "overdrawn household" (chaozhi hu).[88] The important point is that he still received his basic grain ration. In the end, a peasant who earned only one hundred work points could receive the same amount of grain, and therefore the same actual payment, as one who earned one thousand.

Until 1979 the amount team members received in cash was small. Lardy has shown that for the period 1974–1978, annual income distributed in cash averaged only thirteen yuan per commune member. Moreover, the share of collective income distributed in cash fell from 35 percent in 1957 to less than 20 percent in 1974–1978.[89] Peasants in teams that had a small harvest or bad weather or debts and high collective expenses received little or no cash—a problem termed buneng duixian (not able to make ends meet).[90] Some peasants saw no cash income for years, a phenomenon not uncommon during the late 1960s and most of the 1970s when money-making sideline activities were discouraged and severely curtailed.[91]

87. The value of a work point depends on the actual harvest and total income of a team. If a team gives out many work points, the value of each will depreciate because the total number of work points is divided into the team's total distributed income.

88. Parish and Whyte, Village and Family, p. 66, discuss this problem for the earlier periods. Overdrawing continued to be a serious problem at least until the late 1970s, especially in poorer teams. The term "five guaranteed" is usually applied to individuals or households, but some teams were so poor that they were labeled "Five Guaranteed Teams," meaning that everyone in the team was overdrawn and grain-short. See "Nongmin weishenme ruci xihuan shengchan zirenzhi" (Why Peasants Like the Responsibility System So Much), RMRB 14 November 1979:2. It was a vicious cycle; only after official encouragement of profit-oriented sidelines has it been possible to escape. Overdrawing also affected those solvent members of a team because it drained the team's collective wealth. More important, it was a nonincentive for those who managed to stay solvent; chronically overdrawn households continued to get the basic grain rations. Only in the mid- to late 1970s were there signs of change. In some teams, overdrawn households had to pay back at least a certain percentage of their debt by harvest time before the next grain rations were given out.

89. Lardy, Agriculture, p. 161.

90. See "Yao zhuanhao sheyuan de xianjin fenpei duixian" (Pay Close Attention to Paying Team Members Their Cash Distributions), RMRB 28 January 1979:2.

91. Trip notes from Taishan county, Guangdong, 1980. As my other examples will show, this seems to have been a relatively widespread problem. For a discussion in the

The problem stemmed in large part from the way the state paid teams for the sale of their goods. Any cash from collective sales to the state was first channeled through the credit cooperative (*xinyongshe*), which would deduct any past debts owed by the team before paying it for its sales. Because of this, some poor but grain-rich teams (*gaochan qiong-dui*) preferred to take their crops and sell them on the black market, even if the market price was lower than the state's, in order to be assured cash payment. A Hebei county first secretary was surprised to find that peasants wanted to sell their wheat on the free market when the state had offered to buy at a higher price; they did so because the credit co-operatives were withholding funds from teams with outstanding loans.[92]

In short, grain rations represented the bulk of a peasant's wages for collective labor. Consequently, the grain allotment determined not only peasant-state relations but also the incentive for peasants to support the collective system of agricultural production.

Income Ratios and Ceilings.   The amount of grain received and how much of a difference work points made were determined by complex factors outside peasant control. In some areas, the state ruled that the amount distributed as work-point grain should be limited to between 5 and 20 percent of a team's total grain ration allowance.[93] The amount used for work-point grain depended on whether the team was a "grain-deficit" or "grain-surplus" team; the grain-deficit areas would have a lower limit.[94] The limits usually took the form of a ratio that specified the amount of grain distributed as basic grain and as work-point grain. This ratio in effect determined how much the peasant's participation in collective labor was worth in grain. It reflected whether the bulk of the grain was distributed on a per capita basis for simply being a team member or whether one received more grain for more work.

---

press of this, see, for example, "Xianwei shuji," *RMRB* 20 December 1979:2; and "Qubie qingkuang baozheng sheyuan zengchan zengshou" (Distinguishing Different Circumstances Ensures That Team Members Will Increase Production and Income), *RMRB* 20 December 1979:2.

92. "Xianwei shuiji," *RMRB* 20 December 1979:2.

93. For example, in one team in southwestern China work-point grain was limited to under 10 percent. I 3/7480; I 3/15480.

94. I 4/2280. For press accounts regarding limits on work-point grain, see, for example, "Xia liang fenpei caiqu santiao zhengce jiangu guojia yu geren" (Summer Grain Distribution Should Follow the Three Policies, Taking Both the State and Individuals into Consideration), *NFRB* 4 June 1959. It should be noted that limits did not seem to exist in all areas; for example, I 1/12480 said his team had no such limit.

The proper ratio has been an issue since the beginning of collectivization, and it remained an issue until the commune's demise. Perhaps
because the different ratios imply different underlying political views
about the degree of equality that can be achieved in society and the need
for material incentives, different ratios have accompanied swings in the
political pendulum.[95] Following the disaster of the Great Leap Forward
(1958–1961) the ratio of basic grain to work-point grain changed from
5:5 to 3:7 linking the bulk of distribution to work in an effort to spur
production. After the crisis period the balance swung back to 6:4 or
7:3; 6:4 was the preferred ratio. The bulk of the distribution was again
on basic supply.

During the Cultural Revolution (1966–1976) the 6:4 ratio was criticized as putting "work points in command," even though the amount
supplied as basic grain was more than the work points.[96] Consequently,
after the mid-1960s the most common ratio used for grain distribution
was 7:3, although 6:4 continued to be used in a few areas. In some
places, *all* the grain ration was distributed on a per capita basis; no allowance was made for the number of work points earned.[97]

After 1976, when the national leadership attempted to increase peasant enthusiasm and production, the issue of the proper ratio between
basic and work-point grain again came to the fore. "More grain for
more work" was the correct policy. To achieve this, some proposed a
return to the 5:5 ratio, reversing the emphasis on basic supply and
stressing work points.[98] Sichuan province suggested a radical 3:7 ratio,
completely reversing the earlier ratio and making the amount dis-

95. The major exception seems to be the period of the agricultural producers' cooperatives (APCs), when the ratio of supply to work-point grain was 7:3 or 8:2. Denny,
"Rural Policies," p. 111. One of the fullest discussions to date on the supply to work-point
ratio and its negative effect on work incentives is by Peter Schran, *The Development
of Chinese Agriculture,* pp. 167–173, 180–182; unfortunately his research is limited to
the pre-1959 period. Also see Parish and Whyte, *Village and Family,* pp. 62–72, for
the 1970s.

96. Putting work points in command was associated with Liu Shaoqi and the "capitalist roaders." "Zhengque chuli guojia, jiti, geren zhi wenti guanxi" (Correctly Deal with
the Relationship Among the State, the Collective, and the Individual), *RMRB* 18 August 1975:2, criticizes "putting work points in command." This article argued for higher
grain sales.

97. One such case was of a team in Jilin, where everyone got the same amount of grain
regardless of work points. I 8/18680. Parish and Whyte, *Village and Family,* p. 66, found
this for a few areas in Guangdong. They also found the opposite phenomenon, where all
the grain was distributed according to work points. According to my interviews, the latter
was the least common practice.

98. "Renwu laowu, fenpei kouliang fuhe zhengce ma?" (Five Persons Paid as Five Laborers, Does This Method of Grain Distribution Accord with Policy?), *DZRB* 27 March
1980:2.

tributed on a per capita basis only 30 percent and the amount based on labor 70 percent.[99] In other areas during 1979 there was strong sentiment to keep the 7:3 ratio.[100] Interestingly, the official policy stated in the New 60 Articles, crafted to increase peasant enthusiasm for production and promote the slogan of "more income for more work," upheld the old ratios of 6:4 and 7:3.[101]

When one understands their significance, it is easy to see why these ratios, 7:3 or 6:4 but particularly 7:3, have been criticized as weakening incentives for collective labor. In low grain-producing areas, grain-short areas, and areas with no cash to distribute, the most important determinant of the amount of grain a household received from the team was neither the number of work points nor the number of family members (termed "labor powers," *laodong li*) participating in collective labor.[102] Grain was distributed according to the total number of people (*kou*, literally "mouths") within an individual household who were entitled to the basic per capita grain distribution.[103] A hardworking peasant with many work points but few mouths to feed sometimes received less grain than a neighbor who did not work as hard but had more children. Of course, I am referring to the bare subsistence without concern for overdrawing or going into debt. The fact remains, nonetheless, that a family with many small children may have actually received more grain even though they had very few working members. The inequity of such a system led some peasants to grumble, only half-jokingly, that "some labor all day in the fields to get their grain, while others labor at night"—meaning that some get their grain by producing more children.[104]

In addition to the limits on the amount of grain distributed as work-

99. "Zai xiashou yu fenzhong kuoda anlao fenpei bili" (Increase the Scope of Using "To Each According to His Work" in Summer Grain Distribution), *RMRB* 3 June 1980:1.

100. A county vice-secretary in Shandong insisted that the ratio remain at 7:3. "Sanzhe jiangu zhengce duixian" (Take into Account the Interests of All Three Parties, Make Good the Policy), *RMRB* 14 July 1979:2. My interviews conducted in 1979–1980 reveal that views like those of the Shandong vice-secretary were not uncommon.

101. "A Document of the Central Committee of the Chinese Communist Party *Chung-fa* No. 4: "Regulations on the Work in Rural People's Communes (Draft)" (hereafter cited "New 60 Articles"), Article 44, p. 108.

102. The term "labor powers" refers to able-bodied adult peasants capable of full-time work.

103. Peasants I interviewed were particularly critical of this practice. Sent-down youth who were assigned to Four Cleans work teams also commented on the inequity of this system, particularly where no distinction was made according to age. Peasants criticized this by saying that the number of work points might continue to go up, but (grain) income does not go up. I 10/12480.

104. This joke was related to me by a Four Cleans work team member, later a sent-down youth for a number of years in southwestern China. Interviewee 17. Only after she stressed this point to me, and other peasants brought up similar points, did I fully realize the importance of family size in determining a family's grain consumption.

point grain, each province and county set ceilings on the basic grain ration and, in some instances, on the total amount of grain an individual peasant could draw from the collective harvest, regardless of labor input. Each county party standing committee, with the approval of the provincial authorities, set grain distribution limits according to area and period.[105] The limits were fairly stable, but, as one county cadre explained, the county might decide to be more lenient one year only to be less lenient the next. The committees argued that if the peasants were given "extra grain" in the first year, then they could do with less the following year.[106]

In Anhui, for example, a 1974 directive limited the basic grain ratio to 450 *jin*. Limits were also imposed on the maximum worth of each work point. These strict limits fit with the Campaign to Criticize Lin Biao and Confucius, couched in terms of opposition to the philosophy of "dividing all and eating all," one of the many negative influences attributed to Liu Shaoqi.[107] Instead of getting more rations, the team had to sell the surplus to the state as "loyalty [to Mao] grain" (*zhongzi liang*). Prior to this, increases in this area's grain ration were more in line with the actual increases in the harvest. The harvest of 1974 was particularly good so the peasants would have received a very large grain distribution, something the state apparently was not willing to condone. Previous years' distributions were between 300 and 400 *jin*.[108]

County officials seemed to have relative autonomy in setting these limits. For example, around 1976 a county first secretary decided that the peasants' basic grain ration should be limited to only thirty to forty *jin* per month. Work team members sent to enforce this ruling considered it quite low for a relatively high grain-producing area, particularly given the liberalizing winds that began to appear in the national leadership at that time.[109] The state's concern with limits on peasant grain rations is, of course, intimately tied to the definition of the surplus. The state's purpose was to ensure that increasing amounts of grain would be left after the distribution of the basic shares. This grain could then be

105. The county party standing committee also set the minimum amounts of grain that a peasant should receive from each harvest. The amount varied annually. From my limited data it is difficult to give any specific numbers. The existence of such limits was confirmed by a number of former county- and provincial-level cadres.

106. I 1/19680; I 1/2680.

107. See, for example, "Chuliang chucao beizhan beihuang" (Store Grain and Straw, Prepare for War and Natural Disaster), *Hongqi* 1969, no. 8, pp. 54–58. Also see "Zhengque chuli guojia," *RMRB* 18 August 1975:2, for a discussion of the overly large amount of work-point grain given in certain areas.

108. I 21/11180.

109. I 1/19680; I 1/2680.

labeled "surplus grain" (*yuliang*) that the state could *legitimately* extract in the form of government purchases.

A DEPENDENT PEASANTRY

The state's ability to define the surplus indicates the power of the Chinese state. Key to this was China's decision to add the element of rationing to the basic Soviet procurement model and create a monopoly for the purchase *and* sale of grain (*tonggou tongxiao*).[110] This effectively controlled the distribution of grain and had broad political and economic implications for China. Rationing devalued money as an effective currency of exchange and tied peasants to the countryside and collectives for subsistence. Markets were restricted, and peasants were confined to closed corporate villages.

Through collectivizing agriculture, closing the grain markets, institutionalizing unified purchase and supply, and, most important, instituting the system of grain rationing, the state separated the peasants from their harvest. A peasant's work effort was no longer sufficient to secure even a subsistence livelihood for himself or his family. The worth of his labor and his share of the harvest was determined by the state and obtained from the collective. A peasant depended on the collective for his economic well-being. At the same time, these regulations inflated the value of grain, making it a currency of exchange.

This chapter has shown that neither the production team as a corporate group nor peasants as individuals had autonomy over the amount left in the village. It is difficult to measure peasant perceptions of fairness in distributing the harvest and whether such perceptions affected their political action. In this chapter I have tried to gauge these perceptions by delineating how the basic shares of the harvest were determined and limited and how the amount affected their subsistence.

Peasant perceptions also depended on how the surplus was apportioned because the state did not simply extract the surplus from the countryside. Once the basic shares had been allotted, the questions of who was going to get the surplus and how it was going to be used remained. The state would certainly procure a portion of the surplus, but teams as well as individual peasants were also supposed to benefit from it. How much would be left for the teams and how much for individual peasant loans? I will examine these issues in the next two chapters.

110. The Soviets have occasionally used food rationing, but this is the exception, not the rule.

CHAPTER 3

The Struggle over the Surplus

Vivienne Shue writes that the state grain procurement system, *tonggou tongxiao,* was well received in the transition to socialism.[1] She argues that the government provided peasants with strong incentives to sell grain to the state, offering competitive prices and security in 1953–1954. Although Shue may be right, the conditions she describes held only for a short period of time. The context in which the procurement system operated changed markedly, but the procurement system itself changed little after its initial implementation; in large part, that is the problem.[2]

When first offered, the state price was competitive with the market price, but this price remained the same for more than a decade. The enticement of extra profits gained from reneging on the private grain contracts was a one-time opportunity. The voluntary nature of grain sales soon took on an oppressive character that has led to calling these sales "forced procurements" and "hidden forms of taxation." The Chinese themselves now admit

> The unified purchase system represented an integration of exchange and paying taxes. . . . When the price purchase and sales system was in force, selling/delivering grain was equal to paying taxes. The state purchase price scheme was like a tax rate schedule.[3]

1. See Shue, *Peasant China,* pp. 214–245.
2. The implementation of the procurement system illustrates Grindle's point about the importance of policy *context*. The policy essentially stayed the same, but the circumstances in which it functioned changed dramatically. Grindle, "Policy Content."
3. Development Institute, Agricultural Research Center of the State Council, "A Memorandum on the Foodgrain Issue," pp. 12, 14.

Under collectivization, peasants increasingly lost control over the distribution of their harvest. As I discussed in Chapter 2, the definition of surplus became one crafted by the state, not defined by peasant or even collective needs. The formation of communes finalized the process whereby the state placed the collective between the peasants and their harvest. Peasant producers no longer had legal right to the harvest; it belonged to the collective. Peasants were the producers, but they could not ensure that their own subsistence needs were met before they had to sell grain to the state. They became dependent on the collective for their share of the grain. The state set the guidelines for the apportionment of the harvest and designated the peasant's share as merely one collective expense. The issue of sales was no longer a matter that peasant households could decide. The production team, as a corporate group represented by the team leader, became the relevant decision maker, who served as the link with the larger polity.

The context in which the grain procurement operated thus needs to be carefully studied to understand the complex reasons for resistance to procurements; it is more than whether peasants were able to decide how much to sell to the state or that procurement prices were low. The following sections examine the procurement process within the economic as well as political context of rural China for the period from commune reorganization in 1959–1960 to the abolition of unified procurement in 1985.

THE QUESTION OF SUBSISTENCE

Underlying peasant resistance to procurements was concern for subsistence. The collectives, and the peasants within them, lacked guarantees that their basic shares would be met. State demands for its supplementary share, that is, procurements, cut into the collectives' and ultimately the peasants' only legitimate claim on the harvest. In grain-short teams or teams with barely sufficient grain—unless they had reserves or could borrow from neighboring teams—any amount the state took directly affected the amount team members could consume that year.

The state made clear in the mid-1950s the priority of its share after peasants, still wary of the state-induced food shortages in 1953, resisted grain sales in 1955 and 1956 and took more than "sufficient" shares of the harvest. The state declared that its claims, both in tax *and* in procurements, should get first priority.[4] The shortages and famine caused by overprocurement during the Great Leap Forward demonstrated the inviolability of this claim.[5]

Not until output dropped and peasant incentive for production was decimated by the shortages and famine of the Great Leap Forward did the state back off and officially deemphasize the priority of its claim. Since the Cultural Revolution, the state has proclaimed "the necessity of taking into consideration the interests of the state, collective, and individual" (*bixu jiangu guojia liyi jiti liyi he geren liyi*).[6] The welfare of the peasants must be respected, and the various regulations for setting sales quotas must be adhered to. A team should not have to sell grain and then buy it back from the state. The state should not take more than a team can afford to sell and "buy over the top grain" (*mai guotou liang*).[7]

Yet, in spite of these later policy statements, there is strong evidence that in the decade before 1979 the shares of the collective and the peasants consistently received second and third priority, respectively. A 1979 indictment of the errors of the Cultural Revolution in *People's Daily* charged that the individual's interest came last after that of the state and

4. See, for example, "Nongyeshe liangshi fenpeide cixu" (The Procedure for Grain Distribution in Agricultural Cooperatives), *Liangshi* 1957, no. 5, pp. 5–6; "Chungeng qianhou xuanchuan liangshi 'sanding'" (Propagate the 'Three Regulations' Before and After Spring Planting), *DGB* 12 March 1957; as well as "Guanyu dangqian liangshi gongzuode zhibiao" (Targets for Present Grain Work) *Liangshi gongzuo* 1956, no. 22, pp. 1–2, which state the proper order of division as (1) taxes and sales (*zhenggou renwu*); (2) seed, basic grain ration, and fodder; and finally (3) work-point grain and grain for sideline industries. Also see "Guanyu muqian xiaoshou he qiuhou liangshi tonggou tongxiao gongzuode zhibiao" (Instructions on Present Grain Sales and Postautumn Unified Purchase and Sales Work), *Liangshi gongzuo* 1956, no. 20, pp. 1–2. For more recent discussions of this point, see, for example, "Jiashanxian dazai hou liangshi da fudu zengchan" (Jiashan County Greatly Increased Grain Production After Natural Disaster), *RMRB* 8 October 1979:2. Donnithorne, *China's Economic System*, p. 348, sees this hierarchy of priorities as a reversal of past practices. I would argue that the state's claim has always come first in practice.

5. See Bernstein, "Stalinism, Famine."

6. See, for example, *Nongcun liangshi*, p. 62.

7. Ibid., p. 79. Grain was resold to teams as collectives. Teams then apportioned shares to individual peasants whose average rations did not meet the minimal twenty-six to twenty-seven-*jin* level to which all peasants officially were entitled. The amount of *fanxiao liang* received by peasants equaled the difference between the amount of grain the peasants actually received from the collective team harvest and the twenty-six to twenty-seven-*jin* minimum. As I have suggested, it was questionable whether the state in all instances sold needy teams this grain and did so promptly. Some peasant informants complained that they could "starve" before the grain was sent. The price the teams paid for *fanxiao liang* was the same price that they received from the state for selling grain. Ibid., p. 133.

the collective.[8] In 1982 Wan Li announced that 150 million people in the countryside suffered from a shortage of grain.[9] Such admissions, with warnings to cadres not to buy "over the top grain," strongly suggest that the peasants' basic share of the harvest continued to be encroached upon regardless of official policy.[10]

The questions are whether such examples were simply exceptions, the result of local excesses and overzealous cadres, or whether they reflect inherent features of the procurement system itself. On the surface the state appears concerned to distinguish between the grain-rich and grain-poor teams. The state categorized teams and brigades according to whether they were "grain-surplus" (*yuliang*), "grain-deficit" (*queliang*), or "grain-sufficient" (*liang zizu* or *buyu buque liang*).[11] Such categorization determined whether teams were liable to sell grain to the state. These ratings were based on the same information used to compute the agricultural tax: the amount of land and its output for both late and early crops divided by the population of that team.[12]

Grain-surplus teams were generally those whose average basic grain ration was at least thirty to thirty-five *jin* of unhusked grain (including all distributions of potatoes, corn, sorghum, legumes, and millet that the Chinese consider coarse and less desirable) per person per month.[13] If the average ration fell below that "safety level" (*baohu xian*), teams technically were not liable for the basic quota sale or any other type of grain sale to the state. Grain-deficit teams were those whose grain rations averaged only twenty-six to twenty-seven *jin* of unhusked grain per month; these teams did not have to sell any grain to the state and

8. "Jiashanxian," *RMRB* 8 October 1979:2.
9. "Jinyibu fazhan," *RMRB* 23 December 1982:1.
10. See, for example, *Nongcun liangshi*, p. 62.
11. Ibid., pp. 78–79; I 4/12280. Similar categories were given to households, mutual aid teams, and collectives prior to the formation of communes in the early to mid-1950s. See Donnithorne, *China's Economic System*, pp. 346–347.
12. I 4/30180; I 3/15480.
13. *Nongcun liangshi*, p. 81. These figures vary and even then guidelines were not always strictly followed. An official granary handbook from Guangdong, for example, states that for most areas if the average distribution of grain per person does not reach thirty *jin* (including corn, legumes, and potatoes), then the team does not have to sell the state grain; *Nongcun liangshi*, p. 81. Former residents of Guangdong said the limit was thirty-five *jin*, I 5/4380. The figures more than likely varied from one region to another, even within the same province, as did the guidelines for issuing relief, and depended on previous levels of grain consumption in an area. Some areas received special consideration because of their economic specialization. The average grain ration in key grain-producing regions could reach forty-five *jin* before teams had to sell quota grain, but key forestry and cash crop areas and those engaged in freshwater fish breeding were allowed quotas of only thirty-five to forty *jin*. *Nongcun liangshi*, pp. 84–85.

TABLE 7.   GRAIN CLASSIFICATION OF PRODUCTION TEAMS

Classification	Minimum Grain Ration, Average per Person (*jin*/month)	Grain Sales Responsibility	Relief Eligibility
Grain surplus	30–35	yes	no
Grain sufficient	28–29	no	no
Grain deficit	26–27	no	yes

were eligible for relief.[14] Grain-sufficient teams were those that were neither grain-deficit nor grain-surplus. Grain-sufficient teams did not need to sell grain to the state, but they were also not automatically eligible for relief (see Table 7).[15]

The problem was that a team's official grain classification, like the agricultural tax rates, failed to be modified periodically as conditions changed. For example, areas in Fujian kept the same designations from at least the start of the Cultural Revolution in the mid-1960s until 1978 in spite of production changes.[16] Those brigades or teams, originally listed as grain-surplus but later grain-deficit, still had to bear the burden of selling grain to the state; likewise, those teams that were originally grain-short but later improved production legally did not have to sell grain to the state. As a result, on the one hand, an unfair burden was put on newly grain-deficit teams, and, on the other, the state lost grain. One doubts, however, given the annual assessment system, which I will discuss below, whether teams that increased their grain output could often avoid grain sales. The more common problem involved grain-deficit teams forced to sell grain.

Policy aberrations aside, the procurement system had inherent problems that affected all production teams, not just grain-deficit ones. Although there is disagreement as to what constitutes an adequate level of subsistence, the discrepancy between China's definition and the one widely accepted by international relief organizations is significant. Aid organizations and economists generally define "self-sufficient" as equiv-

14. My interviewee (I 4/12280) came from a team that was categorized as grain-deficit and did not sell grain to the state.
15. *Nongcun liangshi*, p. 79.
16. Interviews with former team leaders and accountants from that area. I 4/3180; I 3/15480.

TABLE 8.   CHINESE AND INTERNATIONAL
DEFINITIONS OF SUBSISTENCE

	Deficit	Self-Sufficient	Surplus
	(per capita distribution of unhusked grain in *jin*/month)		
International	44	45–51.5	51.6
Chinese	26–27	27–29	30–35

SOURCES: Walker, *Food Grain Procurement*, p. 3; *Nongcun liangshi zhengce zhaibian*, pp. 79–81.

alent to 45 to 51.5 *jin* of unhusked grain per month, providing 1,700 to 1,900 net calories per day; "surplus" is defined as beginning at 51.5 *jin* of unhusked grain per month, providing 1,900 to 2,100 net calories per day.[17] As indicated above, Chinese guidelines defined a team as having "surplus" when peasant grain rations were between 30 and 35 *jin* per month—at least 20 *jin* less than international standards (see Table 8). Levels considered below subsistence internationally were considered above the surplus level in China. Peasants who received such rations were expected to sell the surplus grain to the state.

Not surprisingly, Kenneth Walker, who used standard definitions of surplus, concluded that "there was no obvious 'cut-off' level of per capita output at which provincial surpluses ceased." For the period 1953–1957 the state procured grain

in all the "rich" provinces where per capita output exceeded 309 kilograms (51.5 *jin*), in most of the provinces falling within the hypothetical "self-sufficiency" range of 275–309 kilograms (45–51.5 *jin*) per head, and even in three out of four provinces where per capita output was in the "deficit" range (below 275 kilograms, i.e., 45 *jin*).[18]

The Chinese simply did not view such areas as grain-deficit.

One should not, however, confuse these figures with a peasant's actual annual grain consumption. As later chapters will show, the collective and the peasants also had means to secure a share of the surplus to supplement their officially allotted basic rations. My purpose here is to

17. See Walker, *Food Grain*, p. 3, where he notes that Chen Yun cited 280 kilograms of grain per head of rural population (per month) as "sufficient" for all uses. For a technical discussion of the nutritional intake by Chinese peasants, see Vaclav Smil, "China's Energetics" and his "China's Food Availability"; also see Piazza, *Trends*.
18. Walker, *Food Grain*, p. 72.

establish that the amount of grain the state defined as sufficient for the peasant ration before it took its second share of the harvest was in practice insufficient by most standards. Some peasants resisted increasing grain sales to the state for this reason. Some peasants were fighting for subsistence.

Whether peasants felt that the state was depriving them of their "fair share" is a complicated question. For those whose subsistence was threatened, the answer is fairly clear. The more difficult case is grain-surplus teams where the state might not have reduced the grain ration but failed to increase the rations as harvests increased.[19] The resistance of grain-surplus teams to sell grain poses the most perplexing question: why would such teams keep their grain rather than sell it to the state?

PROCUREMENT PRICES

What happened to the economic incentives, which Shue describes, that were built into the procurement system? As the system developed, the state increasingly differentiated the type of sales and provided grain-surplus teams with a variety of sales options based on their grain situation and needs. Procurements were divided into quota sales and over-quota sales; the post-1979 reforms added a third category, negotiated sales.[20] Overquota sales were further distinguished by the kind of incentive offered by the state, with prices keyed to the category of sale.

The problem was the reward structure. As the terms of the various sales described below will make clear, the state used other than economic incentives for the bulk of their purchases. The state closed the free grain markets in 1957 and proceeded to implement a grain monopoly that forced peasants to sell grain only to the state and at state-fixed prices that increasingly became inadequate and certainly much lower than those on the black market. Thus, the one-time high price, competitive with the market in 1953–1954, was soon perceived as unfairly low. Rather than being allowed to float, procurement prices were fixed. Price increases occurred only in 1961, 1966, and then not again until 1979.[21]

---

19. Steven Butler found that the peasants he studied accepted the responsibility of increasing sales to the state largely because in that particular village peasant consumption improved and income increased. But that was in 1980; it is unclear if the same situation prevailed in the pre-1978 period as well. Steven Butler, "Price Scissors," p. 102.

20. *Nongcun liangshi*, pp. 79–86.

21. See Chapter 8.

The average procurement price of grain per 100 *jin* averaged six *yuan* in 1952, nine *yuan* in 1961, and thirteen *yuan* in 1979.[22]

The majority of sales were achieved through administrative measures and political pressure. Grain sold under the basic quota was based on administrative pressure; overquota sales were based on peer pressure and political pressure from superiors; political sales were based on mobilizational pressures. Only the barter sales offered the peasants a material incentive for selling grain.

BASIC QUOTA SALE (*gouliang*)

Each grain-surplus team had to sell at minimum state-set prices (*paijia*) a fixed basic quota of grain to the state. This, along with the agricultural tax, was known as the "tax and sales responsibility" (*zhenggou renwu*).[23] This basic quota originally was set for three years; after 1970 it was set for five years.[24] A team was obligated to sell this amount unless it faced a disaster of sufficient severity to merit an exemption or reduction.[25] The inevitability of this sale has caused this procurement to be termed "forced delivery" or a form of "hidden taxation." Such labels capture the impact of such sales on the peasants but are technically incorrect. Contrary to the impression some analysts have given, peasants were paid for this part of their responsibility to the state; only grain for the agricultural tax was taken from the peasants without compensation.[26]

OVERQUOTA SALES (*chaogou liang* or *sanchao liang*)

Overquota sales became the major issue of contention each year between the state and the peasants. Unlike the quota sales, there were no

22. Zhou Jiarang, "Nongchanpin jiage zhizhi jiangzuo: zonglun" (Lectures on the Price of Agricultural Products: General Discussion), *Jiage lilun yu shijian* (Theory and Practice of Price), 1985, no. 1, pp. 50–55.

23. This was also referred to as selling surplus grain (*yuliang*). Maxwell and Nolan call this the fixed-quota purchase (*dinggou*). Neville Maxwell and Peter Nolan, "The Procurement of Grain," p. 305.

24. *Nongcun liangshi*, p. 79. Maxwell and Nolan, "The Procurement of Grain," state that the quotas were set for five years starting in 1953. My interviews with a Guangdong granary manager indicate that the five-year figure only dates from 1971; from 1953 to 1970 the quotas were set for three years. I 5/4380. This is confirmed by *Liangshi jingji* (Grain Economics), pp. 63–65. In 1982, policy again changed back to three years; ibid.

25. According to one source, the harvest loss had to equal 30 percent before a reduction of the basic sales quota was granted. I 5/3580.

26. See, for example, Walker, *Food Grain*, pp. 49–51.

predetermined annual targets for overquota sales; they were based on "negotiation."[27] Originally this was just the amount of grain sold to the state above a team's basic quota, at the same low basic quota price.[28] Peasants were expected to make these sales for political and patriotic reasons. Particularly during the early 1950s and the Korean War, when there was a campaign to "resist America," peasants were called upon to sell "patriotic surplus grain" (aiguo yuliang). The state did not offer a higher price for this procurement until around 1960.

Bonuses became necessary after the dramatic decrease in output caused by the Great Leap Forward, but they disappeared in 1966 when a general increase in the basic procurement price was instituted. Price incentives were not offered again for overquota sales until 1971,[29] when they were priced 20 to 30 percent above the basic procurement price.[30] In addition, a bonus system was reinstated, including awards such as extra fertilizer, fodder, cloth rations, bicycles, and tractors, for teams that sold the most grain.[31]

Before a team was eligible for overquota prices, it officially had to fulfill its basic quota sale[32] and allow an average monthly grain ration of fifty jin per person in key grain-producing areas (i.e., areas where each person sold more than 700 jin of unhusked grain to the state).[33] In practice, as with the basic quota sales, the figure for average minimum rations varied.[34]

27. Nongcun liangshi, p. 92.
28. Maxwell and Nolan, "The Procurement of Grain," p. 304. The precise date this system began is not clear. One source gives 1960; Liangshi jingji, p. 107. Another gives 1965; Zhang Ruhai, Nongchan jiage wenti yanjiu (Research on the Problem of Agricultural Prices), pp. 134–135.
29. Maxwell and Nolan, "The Procurement of Grain," p. 304, date the price increase to 1972–1973.
30. Nongcun liangshi, pp. 80–81. Zhang, Nongchan, pp. 134–135. The official regulations state that, in addition to the 30-percent higher price, teams that sold this overquota grain would also be allowed to buy extra fertilizer—25 jin of chemical fertilizer for every 100 jin of rice (dami). Nongcun liangshi, pp. 80–81. Some informants said the price differential might be even larger, depending on whether they sought extra fertilizer. Other peasants said that no fertilizer was given for overquota sales, only for grain sold as barter sales. See the following category of sales.
31. I 21/13180; I 15/12180. Liangshi jingji, p. 108.
32. A team leader from Guangdong said that when grain was delivered to the state granaries, it could be designated as any of the above types of sales or as tax grain, if it were of sufficient quality; but this is contrary to official regulations. Apparently in this area there was no set priority of which type of grain sale had to be completed first. In his area only for the negotiated grain sales (yigou liang) did there seem to be strict rules on the necessity of fulfilling the basic and overquota sales first. I 1/24680.
33. Nongcun liangshi, p. 85. Limits of 420 jin of unhusked grain or more are also given; ibid., p. 80.
34. For example, a granary manager (I 5/4380) insisted that the minimum ration figure was forty-five jin, when the granary handbook for his province cited fifty jin.

BARTER SALES (*huangou liang*)

This was a variant of overquota grain sales and like other overquota sales[35] could be transacted only after the basic quota sale had been met.[36] Teams did not get a discount price on the items they wanted in exchange for the grain sale. The existence of this barter sale is a good example of the limited use of money in the commune economy and the value of grain as a currency of exchange. The incentive was the opportunity to purchase larger quantities of rationed goods, such as fertilizer, sugar, cooking oil, and cloth, otherwise unavailable at state prices. For example, if a team sold one hundred *jin* of grain to the state under this arrangement, it would receive the cash for the sale and the right to purchase an extra ten *jin* of oil. If three hundred *jin* of grain were sold, then a team might be able to buy an additional one hundred *jin* of fertilizer. The precise terms of trade were decided after a team submitted an application to the county government. In some areas, fertilizer was the hardest to secure, and oil and sugar were much easier to obtain.

The price teams received for grain sold under barter agreements varied. According to some reports, it was lower than the overquota grain price, even though this grain could be used in overquota sales. In some areas, the procurement price for barter sales was the same as the basic grain quota sales price; in others, the price was lower than overquota but higher than the basic quota price.[37]

POLITICAL SALES

This category of sales is not mentioned in any official handbook. I have chosen to name certain sales political to highlight the pressures placed on teams to sell grain, but technically they are subsumed under the category of overquota sales. The price teams received was slightly

35. Lardy, *Agriculture*, p. 34, refers to "exchange purchase" (*huangou*) as grain that peasants delivered to the state in exchange for the right either to repurchase the equivalent quantities of grain at a later date or to purchase a different type of grain. According to my understanding, that type of transaction was not *huangou liang* but *zhouzhuan liang* (circulation grain). This system was pushed in the late 1950s when the state was making a big effort to build grain reserves. See Chapter 4.

36. According to *Nongcun liangshi*, p. 91, this category did not exist in the mid-1970s. A cadre (Interviewee 21) from north China also said it did not exist in his area. But according to most other peasants as well as to a granary manager from Guangdong, this type of sale did exist. In the case of fertilizer, peasants in certain areas probably just sold extra grain as overquota sales and took the bonus of fertilizer according to official regulations, as I described above.

37. I 5/3480; I 1/6680.

higher than for basic procurements but not necessarily as high as for other overquota sales.[38] The "war preparedness" grain (*zhanbei liang*) and "loyalty to Mao" grain (*Mao Zedong zhongzi liang*) are examples of this category of sales. Such sales were at their height from 1969 to 1971, but in some places they were still implemented as late as 1974.[39]

Nominally voluntary, quotas were not usually sent down from the upper levels. In practice, significant political pressure was used to compel teams to make such sales. Grain sales became a measure of a team's "loyalty" and "redness." Teams were mobilized to sell "loyalty to Mao" grain with little regard for levels of individual peasant grain consumption. Grain-surplus teams, barely grain-sufficient teams, and sometimes grain-deficit teams were subjected to these pressures. Fear of being accused of lacking loyalty prompted some team leaders to vie with one another in making loyalty sales. In some cases, they pledged so much grain that team members were left with insufficient rations.[40] In some areas, the amount sold under pressure was incorporated into the regular quota sales teams were expected to sell the following year. The state assumed that if a team could sell extra grain one year, it could sell it the next.[41]

THE SCISSORS EFFECT AND THE COSTS OF PRODUCTION

Inadequate procurement prices are most apparent when viewed in the context of grain production cost. Former team leaders and peasants alike complained that the cost of production was more than the procurement price of the grain. Western economists and researchers have come to similar conclusions.[42] In his field work in Dahe Commune in Hebei province, Butler found that grain yields doubled but that income distributed, as well as net production team income during the same period, stagnated.[43]

38. I 21/11180.

39. In 1971 and 1972 one team in Anhui each year sold 5,000 *jin* of "loyalty to Mao" grain. This was done under pressure from the brigade leaders and party secretary. Then in 1974 a limit of 450 *jin* was set as the maximum amount of grain that peasants could receive from the harvest. The extra surplus was then sold to the state as "loyalty to Mao" grain. I 21/11180.

40. I 5/3680; I 21/11180.

41. "Hexian shedui yingyou de zizhuquan nongye shengchan jiang geng kuai fazhan" (The Communes and Production Teams of He County Should Have Autonomy, Agricultural Production Will Rise Even Faster), *RMRB* 6 February 1979:2.

42. See, for example, Lardy, "State Intervention."

43. Butler, "Price Scissors," p. 98.

Grain production became so unprofitable largely because the costs of agricultural inputs, such as chemical fertilizer, increased relative to the low procurement price of grain. Chemical fertilizer is a key input for higher yields, but it is expensive and scarce. Peasants commonly complained that the marginal cost of the extra fertilizer was more than the profit from the increased grain sales. One team leader said that chemical fertilizer consumed 15 percent of the team's total income. Many a cadre summed up the situation with the comment, "To get higher yields, a team has to buy chemical fertilizer; growing grain is money-losing (*peiben*)."[44]

Since the decision to reform agriculture in late 1978, such complaints have been openly discussed in the press. In Gaocheng county, Hebei, during 1971–1977, when grain production was stressed at the expense of cash crops and sidelines, costs of production increased from 35 to 47 percent of the team's total income.[45] A 1976 Chinese study showed that of the five types of grain—rice, wheat, corn, barley, and sorghum— only rice was profitable. Even so, the profit margin was a mere 7.6 percent (see Table 9). All economic crops, in contrast, were profitable. From 1965 to 1977, total production costs per *mu* rose by 50 percent while production increased by only 30 percent. During the same period, the average price of the twelve main agricultural products increased by only 13.6 percent, while costs increased by 20 percent.[46] From such calculations the state increased the basic procurement price of grain (to 11.56 *yuan* per 100 *jin* in 1979) so that peasants could have a profit margin of roughly 30 percent.[47]

The limited value of money as a currency of exchange due to rationing and the closure of free markets further undermined the sales incentive system and encouraged peasants to resist sales to the state. In many instances, grain in kind was more valuable than its cash equivalent. Peasants preferred to sell goods for grain tickets rather than money; in Chapter 6 I will further explore grain's use as a currency. It makes sense that peasants, especially poorer ones who have experienced food shortages, preferred to store grain rather than money. Grain could always be

44. I 10/12480; I 19/3680; I 8/18680.

45. "Gaochengxian zenyang gaibian 'gaochan qiongxian' zhuangkuang" (How Did Gaocheng County Change Its Situation of "High-Yield Poor County"?), *RMRB* 8 July 1979:2.

46. Zhang, *Nongchan*, pp. 18–21. A separate study of south China found that for every 100 *jin* of paddy, production costs and agricultural tax averaged 8.97 *yuan;* the average price paid to peasants until 1979 was 10.6 *yuan;* the median price was 10.4.

47. Materials = 4.67 *yuan;* wages = 3.80 *yuan;* agricultural tax = 0.80 *yuan.* Zhou, "Nongchanpin jiage," p. 51.

TABLE 9.   AVERAGE PROCUREMENT PRICES AND
PRODUCTION COSTS FOR AGRICULTURAL PRODUCTS, 1976

Crop	Procurement Price	Production Costs	Profit/Loss
	(*yuan* per *dan* when grown as main crop)		
Grain crops			
Paddy	10.57	9.82	+0.75
Wheat	13.50	14.02	−0.52
Barley	9.23	9.37	−0.14
Maize	9.29	9.33	−0.04
Sorghum	8.77	10.25	−1.48
Average	10.75	10.89	−0.14
Oil-bearing crops			
Peanuts	25.53	23.29	+2.24
Rapeseed	27.70	30.41	−2.71
Sesame	41.56	26.42	+15.14
Average	29.41	26.32	+3.09
Economic crops			
Cotton	107.29	108.10	−0.81
Tobacco	68.82	41.95	+26.87
Hemp[a]	64.37	34.49	+29.88
Sugar[b]	2.46	1.49	+0.97
Average		n.a.[c]	n.a.[c]

SOURCE: Zhang Ruhai, *Nongchanpin jiage wenti yanjiu,* pp. 20–21.
[a] Average of 4 types of hemp.
[b] Data on sugar are incomplete.
[c] Not available because of the incomparability of different economic crops.

exchanged for money, whereas money could not always be exchanged for grain. State procurement prices made it more advantageous to keep the grain, use it for sidelines, or sell it on the black market, where they would receive at least twice the state price. Only the barter sale of grain, which allowed peasants to buy the desired items in short supply, served to improve the peasants' material well-being.[48]

THE POLITICS OF EXTRACTION

Why then did teams, harvest after harvest, "voluntarily pledge" grain sales to the state, when they wanted and needed to keep more grain for

48. Stavis, *People's Communes,* presents a much more positive view of the procurement process. He does not fully appreciate the problem of getting goods in China even when one has money.

TABLE 10.   SETTING OVERQUOTA SALES

Before the Harvest: Top-Down
1. Provincial meeting of prefectures to divide target, based on prefecture harvest estimates
2. Prefecture meeting of counties to divide amended target, based on county harvest estimates
3. Counties issue targets to communes based on commune estimates
4. Communes issue targets to brigades based on brigade estimates
5. Brigades issue targets to teams based on team estimates

After the Harvest: Bottom-Up Sales Pledges and Deliveries
1. Team decides on sales pledge
2. Brigade meeting of team leaders: (a) each team announces its sales pledge; (b) team leaders discuss and amend each team's pledge; (c) brigade finalizes and approves each team's pledge
3. Commune meeting of brigade heads: repeats process 2 a, b, c, at brigade level
4. County meeting of commune heads: repeats process at 2 a, b, c, at commune level
5. Communes send totals to prefectures and province: final approval given
6. Teams deliver grain

consumption and personal or collective use, when prices were low and sales incentives were few? The answer lies in the political process by which the sales quotas were set and the pledges made.

This process is important in understanding how the procurement system worked, but it also sheds light on the character of the larger political system, particularly the dynamic of its bureaucratic politics, and reflects both the strength and weakness of the state's ability to implement unpopular policies. From an analytical perspective this process is important because it reflects the room that exists for "negotiation" in the Chinese political system, a system traditionally understood as a command economy.[49] At the same time it shows how the state allowed negotiations but not compromise of its ultimate objectives.

The key to the state's ability to force teams to pledge increasingly large grain sales centered on the use of political coercion, which more than compensated for the lack of economic incentives. Officials at each level of the agricultural hierarchy were pressured to meet the state's procurement targets and applied similar pressure to subordinate levels. The behavior of each level, however, differed depending on its position in the bureaucratic hierarchy. Those higher-level cadres, paid by the state and

49. See David Michael Lampton, "Chinese Politics," pp. 11–41, for a useful analysis of bargaining in the Chinese bureaucratic process.

not dependent on the well-being of the local levels, were less likely to be torn by conflicting loyalties and more content to simply pass on the targets. Those lower down the administrative hierarchy, such as brigade and especially team leaders, had to meet state targets but also to protect their local interests. The result was a mix of administrative pressure, top-down targets, bureaucratic bargaining, and grass-roots manipulation, evasion, and participation.

The administrative hierarchy from the province to the production team submitted complex reports and participated in a series of meetings that finalized target quotas and amended quotas, pledges, and actual deliveries. The process can be divided into two phases, as Table 10 illustrates. In the first, before the harvest was in and after crop estimates had been sent from lower levels, targets were set and sent from the "top down"; in the second, after the harvest was in, grain sales pledges went from the "bottom up."

TOP-DOWN TARGETS

The first step toward setting the annual quota was to have teams estimate their current year's yield (*guchan*).[50] This occurred each season about two weeks prior to the actual harvesting. The team leader along with his accountant, accompanied by a brigade cadre or higher-level official, went to the fields to inspect the crop and estimate the potential yield.

Higher-level officials would sometimes use a divide-and-rule strategy and send other team leaders along to ensure accurate estimates. After this on-site inspection, the team accountant and team leader had to prepare an estimate of the team's yield and send it to the brigade. The accompanying brigade cadre made his own record of the expected harvest. The upper levels used these annual estimates of the harvest to set their grain procurement targets.

After receiving all of the teams' estimates, the brigade sent them to the commune. The commune then used these figures in the preliminary planning meeting (*guchan jihua huiyi*) called to discuss grain sales. Afterward, the commune aggregated these figures and sent a report to the

50. Press accounts are vague about this process. See, for example, "Xibei gongshe wancheng jiaoshou liangshi renwu" (Xibei Commune Completes Its Grain Procurement Task), *RMRB* 20 October 1961:3; and "Quanmian guanche zhengce, jishi zhenggou qiuliang" (Thoroughly Implement Policies, Procure Autumn Grain in Time), *DGB* 16 October 1961.

county. The county, however, only saw the aggregated figures prepared by the communes; it never saw the raw data for the individual teams and was thus unaware of bad harvests in any particular team, when preparing its initial procurement targets. The county's job prior to harvesting was to conduct a telephone conference with all the communes to spur them in their work and encourage a safe and successful harvest, warning against fire and theft.[51]

Then a series of meetings was held, at the province and succeeding levels of the bureaucracy down to the brigade, to decide and apportion the procurement targets.[52] At the provincial level the prefectural grain bureau met with the provincial party secretary and representatives from other ministries and bureaus involved. The provincial party secretary divided the provincial target among the different prefectures (*diqu*). In a telephone conference the provincial finance office notified prefectural heads of their agricultural tax quota, which would be collected along with the procurements. The provincial grain bureau might also call a meeting of the prefectural grain bureau heads from the most important grain-producing areas (*zhongdian diqu liangshi juzhang huiyi*) or a provincewide grain work conference (*quansheng liangshi yewu gongzuo huiyi*).

By this time, each prefecture had already formulated a grain sales pledge, based on the production estimates it had received from its counties. The total of all the prefectural pledges for the province was calculated, and, if necessary, a compromise figure was negotiated between provincial and prefectural officials. This compromise figure became the final planned grain procurement quota, what I call the amended quota. This quota was then divided among the prefectures and finally among the lower levels. Each prefecture head, in turn, called its own county cadres together to discuss and divide the prefecture's quota.

At this level there was little debate among the county cadres themselves over the apportionment of the quota. The prefectural officials simply allocated the quotas to each county head. Unlike team and brigade cadres, the cadres at these higher levels are state cadres who received set grain rations and set salaries independent of the local grain

51. For the importance of phone conferences as a mode of communication in China's bureaucracy, see Michel Oksenberg, "Methods of Communication."

52. Printed sources contain little information about the quota-setting process. For an exception, see "Zhenggou renwu tanpai banfa" (Measures for Distributing the Procurement Quotas), *DGB* 2 June 1959. My account relies heavily on interviews with former cadres who had direct experience with the annual quota-setting process, especially informants 1, 5, 21, and 29 of my 1979–80 interviews (see Appendix B).

harvest. Their immediate economic welfare was not directly tied to grain sales. They were mainly concerned that enough grain be retained for their level's administrative needs, not that the amounts sold by their administrative level were so high that peasants would have less to eat. At these higher levels the important consideration was whether the cadres realistically thought their subordinate levels would be able to fulfill the targets.

Throughout this process top-down targets were sent, level by level, to the production team. These were the quotas each level was supposed to meet, but the actual amount sold by each level was determined after the harvest. Production teams remained uncertain of the total amount they would have to sell until after the harvest was in.[53]

BOTTOM-UP PLEDGES AND DELIVERY

In the Team. After the harvest, production teams would calculate their anticipated costs and needs. Grain for each fund was put aside; the tax grain and seed grain received first consideration. Teams budgeted simultaneously such expenses as fodder and rations while keeping in mind their anticipated sales quotas. Team leaders did not have free rein in making this budget; it had to be approved by the brigade to ensure compliance within the county limitations and guidelines.

This accounting formed the basis of a team's grain sales pledge to the state. Theoretically, this figure was the outcome of team discussion, but in most cases the decision was the team leader's in consultation with the accountant and possibly the granary manager. The amount that a team actually sold to the state was decided in a series of meetings beginning at the brigade.

At the Brigade. Team leaders attended a meeting of all teams called by the brigade secretary and brigade leader. These brigadewide meetings determined each team's sales. The meetings lasted from one to two weeks after the harvest was completed, when team heads could be spared from directing production and planting for the next crop was well under way. Each team leader presented his sales pledge, and

53. Stavis, *People's Communes,* pp. 70–71, implies that the quotas were set prior to the harvest and that therefore the peasants knew in advance how much they would sell. My research shows that this was not the case. The teams only knew the basic sales quota, which was set for five years. (The overquota sales were set annually after the harvest.) They were not able to keep the grain over and above this amount.

the other team leaders in the brigade discussed whether the pledge was sufficient.

Each team leader was faced with a zero-sum situation. For every *jin* of grain that one team managed not to have to sell, some other team would have to sell in order to fulfill the brigade's quota and comply with the commune's planned procurement. Each team leader thus felt considerable peer pressure to sell as much as possible. All the participants were local peasants with firsthand knowledge of each other's grain situation. If a team leader pledged too small an amount, others would quickly point out that they had personally seen the fields in question and estimated a much bigger harvest.

These meetings were marked by heated discussions, which sometimes turned into shouting matches where red-faced team cadres argued over who should sell how much grain. The brigade secretary's job was to ensure that every team sold at least its minimal share and to settle arguments. If necessary, the brigade secretary would have a heart-to-heart talk with individual team leaders when he felt their pledges inappropriate.

A team leader who wanted to qualify for a lower quota and put the burden on the other teams was caught in a delicate situation. He had to minimize the team's harvest in such a way that he could placate various interests while not appearing to be a poor leader or inept manager who warranted the label of "backward element" (*luohou fenzi*). He had to impress his superiors with evidence of good management, showing increased production and pledging large grain sales. But he also had to keep the team's sales quota as low as possible in order to placate his team members, who expected him to represent their interests and keep more grain in the village. Unlike state cadres, who were paid by the state and were not immediately responsible to the peasants, a team leader had dual roles with conflicting interests: he represented the interests of both the state and the local peasants. In addition, a team leader had to consider his own interests: he needed to keep the quota as low as possible to pay for the team's unauthorized expenses, finance its sideline industry, allow some extra investment in equipment, or simply use as its emergency fund by providing some financial slack.

The most effective way to get a reduced quota was to go outside the formal policy-making arena. A team leader could maneuver only so much within the context of the formal meetings. At most he could argue that his team was plagued by some specialized problem or suffered some special hardship and therefore needed special consideration and a reduced quota. An experienced team leader would likely supplement or even bypass the formal channels of participation to pursue his interest and rely on backstage bargaining and lobbying. Before the quotas were finalized, a team leader might talk informally in the fields or lanes of the village with the brigade cadres, outside both the formal decision-making arena and the presence of other team leaders. A team leader might also rely on a special personal tie with the brigade cadre to persuade him to accept a lower compromise quota.

There were, of course, limits to these informal personal channels of influence. Most brigade secretaries could bend only so far; the pledges, at least in theory, were subject to the other teams' criticism. Most had to be careful not to show too much favoritism. Yet if a team leader got on well with the brigade cadres, chances were good that they would be more receptive to excuses and stories of hardship and poor yields when the team leader publicly argued for a reduced quota. Because brigade cadres played the key role and had the final say at the formal meetings, if a brigade secretary wanted to give a production team a slightly reduced quota, so be it.

Chapter 6 will examine further the discretion exercised by brigade secretaries and the factors that determine which teams benefit from this power. But here one example of a cadre who reduced a team's procurement quota is in order. The brigade cadre's rationale in this case went beyond merely giving the team a break; rather, it signified personal interest because his daughter worked for this team. The team had treated her well and had given her jobs with high work-point values. The team took care of the brigade secretary's daughter, and the brigade secretary took care of the team.[54]

At the Commune and the County.   The team leader's role in negotiating the sales quota ended after the meetings at the brigade. The matter was then out of his hands and left to the brigade secretary, who used the total team pledges as his brigade's sales pledge to the state. The brigade secretary, however, tried to ensure that this figure was in line with the brigade's apportioned target before he presented it to the other brigade secretaries at the next round of meetings, in a process similar to that which took place among the team leaders.

Next, the county's commune secretaries held a meeting to negotiate the amount each commune would deliver. As suggested earlier, these are

54. I 21/22280.

the last meetings where any real debate occurred. At the prefecture and province levels the process involved less bargaining and more planning and dividing. Once the communes' pledges were finalized and tallied by the county, the total became the county's sales pledge. Through this series of meetings, postharvest pledges were made to mesh with preharvest targets. Only after this series of meetings was completed did individual teams actually know how much they would have to deliver to the state that harvest.

Once the targets were finalized, teams had to bear the costs of transporting the tax grain and the basic grain sales to the state granaries. The amount that teams had to move without compensation is called the "public service grain transport figure" (*yiwu yun liang shuliang*). The state was responsible for the transport costs of overquota sales, but it did not pay for the transport of barter-sale grain, grain the state granary kept for the production team (*zhouzhuan liang*), or grain in repayment of a debt (such as back taxes) to the state.[55]

THE PROBLEM OF COMPLIANCE

The success of the state's grain procurement policies relied on a mix of political pressure and discussion. The process may be seen as an example of the bargaining that Lampton attributes to the Chinese political system.[56] At the same time, it highlights an aspect of the political system that is obscured by the use of the term bargaining. Understand that sharp limits are determined by the higher levels that constrain and define the extent to which bargaining occurs at any particular level. The process may be termed bargaining, but it is bargaining in which one's gain reflects another's loss; both cannot win. What one team escaped selling, another would have to make good.

At each level the state employed a divide-and-rule strategy that played teams off each other to attain its needed procurements. Production team leaders, at the bottom of the agricultural bureaucracy, were the key political actors in this process. They were allowed to discuss their sales quota, but the political pressure combined with the peer pressure from other team leaders in the brigade forced them to agree to sell at least a minimum amount of grain to the state.

55. *Nongcun liangshi,* pp. 89–90, provides details on distances and weights carried by peasants using different means of transport.
56. Lampton, "Chinese Politics."

TABLE 11.   PER CAPITA GRAIN PRODUCTION AND
PROCUREMENT, 1952−1978

Year	Per Capita Production (tons/person)	Per Capita Net Procurement (tons/person)	Change in Per Capita Net Procurement (percent)
1952	.326	.056	—
1953	.327	.070	25.0
1954	.326	.061	−12.9
1955	.346	.068	11.5
1956	.359	.054	−20.6
1957	.357	.062	14.8
1958	.362	.076	22.6
1959	.310	.087	14.5
1960	.270	.058	−33.3
1961	.278	.049	−15.5
1962	.288	.046	−6.1
1963	.296	.050	8.7
1964	.326	.055	10.0
1965	.327	.057	3.6
1966	.350	.063	10.5
1967	.347	.060	−4.8
1968	.323	.059	−1.7
1969	.317	.051	−13.6
1970	.350	.061	19.6
1971	.355	.057	−6.6
1972	.333	.047	−17.5
1973	.359	.056	19.1
1974	.366	.058	3.6
1975	.372	.058	0.0
1976	.370	.053	−8.6
1977	.361	.048	−9.4
1978	.386	.054	12.5

SOURCES: Computed from statistics presented in *Zhongguo tongji nianjian 1984*,
p. 370; *Zhongguo tongji nianjian 1985*, pp. 185, 482.

The system was effective, but only up to a point. Official statistics indicate that the state failed to procure the maximum amount of the surplus. Kenneth Walker, among others, has shown that between 1953–1957 and 1977–1980 purchases declined as a percentage of the total output, from 17.1 percent to only 14.7 percent, even though there was an increase of 50 percent in the absolute amounts procured. By the late 1970s there was a national procurement sales deficit of 4.24 million tons per year compared to a surplus in 1953–1957 of 4.96 million tons.[57] The amount of grain that remained in the countryside and the amount of grain per capita of rural population after gross and net procurements increased (see Table 6).

One might argue that the state's decreased procurements can be explained by drops in production or population increases. Neither explanation, however, fully accounts for the decrease. For the periods 1953–1957 and 1977–1980, production increased by 70 percent while gross state extractions (taxes and purchases) rose by only 18 percent.[58] Table 11 shows that per capita production was relatively stable, and during certain years it showed an increase. Population did increase over the period (see Table 12), but relatively steady rates of per capita net procurement rule this out as an explanation (see Table 11).

These statistics beg the question of why the state would go to great lengths, as described in the last chapter, to limit the peasant and collective shares in the initial distribution of the harvest to create a maximum surplus and then not extract that amount in procurements. One answer is that this decreased procurement reflects the weakness of the Chinese state in pursuing its policy objectives. Another possibility is that the state consciously decided both to adopt a more flexible policy for controlling the surplus and to use alternative methods to control the grain surplus it did not procure.

This chapter has looked at the first of these possibilities, focusing on why peasants and collectives resisted grain sales to the state. I have shown that, in theory, the state based the procurement process on local interests and negotiation, used detailed guidelines to distinguish between grain-surplus and grain-deficit teams, procured grain under different categories and prices depending on the amount of surplus a team possessed, and relied on "voluntary pledges" from production teams to

57. Walker, *Food Grain*, p. 179.
58. Ibid.; similar findings are documented in Lardy, *Agriculture*, chaps. 2 and 3.

TABLE 12.   RURAL POPULATION CHANGE FOR
SELECTED YEARS, 1949–1978

Year	Rural Population (million persons)	Difference from Previous Year Listed (million persons)	Percentage Change
1949	484.02	—	—
1952	503.19	19.17	4.0
1957	547.04	43.85	8.7
1962	556.36	9.32	1.7
1965	594.93	38.57	6.9
1970	685.68	90.75	15.3
1975	763.90	78.22	11.4
1976	773.76	9.88	1.3
1977	783.05	9.29	1.2
1978	790.14	7.09	0.9

SOURCE: *Zhongguo tongji nianjian 1985*, p. 185.

sell grain to the state. In practice, these policies masked the continued priority of the state's interests, which were achieved through administrative fiat and political pressure. Chapter 4 will consider a second explanation: the state had an alternative strategy for *controlling* rather than procuring the surplus.

Local Grain Reserves as a State Strategy, 1956–1978

The brutality of Soviet collectivization and the procurement crisis that followed has caused Westerners to use the imagery of Stalin thinking of the countryside and the peasants as merely the "milking cow" to satisfy the needs of rapid industrialization. Students of China have resisted that image in describing the Chinese Communist party's relationship with its peasantry; in fact they have made a point to distinguish it from the relationship that existed in the Soviet Union. Shue's book on the use of incentives to smooth the socialist transition is within this tradition, as is Bernstein's early comparative work on Chinese and Soviet collectivization.[1] The main theme in Chapter 3—that the state decreased the percentage of the harvest it extracted in procurements after the disaster of the Great Leap Forward—fits nicely with the image of China as a less brutally extractive regime. The increased amounts of grain left in the village as well as the guarantee of a basic grain ration further contribute to that picture.

Yet one cannot judge the impact of the state or the situation of the peasantry by looking only at how much was taken in procurements and how much remained in the countryside. To reiterate an earlier point, one cannot assume that peasants have access to grain left in the village. One must look closely at the peasant's entitlement from that amount. I have already shown how the state strictly limited collective expenses to ensure a maximum surplus. In this chapter I will show how the state

---

1. Shue, *Peasant China;* Thomas Bernstein, "Leadership."

then extended its authority to control that part of the surplus stored in production teams.

One cannot conclude from the procurement statistics that the state had lost the struggle for grain and was unable to control the remaining portion of the surplus. Procurements are only one measure of effectiveness. The state also had indirect methods to control the surplus it failed to procure. After initial problems with procurements in the early to mid-1950s, the state exhibited impressive flexibility in trying a number of ways to induce peasants to turn over more grain.[2]

One method was the "circulation grain" (*zhouzhuan liang*) program; it offered to buy extra grain from the peasants and allowed them the option of repurchasing equal quantities of the same type and quality at any time. Peasants, however, soon became suspicious of this system when they either had difficulties buying back their grain or were given grain of a different quality or type from that which they had sold to the state. Peasants who sold unhusked grain to the state were returned husked grain, depriving them of fodder.[3] Other peasants complained that when they needed to buy back their grain from the state, they were treated as if they were asking for state relief and trying to buy supplements (*fanxiao liang*) rather than exercising their right to buy back what had been officially guaranteed as theirs on demand.[4] The system was further discredited when in some places the amounts sold as circulation grain after one harvest were used as guidelines for increasing the next harvest's sales quotas.[5] These problems reinforced the peasants' fears that any grain taken out of their village would be out of their control.

At this sensitive juncture in peasant-state relations, in the midst of collectivization, the state instituted the local grain reserve system. Having villages keep local reserves did not directly increase the size of the state reserves, but it could shield existing national stockpiles from further reductions. Once local reserves were established, the central

2. As Table 11 shows, after an initial rise in procurements there was only meager growth. In addition, resales to the countryside averaged 8.5 million tons between 1953 and 1957.

3. "Zhouzhuan liang yiding yao mai dami ma?" (Do We Have to Buy Rice When We Repurchase Our Circulation Grain?), *MBRMB* 28 February 1957.

4. "Jiejue nongcun liangshi goushou gongzuo de jiewei wenti" (Solve the Peasants' Problems in the Final Stages of the Grain Purchase Process), *DGB* 12 February 1957.

5. For warnings against keeping the *zhouzhuan* sales separate from quota sales, see "Shiying xin qingkuang zuo hao jinnian de xialiang tonggou he ruku gongzuo" (Adapt to the New Environment, Do Well the Work of This Summer's Grain Procurement and Storage), *Liangshi gongzuo* 1956, no. 10, pp. 17–19.

state could legitimately hold back its reserves and tell the peasants that they should first rely on their own local reserves. Over time this policy became the major excuse for curbing peasant use of that portion of the surplus the state failed to procure.

ESTABLISHING LOCAL RESERVES, 1956–1961

By instituting a system of local grain reserves, the contemporary Chinese state continued an imperial tradition that originated in the Han dynasty, continued through the Qing dynasty, and existed in modified form during the Republican period.[6] Like other governments before them, the communist state saw national reserves as a source of peace and stability.[7] Such local grain reserve systems have been understood as insurance mechanisms for the poor; they integrated rural society by binding poorer peasants to the landlord and gentry classes through grain loans in times of shortage.[8] The traditional Chinese system of local reserves is often cited as a prime example of a "subsistence guarantee" that gave legitimacy to authority relations in peasant villages.[9] Whether this was true in traditional China cannot be determined here, but in contemporary China the local grain reserves provided strong disincentives for production. The policy was abandoned as part of the Third Plenum reforms of 1978 to increase enthusiasm for production.[10]

The fate of the local grain reserves does not necessarily disprove previous theories about either the usefulness of reserves or peasant appreciation of them. Like those of past dynasties, these reserves served many purposes. As the following sections will show, local reserves were part of the local welfare system, but the state also used the policy to control

6. See, Hsiao Kung-chuan, *Rural China*, pp. 549–552, 144–185; a book-length study of the Qing civilian granary system is R. Bin Wong and Pierre Etienne Will, eds., *Nourish the People*.

7. The classic Confucian view, as stated by Mencius, also expresses a strong connection between legitimacy and food supply; see James Legge, trans. and ed., *Mencius*, pp. 239–240. The Chinese communists, however, instead of quoting Mencius or Confucius, quote Lenin on the importance of reserves. See "Woguo liangshi zhanxian de weida shengli" (The Great Victory of Our Grain Front), *RMRB* 1 October 1971:2. Also see Chen Yun, "Speech at National Conference of Party Delegates (23 September 1985)," *Hongqi* October 1985, no. 19, pp. 35–37, translated in *JPRS-CRF* 12 December 1985: 61, where he talks about the political consequences and social disorder of grain shortage.

8. See, for example, Barrington Moore, Jr., *Social Origins*, pp. 162–227.

9. See James Scott, "The Erosion," or James Scott and Benedict Kerkvliet, "Traditional Rural Patrons."

10. The reserves were not actually abolished but simply made completely voluntary, which resulted in none being kept. See Article 43, "New 60 Articles," p. 108.

increased amounts of the surplus that it failed to extract through taxes or procurements. The grain remained in the teams, but the state and not the teams regulated when and how the reserves could be used. Peasants were not only deprived of larger shares of the total harvest to fund the team reserves, but they were also subsequently prohibited from using the grain in their reserves.

The state's hidden agenda in promoting the local grain reserve system is most apparent in the timing of the policy changes with regard to the reserves. Local grain reserve policy changed according to procurements, the amount of grain left in the village, and the size of national reserves.

The initial regulations for local grain reserves were vague and re-sulted in little or no action.[11] Reserves were for "emergency use," but no definition of an emergency is given.[12] In mid-1957 a few provinces es-tablished local reserves, calling them *yicang* rather than the later desig-nation *chubei liang*.[13] *Yicang,* the traditional term for charity granaries that existed as late as the Republican period, may have been adopted to suggest a familiar system of welfare, a relief rather than a threat to the peasants. The 1957 regulations were vague about who would form the responsible reserving unit, but one is left with the impression that it was supposed to be the agricultural producers cooperatives. No information is provided on the amount of grain the collectives stored or how it was used.[14]

The first hint that the state was ultimately concerned with control over the surplus came in 1958, when the leadership expected an excep-

11. First draft of the Twelve-Year Agricultural Program, "The Draft Program for Ag-ricultural Development in the People's Republic of China, 1956–1957," Article 7, trans-lated in Robert Bowie and John Fairbank, eds., *Communist China*, p. 122. An earlier document mentions a similar fund, but the terms are extremely vague and imply that local reserves were to be used for production expenses as well as welfare. See "Decisions on Agricultural Cooperation," translated in Bowie and Fairbank, eds., *Communist China*, pp. 106–107.

12. Bowie and Fairbank, eds., *Communist China*, p. 122. The article added that "dur-ing this same period the state too should store sufficient reserve grain for one or two years for use in any emergency."

13. "Jizao yufang ziran zaihai" (Start Early to Prevent Natural Disaster), *RMRB* 30 May 1957. There were earlier reports of *yicang,* but these were owned by the prefec-ture or the district; see "Changwei zhuanqu xingban yicang de chubu tihui" (The Initial Experience of Changwei Special District in Building Granaries), *DZRB* 19 December 1952:2. The pre-1949 charity granaries (*yicang*) were similar to the community granaries (*shecang*), but the charity granaries were established in larger towns rather than in the local peasant communities. On the socialist *yicang* see "Fengshou mo wang huangnian" (Do Not Forget Disastrous Years When Having a Good Harvest), *RMRB* 18 October 1957, and "Jigu fangji shou huanying" (Storing Grain to Guard Against Hunger is Well Received), *ZGQNB* 9 October 1957.

14. Article 25 in "Revised Draft Program," translated in Chao Kuo-chün, *Economic Planning*, p. 173.

tionally large harvest.[15] The state initially responded by increasing grain procurement quotas by 20 percent; but it calculated that a sizable amount of the expected harvest would still remain in the villages. In July 1958, just before the formation of communes, the grain bureau heads of eight provinces met and decided that any remaining surplus should be apportioned first for enriching the collective reserves and added to the public investment funds (*gonggong jilei*). Only then, if any was left, could it be given to peasants as bonuses.[16] No firm guidelines stipulated the exact proportion for each use.[17] But it was quite clear that the surplus was not to be squandered in increased rations to the peasants. The state was determined to control the grain it did not extract.

RESERVES AS INCENTIVES, 1962–1968

The state never lost sight of its goal of controlling the surplus, but it was also realistic and flexible. After the disastrous Great Leap Forward and the famine of the "three lean years" (1959–1961), the state put aside its concern with the surplus, fully aware there was little grain in the villages, and concentrated on raising peasant enthusiasm for production. The state both reduced procurements and authorized expanded use of local reserves. Instead of an unspecified amount or the 15- to 20-percent figure sometimes used in 1958 and 1959, in 1962 local reserves were limited to 1 or 2 percent of the distributable harvest.[18] This kept to a minimum the amount taken from the collective

15. Eight provinces reported an increase of 64 percent. In one area of north China there was such confidence in the size of the harvest in 1958 that large amounts (30 to 40 percent) of the sweet potato crop were left to rot in the fields. Waste due to haphazard harvesting is often cited as contributing to the later food shortages. I 29/26680.

16. "Fengshou bu wang qiannian xiaofei bu wang jilei" (When Having a Rich Harvest Do Not Forget the Bad Years, When Consuming, Do Not Forget to Build Reserves), *RMRB* 2 July 1958.

17. A report from Qinghai states that 15 percent of the grain production was put aside as local reserves. Of that amount 70 percent was held by the cooperative and 30 percent by the individual households. A Guangdong report cited a requirement that 20 percent of increased output be kept as reserves. For Qinghai see *Red and Expert* 1 October 1958, no. 4. The USDA Clipping Files, where I found this article, stated that this journal was the Qinghai equivalent of *Red Flag*. For other examples see "Fenpei liangshi xian ti banfa Shantou zhuanqu yijing tichu" (Shantou Special District Has Already Proposed Concrete Methods to Distribute Grain), *TKP* 18 June 1958. Similar reports exist in *RMRB*; see, for example, 5 December 1959:1. In 1959, 21.1 percent of a Shandong brigade's harvest reportedly went toward collective reserves; see *RMRB* 10 May 1959.

18. Rules and regulations governing the implementation of the policy and the use of reserves were included in the "Regulations on the Work," p. 712; hereafter cited as "60

and increased the surplus that could be distributed to peasants, thus linking reward more closely to labor input. Moreover, the state made it clear that only teams, the lowest level of collective organization, were to reserve and use the grain, and then according to democratic discussion.[19]

The state hoped that by giving the peasants extra grain, it could increase production and at the same time rebuild its image as a benevolent and able ruler. The 1962 statement defined reserves as having a broad welfare function and explicitly authorized their use for the peasants' benefit. Reserves were no longer directly funneled into the production and investment funds; they could legitimately be loaned to grain-short families and used to support needy households.

The liberal policies, however, did not last long. Once production increased, the state again expressed concern about the surplus. In 1962, and in some places as early as late 1961, when the economy showed the first signs of improvement and output increased, the state was quick to stress the importance of local reserves as a necessary step to curb the "undisciplined use" of grain by the peasants for celebrations, feasts, and entertainment.[20] But because production had not yet fully recovered, the articles were moderate in tone and intended to calm peasant fears about withholding grain to build reserves.[21]

By 1962–1963 the press contained a number of articles encouraging teams to build reserves, but it is unclear how many actually established

---

Articles." The 60 Articles stated clearly and precisely the terms of ownership, operation, and function of local reserves:

> A proper amount of reserve grain may be set aside by the production team as crop conditions may permit and as determined by the general meeting of commune members, so as to be prepared against natural disasters, and [so] that grain-short families may borrow grain from those that have surplus, [so] that grain may be borrowed or taken on loan and returned, and [so] that proper care may be given the families which experience difficulty of living and also the five guarantee families. The amount of reserve grain must in general not exceed 1 percent of the total grain left over after the state collection quota has been met by the production team, but in no case should it exceed the maximum 2 percent.

19. "Keqin kejian chuliang beihuang" (Be Industrious and Frugal, Store Grain to Prepare for Natural Disaster), *RMRB* 27 November 1962:2, translated in *SCMP* 14 December 1962, no. 2880, pp. 2–5.

20. See, for example, ibid. Also see "Majiawan shengchandui shouji jige fangzai beihuang" (Maijiawan Production Team Reserves Grain to Prepare for Natural Disasters), *RMRB* 27 November 1962:2, translated in *SCMP* 14 December 1962, no. 2880, pp. 5–10.

21. One model brigade had saved 1.6 percent of its total distributable harvest. "Zhazha shishi anpai hao sheyuan shenghuo" (Reliably Arrange Well the Peasants' Livelihood), *DGB* 6 December 1961:1.

reserves so soon after the three lean years.[22] Interviews confirm that local reserve programs were established in a few areas of north China prior to 1963, but these seem the exception. Local reserves were not widely established until 1969.

The state did not take direct measures to regulate the growing amounts of grain that remained in teams until 1964, when production showed a marked increase. Even then there seemed to be a lack of consensus among the policy makers, perhaps reflecting the ongoing dispute between the more radical and the more conservative views on the best way to develop socialism. On the one hand, articles in the national press indicated concern about increasing production and gaining peasant support.[23] And the 1964 regulations further expanded the use of local reserves to include production expenses, such as financing purchases of chemical fertilizer, and circulation grain to be sold for cash or exchanged for goods.[24] These same rules also authorized reserves for use as supplementary ration grain, seed, and fodder for collective members in economically bad years.

On the other hand, there are indications that some wanted to tighten control over the steadily increasing amounts of grain remaining at the local levels as harvests improved. A mobilization effort was launched in Shanxi in December 1963 to build local grain reserves; 1,500 cadres were called together to study and organize the effort to build reserves.[25] For the first time approval was needed from the commune authorities before reserves could be used; the 1962 regulations only specified that use should proceed from democratic discussion.[26] Furthermore, all activities had to be reported to, and thus approved by, the county government. Reserves were not to be used wantonly, and storage required stricter attention. Special grain reserve management committees were created in each team to guard against insects, pests, rats, and spoilage.[27]

22. A 1962 *RMRB* editorial stated that in 1962 a Shanxi team reserved 150,000 *jin* of grain while output increased by 15 percent. It further claimed that in 1960 the team had reserved 27,000 *jin* and that output increased 37 percent in 1961 over 1960.

23. See, for example, "Lingchuanxian dabufen shengchandui you chubei liangshi" (The Majority of Production Teams in Lingchuan County Have Grain Reserves), *DGB* 26 October 1964:1, translated in *URS* 37:238–242; and "Jianli shengchandui de jiti liangshi chubei" (Build Up the Collective Reserves of Production Teams), *DGB* 26 October 1964:1. "Qufu liangshi bumen dai cun shengchandui chubei" (The Grain Bureau of Qufu Stores Grain for Village and Production Teams), *DGB* 27 October 1964:1.

24. See "Lingchuanxian," *DGB* 26 October 1964:1.

25. Ibid.

26. See "Keqin kejian," *RMRB* 27 November 1962:2; and "60 Articles."

27. "Lingchuanxian," *DGB* 26 October 1964:1.

The government took the additional step of offering to store grain for teams.[28] The stated purpose was improved storage efficiency and diminished losses.[29] A number of different storage options were offered to the brigades, teams, or individuals who allowed the government to store their reserves.[30] Each method allowed the reserving unit the right either to withdraw the reserves at will or to buy back the reserves if in the intervening time the reserving unit had decided to sell the reserves to the state for cash as circulation grain. At that time there was no mention of securing upper-level approval for withdrawals. When teams or individuals brought grain for storage, the state gave them a receipt stating the amount, grade, and quality of the grain, which was divided into three grades for this purpose; when teams or individuals withdrew grain, it was to be of the same quality and type. Each withdrawal of grain would be listed on this same receipt. Teams at any time could sell the reserves as an overquota grain sale or conveniently use it to pay the agricultural tax. The government also offered to mill the grain at no charge if it could keep the husks (liangpi) to sell as fodder.

One must ask why the central government undertook such a program to help production teams if not simply to gain direct control of more grain. The state had a long-standing shortage of proper storage facilities. In the 1950s, when the central authorities had little choice,

28. To stress a point made earlier, it should be noted that the manner in which this policy was presented suggests some differing opinions regarding the desirability of such a policy. See the conflicting accounts in ibid.; "Qufu liangshi," DGB 27 October 1964:1; and "Liangshi bumen de yixiang xin renwu" (A New Task for Grain Bureaus), DGB 27 October 1964:1. They reflect different opinions about whether central storage is preferable to central control over the use of locally stored reserves. However, despite initial disagreements, the state's offer of storage became a call for all teams to turn their reserves over to the state for safekeeping. Later articles from 1964 are more specific: peasants should be given grain certificates (pingzheng), which deducted 2 percent of the grain for a spoilage fee. "Guojia dai shengchandui baoguan chubei liang haochu duo liangshi bumen yingdang jiji kaizhan zhexiang gongzuo" (State Storage for Production Team Reserves Has Many Advantages, Grain Bureaus Should Enthusiastically Carry Out This Work), DGB 11 December 1964:1.

29. Citing an average loss rate of 5.3 percent for team-stored grain, the state promised to bear any loss over 0.5 percent of the grain turned over for government storage. "Qufu liangshi," DGB 27 October 1964:1. Two months later, the state modified the offer and specified that 2 percent of the grain turned over would be deducted for spoilage. "Guojia," DGB 11 December 1964:1. The precise standards for judging loss are unclear. Florence Dunkel, Z. T. Pu, and C. Liang, "The Conditions," found that in China in 1980–1981 an average team spoilage rate was 29 percent. One must wonder whether the figures cited during the earlier 1950s, presented as high rates of loss, were accurate.

30. See "Jianli," DGB 26 October 1964:1. The state also offered the same storage program to individual peasant households. In some areas of the countryside the reserving unit was the brigade. I 29/24680.

they commonly left grain in the villages for storage by collectives; this resulted in losses because peasants used this grain as their own.[31] In 1950, for example, excluding the northeastern provinces, China had more than a two-billion *jin* storage capacity, but most was unsuitable for grain. Of the state's agricultural tax grain, 90 percent was stored in people's houses, temples, halls, and open-air shelters.[32] From a survey of one Sichuan county in 1955, "civilian granaries," including old houses and temples, made up 69 percent of the county's three "state granaries, rather than structures specially built for storage purposes."[33] Large amounts of grain were lost to animals, rodents, and insects, to the lack of storage space, and to deficient makeshift shelters that left grain out on the road covered only with a tarp.[34] Rats and insects alone were responsible for almost 30 percent of all grain losses in 1954.[35]

Damage and loss rates reportedly improved, but problems continued to be serious, particularly damage due to moisture and foreign particles.[36] As late as 1958 a 30- to 40-percent shortage of grain storage

31. See, for example, "Zhidu buyan liangshi bei nuoyong daoqie" (Because the System Was Lax, Grain Was Embezzled and Misappropriated), *GXRB* 24 March 1957, and "Buneng dongyong guojia cunfangde liangshi" (Cannot Draw on State-Stored Grain), *XHNB* 24 February 1957. Much of this grain was "circulation grain" that the state purchased from the peasants but did not take out of the village.

32. "Ba liangshi chuyun gongzuo zai tigao yibu" (Further Improve the Work of Grain Storage and Transport), *RMRB* 20 October 1950.

33. "Jiaqiang dui liangshi daiguan gongzuo de lingdao" (Strengthen the Leadership in the Work of State Management of Team Grain), *DGB* 22 August 1955.

34. See, for example, "Lutian liangcang laoshu wo" (Lutian Granaries Are Rat Nests), *JFRB* 27 April 1955; "Rehe gongliang sunfu yanzhong" (Severe Losses in Rehe Tax Grain), *RMRB* 11 March 1950; "Shandong Kuyu diqu dapi liangshi zao chong shi meilan" (Large Amounts of Grain Spoiled in Kuyu District of Shandong), *RMRB* 25 April 1952.

35. "Zuo hao liangshi baoguan gongzuo" (Maintain Stored Grain Well), *DGB* 16 March 1954.

36. See "Jinyibu kefu liangshi baoguan zhongde langfei xianxiang" (Further Overcome the Waste in the Storage of Grain), *DGB* 17 May 1955; "Zuo hao liangshi baoguan," *DGB* 16 March 1954; "Liangshi meibian de yuanyin zai nali?" (What Are the Causes of Grain Spoiling?), *DGB* 15 May 1955; "Quanguo chuxian liuwanduoge siwu liangcang, chuliang sunshi jiangdi jin liangcheng" (Nationally 60,000 "Four No" Granaries, Reduced Storage Losses Nearly 20 Percent), *DGB* 5 February 1957; and "Jinyibu jiaqiang dui liangshi gongzuo de jiandu he jiancha" (Go Forward and Strengthen the Supervision and Inspection of Grain Work), *Liangshi* 3 July 1957, pp. 20–21, for details of widespread spoilage by moisture, mildew, and insects. The seriousness of the state's problems is painfully evident in the stories former urban residents tell of having to buy "patriotic grain" (*aiguo liang*)—bitter-tasting, mildewed grain—as part of their allotted grain rations during this period. See "Aiguo de miaoyong" (The Ingenious Use of Patriotism), *RMRB* 19 August 1956; "Wuchengxian liangshiju lingdao tongzhi gongzuo bufuze dapi xiaomai meilan" (The Leadership of Wucheng County Grain Bureau Irresponsible, Great Amounts of Wheat Mildewed and Spoiled), *DZRB* 2 February 1953:2; and "Henan Dongming liangshiju hushi baoguan meilan dapi yumi" (Dongming, Henan Grain Bureau Ignored Storage Work, Great Amount of Corn Mildewed and Spoiled), *DGB* 1 June 1955.

facilities still affected the country as a whole, in addition to problems in storage technique.[37] It is unlikely that between 1958 and 1964—the years of the Great Leap Forward, shortage, and retrenchment—great improvements were made in granary facilities.

Not only were technical and physical problems rampant, but also personnel problems abounded. When the state first announced its policy of low-cost state storage for brigade, team, and individual private grain stocks, state granary cadres resisted assuming that responsibility added to their regular care for the state's reserves. Intensive education and mobilization of state granary workers were necessary before they "understood" the importance of their new task.[38]

Moreover, the added costs for centralized storage must have been substantial. In 1956 the costs to the state for storing grain for more than three years was equal to the value of the grain itself. Unless conditions had improved dramatically, costs must have been still fairly high in 1964.[39] But the state stored these reserves for the teams cost-free, deducting only a 2-percent spoilage fee. One assumes that the state officials supporting this policy thought only in terms of the extra grain placed in state granaries, not the costs involved.[40]

This suggests that when the state introduced the 1964 policy, it had not necessarily solved its storage problems. Moreover, this corroborates later government reports of continued difficulties in state storage in 1969 and the early 1970s during the campaign to build small collective granaries.[41] The problems, in sum, had never been solved.

A more likely explanation is that the state was merely trying to replenish its reserves depleted by the Great Leap Forward. The state did

37. "Liangshi baoguan gongzuo de xin renwu" (The New Tasks of Grain Storage), *DGB* 11 July 1958.

38. "Jinzhong zhuanqu liangshi bumen kaizhan daicun chubei liang yewu" (Jinzhong Special District Grain Department Starts the Work of Storing Reserve Grain), *DGB* 10 January 1965:2.

39. See "Kaizhan 'siwu' jingsai, zuo hao liangshi cangchu gongzuo" (Promote the "Four Nos" Competition, Do Well the Work of Grain Storage), *DGB* 5 May 1956, and "Quanguo cun liang sun hao lü dada jiangdi" (The Entire Country Is Storing Grain, the Loss Rate Is Greatly Decreasing), *DGB* 9 September 1957.

40. Another possible and complementary explanation is that they wanted to overcome the speculation, hoarding, and general corruption involving grain that took place after the Great Leap Forward and became targets of the Four Cleans Campaign in 1963–1964. On the Four Cleans, see Richard Baum and Frederick Teiwes, *Ssu-Ch'ing.*

41. "Chuliang jiancang beizhan beihuang" (Reserve Grain, Build Granaries, Prepare for War, Prepare for Disaster), *RMRB* 5 August 1971:2, gives details of losses and damage of grain left out in the open due to lack of storage facilities. The state freely admitted to these problems during this period because it wanted to stress the need to build small local collective granaries.

not care who owned the grain stocks; the important thing was to have the grain in the state granaries. Once there, the state could then use the local reserves as part of its own without increasing taxes or procurements. If the state held the grain, it could use the extra stocks to bolster its own state reserves, more profitably sell the grain as "circulation grain" (*zhouzhuan liang*), or use it to stabilize grain supplies.[42] Collective and private reserves stored in the state granaries under such a plan became extra capital and security for the state's grain monopoly.

Perhaps equally important, obtaining extra grain stocks reduced the need, if only temporarily, to dramatically increase procurements. The liberal 1964 guidelines on the use of reserves suggest that the state was not yet willing to risk any moves that might endanger further increases in production. The storage program allowed the state temporary control of more grain and helped guard against wasteful overconsumption while allowing teams to use this grain only for projects that the state screened as worthwhile. Reserves could thus be used as both an incentive and a control. The state gave the peasants leeway to increase production, without having to trust peasants either to use the extra wisely or to keep it as reserves. State storage removed the temptation for peasants to overconsume by taking grain out of the villages, without openly alienating the peasants through higher procurement quotas.

LOCAL SELF-SUFFICIENCY, 1969–1978

The state's hidden agenda in instituting the local grain reserve system is next revealed in 1969, when reserves were promoted under Mao's slogans: "Prepare for war, prepare for disaster, serve the people"; "One must have grain reserves, each year reserving a little will result in a lot."[43] Later the slogan "Every team has its reserves, every household

42. See "Jianli," *DGB* 26 October 1964:1. The availability of increased amounts of grain in the state granaries allowed the sale of limited supplies of grain outside of the rationing system (with no grain tickets needed) both to and by restaurants.

43. The call to build reserves covered the front page of *Renmin ribao* on 11 July 1969. Also see "Jixu fayang jianku fengdou, qinjian jieyue de zuofeng" (Continue to Promote the Style of Struggle in Difficult Circumstances, and Practice Thrift), *Hongqi* December 1969, pp. 24–27. The movement had started as early as 1966 in some areas; see "Duidui you chubei, huhu you yuliang" (Every Team Has Reserves, Every Household Has Surplus), *RMRB* 13 November 1969:3. The slogan more commonly known in the West, "Dig tunnels deep, store grain everywhere, and never seek hegemony," was not used at this time; it did not come into popular use until about 1975. See, for example, Chin Shih-ming, "Storing More Grain," *Peking Review* 29 August 1975, no. 35, pp. 14–16, which stresses the importance and implementation of this policy. This same article points out that Mao had a similar slogan in 1933 in *Pay Attention to Economic Work*, where he said, "Set up public granaries and storehouses for famine relief everywhere."

has its surplus grain," was pushed to build household as well as collective reserves.[44] During this third phase, local reserves took on a new character and became a key part of the more general policy of local grain self-sufficiency. Teams were told to build their own local granaries and reduce reliance on state grain storage. Instead of advocating the 1964 program of centralized storage, the state emphasized scattered local team reserves to be used *only* in war or disaster. Press articles openly criticized the state storage policy and implied that it should be abandoned.[45]

Beginning in 1969–1970 the press criticized the use of team reserves for production expenses, sideline activities, and fodder—all those purposes that in 1964 were officially authorized.[46] The grain was to be used only if there were war or disaster, and then only after discussion and approval by the poor and lower peasants association, commune authorities, and reports to the revolutionary committee. Reserve grain was not to be used in financing sideline industries, in exchange for other goods, and in combination with grain used for production, seed, or fodder.[47] Most important for individual peasants, reserves were not to be used for loans to grain-short or overdrawn households;[48] this directly contradicted the 60 Articles and 1964 regulations. In November 1969, after the initial campaign to build scattered reserves, overdrawn households were accused of "eating without first planning." Those who overconsumed and wasted grain became prime candidates for criticism.[49]

Political viewpoints became explicitly linked with conserving and building reserves. Waste and overconsumption became the targets of the later Campaign to Criticize Lin Biao and Confucius, in 1973–1974.[50]

44. "Duidui," *RMRB* 13 November 1969:3.
45. See, for example, ibid.
46. See "Zhonggong zhongyang wenjian" (A Document of the Chinese Communist Party Central Committee, Chung Fa [1971] No. 82), p. 100; hereafter cited as "Central Directive [1971] No. 82."
47. See "Jianchi chubei liangshi renzhen guanhao liangshi" (Insist on Reserving Grain, Responsibly Care for the Grain), *RMRB* 13 November 1969:3; also Yi Fan, "Yijiuliujiunian de zhonggong nongye ji nongcun gongzuo" (Chinese Communist Agriculture and Rural Work in 1969), *Zuguo* March 1970, no. 72, pp. 13–14.
48. "Central Directive [1971] No. 82" pinpointed the problem the state was trying to curb when it stated that "certain communes and brigades are having quite a few overdrawn households and cannot balance their system of distribution. They have reached the point of depleting their collective reserves. . . . a serious problem and must be treated accordingly" (p. 103). See also "Kaizhan jieyue yong liang de jiaoyu Zhengzhoutian dadui xingban xuexiban" (Zhengzhoutian Brigade Sets Up Classes to Save Grain), *RMRB* 13 November 1969:3.
49. "Duidui," *RMRB* 13 November 1969:3.
50. See, for example, "Reserve Grain Must Not Be Forgotten When a Bumper Crop Is Harvested, Economy Must Be Practiced When There Is a Surplus"—Investigation Re-

"Capitalist roaders" were those who wanted to "divide all and eat all," that is, those who opposed keeping a portion of the harvest from collective distribution and building collective reserves. Having reserves followed Chairman Mao's teaching of "taking grain as the key link," while not building reserves and "dividing all and eating all" were signs of Liu Shaoqi's capitalistic influence, which took "money as the key link" and "allowed wealth to take the place of grain (reserves)." The true proletarian line was for "every team to have reserves and every household to have surplus"—in other words, to build both collective and individual reserves.[51]

In contrast to the 1- to 2-percent limit set forth in the 60 Articles of 1962, after 1969 the amount to be set aside as local team reserves was never explicitly stated. Instead, teams were to set aside reserves "according to local circumstances." Interviews with former team leaders and accountants reveal that in some areas "according to local circumstances" meant not only economic circumstances but also the political climate and the degree of pressure from the upper levels to implement the policy. In some areas as much as 20 percent of the harvest was kept as a team's collective reserves;[52] recall that 20 percent was also the figure used in 1958.[53] Post-1978 press reports confirm that some teams were forced through political pressure to reserve a certain portion of their harvest, regardless of their economic situation.[54]

Threat of war with the Soviet Union was the official explanation for the renewed urgency of building granaries and keeping reserves scattered throughout the country. China was engaged in border skirmishes

port on Peichianhsiang Production Brigade of Liaochung Hsien, Liaoning," in *Red Flag* 1 October 1973, no. 10, translated in *SPRCM* 29 October–5 November 1973, no. 761–762, p. 133; also see "A Team Has Its Reserves, a Household Has Its Surplus Grain—Investigation Report on Chaiting Production Brigade, Kuanglin Hsien, Shansi," in *Red Flag* 1 January 1973, no. 1, translated in *SCMM* 29 January–6 February 1973, no. 745–746, pp. 49–53; and "Increase Production, Practice Economy, and Store Grain Everywhere," in *Red Flag* 1 May 1974, no. 5, translated in *SPRCM* 28 May–3 June 1974, no. 775–776, p. 51.

51. "Zhonggong weile beizhan pingming sougua liangshi" (The Chinese Communists Exact Grain from People in Order to Prepare for War), *XDRB* 28 January 1970:4.

52. I 21/10180; I 21/11180. In this particular team 18,000 *jin* was reserved.

53. See "Fenpei," *TKP* 18 June 1958.

54. See "Seriously Study Chairman Mao's Theory on the People's Commune," in *Red Flag* 1 August 1978, no. 8, translated in *JPRS-CRF*-710 September 1978, pp. 124–142; "Gaohao nianzhong fenpei quxinyumin" (Do Well the Distribution Work at Year's End, Gain the Trust of the Masses), *RMRB* 24 December 1979:1; and "Pingjun zhuyi weihai da anlao fenpei haochu duo" (Egalitarianism Has Many Drawbacks, To Each According to Work Has Many Advantages), *RMRB* 14 December 1979:2.

with the Soviets in 1969.[55] Military strategy at the time stressed the importance of readiness to fight a protracted "people's war." Decentralized food supplies kept throughout the countryside were an essential part of the guerrilla war tactic. Keeping team-level grain reserves, along with the campaign to build low-cost small team granaries (*tuyuancang*), became part of China's war preparedness plan and a key part of the general policy of self-sufficiency.[56]

An equally important, if not more important, reason for revamping the local grain reserve policy was rooted in China's domestic problems, particularly in the chaos and weakened effectiveness of the state as a result of the Cultural Revolution. The turmoil in the mid- to late 1960s directly affected state grain stocks. In 1967, shortly after the Cultural Revolution began, Red Guards went to grain stations and either obtained grain or were given vouchers for obtaining grain elsewhere. County grain bureaus, like other units during this period, were divided into factions. Those sympathetic to various Red Guard factions issued grain or coupons accordingly; those granary cadres not so sympathetic also issued grain, given that the alternative was criticism and attack by hostile Red Guards. In other instances, granaries were simply raided and the grain was taken by force. It is difficult to estimate the amount of state reserves lost in this manner or the amount given to Red Guards as they "exchanged revolutionary experiences" across the country. The unrestricted access to grain only lasted a brief period (1966–1968) and the raids were admittedly rare, but they could not have helped the government stockpiles of grain. These, however, were isolated and rather short-lived effects on the state's grain policy. More serious were the long-term effects on both centralized grain storage and procurements.

The policy of "self-sufficiency," regardless of Mao's penchant for pursuing this policy, was a cost-effective means by which the state could abnegate part of its responsibility for interregional grain transfers and supply and reduce the need for increased procurements. The local grain reserve system, as a stable local welfare fund that could be drawn upon only in war and disaster, reduced the central government's need for reserves.

The restricted use of local reserves adopted in 1969 was the state's

55. See Neville Maxwell, "The Chinese Account."
56. See Yi Fan, "Yijiuliujiunian," *Zuguo* March 1970, no. 72. On the movement to build *tuyuancang* see, for example, "Chubei jiancang," *RMRB* 5 August 1971:2, and "Woguo nongcun he liangshi bumen jianzao dapi tuyuancang" (Our Villages and Grain Bureaus Have Built Large Numbers of Granaries), *RMRB* 5 August 1971:1.

response to continued low procurement rates in spite of increased production and peasant resistance to its earlier policy of centralized storage. Those areas that could meet their overquota sales and still have a surplus would be encouraged to build reserves to prevent the "wanton use of extra grain and overconsumption." Indirect control by strictly limiting the use of the surplus was better than no control at all.

The abandonment of the centralized storage policy can be traced to the problems in the state's always limited granary facilities. The Cultural Revolution further reduced the state's capacities by negatively affecting the efficiency of state granary workers; this may ultimately have made centralized storage an unviable option. The evidence is somewhat sketchy, but interviews and press reports suggest that after the Cultural Revolution granary workers (*liangshi ganshi*) became more careless and irresponsible (*bu fuzeren*) in their work, leading to serious losses.[57] In 1974 a whole warehouse of sweet potatoes in Zhejiang rotted from poor storage. From 1965 to 1971 a county grain bureau in Jiangxi had an average deficit of more than 310,000 *yuan* because of poor management and administration.[58] In Guangdong one granary lost one-third of its stocks to rats, mildew, and generally poor management.[59] Into the late 1970s reports continued to describe problems in state grain storage.[60] State granaries in Shandong in 1980 still had to rely on makeshift open-air shelters for grain stocks. Similar problems were also found in Heilongjiang.[61]

Part of the reason for the deteriorating situation was the reduced accountability of granary cadres for losses. According to those familiar with the granary system, prior to the Cultural Revolution granary cadres were personally responsible for all losses other than those purely accidental. Thus, regulations on granary conditions were followed more closely and the temperature checked daily. But with the disillusionment and cynicism that existed during the Cultural Revolution and the general weakening of state control, cadres were less concerned about fol-

57. See, for example, "Bixu ba liangshi zhuajin" (Must Pay Close Attention to [Grasp Tight] Grain Work), *RMRB* 5 November 1977:3.
58. "Yujiangxian liangshiju lianxu liunian yingli" (The Grain Bureau of Yujiang County Has Consistently Made Profits for Six Years), *RMRB* 10 April 1978:3.
59. I 5/13380. The incident took place around 1969.
60. "Shi liangshiju 'siwu' liangcang yuelaiyueduo" ("Four No" Granaries of Municipal Grain Bureau Ever Increasing), *GRB* 18 July 1973:2.
61. See "Da zhua kexue baoliang quebao chuliang anquan" (Greatly Promote the Scientific Storage of Grain, Ensure the Safety of Reserves), *DZRB* 24 April 1980:2, and "Liangshi da duole ye fachou" (In Good Harvests We Still Have Anxiety), *RMRB* 24 November 1979:3.

lowing directives, and likewise those assigned to check implementation were lax in their tasks.[62]

If the state's interests in instituting the state storage program were rooted in its need to replenish national grain stocks depleted by the Great Leap Forward, then after the particularly critical period was passed in the mid-1960s and state reserves were sufficiently replenished, it would no longer have been in the state's interest to shoulder the burden of storage. The costs of the state storage program may have started to outweigh its benefits. In those areas where state storage had taken root, the government may have found the program too costly, given that it was no longer desperate for reserves and that output had steadily increased. Total grain harvests improved from 295 billion *jin* in 1961 to more than 418 billion in 1968.[63] In at least one grain-rich area in Guangdong where collectives and peasants had accepted the state's storage offer, the state took direct measures to rid itself of this extra storage burden. According to a commune-level granary head from the area, teams and peasants were given notice in 1975 by the central grain authorities (*zhongyang liangshibu*) that the collective and private grain in state granaries had to be removed.[64]

During this same period, however, in a poor area in Anhui, the state encouraged teams for the first time to turn grain over for state storage, using the same arguments put forth in 1964–1965. These conflicting examples are not just cases of regional variation in policy implementation; rather they suggest that the state was selective in abandoning the policy of centralized storage based on levels of procurement and regional grain supplies. In areas such as Guangdong that had significantly increased production and sales to the state, where the regional grain stocks held by the government were sufficient, the state decided to unburden itself of the costs of centralized storage. Rather than directly control the grain, it was content to restrict peasant access to the surplus by strictly regulating its disposition. The stocks would be available for state use, but the state would not have to worry about storage or transport costs; the teams would store the grain and absorb the costs themselves.

But in poor areas such as Anhui where grain production was historically low, regional stocks were still lacking, and extra reserves would

62. I 27/2480; I 5/13380.
63. *Zhongguo nongye nianjian 1980*, p. 34.
64. I 5/13380. This action was taken after the authorities had tried to launch a movement to build more local granaries. Some of the teams did, but others did not and continued to use the state's facilities.

not create an excessive burden, the centralized storage remained attractive, especially given the alternative to allow the newly increased harvest to be wasted in increased consumption. Thus, in 1975, when teams in Anhui finally experienced a bumper harvest and were expecting to increase their grain distribution to team members, they were called upon to use the centralized storage system.[65] Likewise, teams that failed to meet their procurement targets or owed state taxes were explicitly prohibited from keeping grain for reserves and using the policy as an excuse for retaining extra grain.

The logic of the state's local grain reserve policy is summarized by a former work team member:

> The state's chief objective was to have teams sell more grain; reserves were only of secondary priority. The state would not encourage reserves in teams that could barely meet the minimum state levies. Peasants would gladly reserve grain, but the state does not allow this when it has not received its full share.[66]

A FLEXIBLE STATE STRATEGY

The findings of this chapter and the last chapter pose important questions about the nature and effectiveness of communist rule. Does the poor performance of China's state procurement system suggest that the state was weak and ineffective in achieving one of its major policy objectives? Or do lower procurement rates and the state's manipulation of local granaries suggest strategic flexibility?

My analysis favors the latter interpretation. The state intentionally decided not to follow the draconian route of Stalin to extract maximum amounts of grain at any cost. When the state began to experience difficulty, particularly after the Cultural Revolution, it chose to adopt local granaries, under the slogan of "local self-sufficiency," to control that part of the surplus it failed to procure. Thus, on the one hand, the Chinese party was different from the Soviet; it was less willing to alienate the peasants by forcing the issue of procurements. Yet, on the other hand, the end result was similar—peasants were denied access to a larger portion of the harvest.

Mao's policy of local self-sufficiency and local granaries can be viewed as a conscious strategy to decentralize grain production and storage. It

65. I 21/11180.
66. I 1/16680.

was a preferable political alternative to increasingly harsh measures of procurement. It also saved on costs of interregional grain transfers in an era of political disruption when they were difficult to administer. The net result, whatever the state's calculation, would be to give the state greater control over the disposition of the surplus—if, that is, the state could effectively limit the use of the local reserves. This is a big question, as Chapter 5 will show.

Bureaucratic Strategies of Control

Control by the Chinese communist state does reach to the grass roots, as the totalitarian model stresses, but the question is whether it does so effectively. Previous research on the Chinese countryside suggests that the system could be circumvented, that peasants and cadres have been able to cheat the state and pursue their own interests.[1] In the last two chapters I have shown that grain procurements declined over time and that the state employed alternative strategies of control. This chapter examines the forms and mechanisms of state control in an attempt to understand how the local levels could thwart the state's policy goals and keep more grain in the collective. This is the first step in understanding how the local levels are able to influence the implementation of policy. Although the mechanisms of control I will focus on are peculiar to the state's grain policies, the forms they represent are similar to those throughout the Chinese political system, in both urban and rural areas.

The control system in the countryside is important for the Chinese state because it doubles as the means by which the central planners receive the information necessary to formulate the plans and set the procurement targets. The famine created by false reporting during the Great Leap Forward is an example of the worst consequences of sabotaging that system.[2] Here I will look systematically at state control on the local level to try to understand how the local levels routinely are

---

1. See, for example, Bernstein, "Cadre and Peasant" and "Stalinism, Famine," and Ezra Vogel, *Canton Under Communism.*
2. Bernstein, "Stalinism, Famine."

able, for their own purposes, to both overreport *and* underreport the harvests.

The extent to which the bulk of the state's control mechanisms hinged on the loyalty and efficiency of *local* cadres, particularly team leaders and brigade cadres, will be apparent. The team leader occupied the key position in the production and reporting systems. He, more than anyone else, had the most accurate information on the condition and size of the harvest. But these cadres had conflicting interests. The political behavior of grass-roots cadres was bounded by administrative demands from the higher levels, but the cadres' personal loyalties and ties with those they were assigned to regulate encroached on those bounds. The economic interests of local cadres were rooted in the well-being of their corporate units. This chapter defines the responsibility of cadres at each lower level in the administration of policy to highlight the areas of cadre discretion that served as the basis of clientelist politics. The next chapter will describe the behavior of local cadres as they faced conflicting demands over the harvest.

ROUTINE REPORTS AND INSPECTIONS

The Chinese state used both *routine* and *nonroutine* forms of control to regulate its policies. Routine controls consisted of reports and inspections by local cadres; nonroutine controls consisted of intervention and inspection by outside work teams. The major differences between the two lie in their predictability and personnel.

This section will examine the points at which the state routinely applied checks to ensure that its policy goals were properly implemented. The checks can be divided into two categories: some rely solely on the cooperation of the team leaders; and some rely on both team leaders and on-site inspection by brigade- and commune-level cadres. I will first consider those routine reports submitted by the team leader; these reports formed the base of all other information gathered on the harvest.

TEAM REPORTS

A series of reports, some of which I have already mentioned in Chapters 2 and 3, submitted by each team leader to the brigade and then processed for the commune, county, and provincial authorities formed the first layer of controls, the most important means by which the state

TABLE 13.   TEAM REPORTS ON THE HARVEST
SUBMITTED TO THE STATE

Report	Timing	Purpose
Estimation of harvest	After the estimation of the harvest	Forecast the harvest —*For the upper levels:* 1. check false reporting 2. guide harvest apportionment 3. lay basis for quotas
Proposed budget	After the harvest, prior to distribution	Plan allocations of the team's harvest —*For the upper levels:* 1. justify state's notion of "surplus" 2. allow rational allocation of quotas —*For the team:* 1. justify sales pledge
Final budget	After the distribution of the harvest	Record the distribution of the harvest —*For the upper levels:* 1. update records 2. check apportionment and use 3. set next year's apportionment guidelines

gathered information. The most crucial were submitted to the brigade three times each growing season: after the estimation of the harvest; after the harvest but prior to the actual distribution; and after the distribution to the state, team, and individual peasants (see Table 13).

The harvest estimate was the first report submitted. Completed prior to the harvest, it served a number of functions. First, because it was filed while the grain was still in the fields, it facilitated on-site inspections by brigade or commune officials and reduced the chances of false reporting. Through careful field inspections an accurate estimate of each team's harvest could be made. Second, the provincial and county levels used this harvest estimate to plan its strategy to set the size of peasant rations and control the surplus. A bumper crop, for example, might lead to a request that teams build local reserves instead of increase rations. These reports provided the provincial and county officials an idea of the maximum amount of grain they could hope to procure. Third, these reports provided the basis from which team leaders might argue for a lower sales quota. Consequently, this estimation of the harvest was not only important for the state in setting its initial targets, but it was also an equally important first step for teams trying to bargain about procurement quotas.

Teams submitted a second report after the harvest; this preliminary budget of the planned disposition of its harvest included both the team's proposed grain sales pledge and proposed expenditures for seed, fodder, and basic grain rations. This accounting justified its proposed sales by showing quantitatively why a team could sell to the state no more than its pledged amount of grain. Teams had to secure approval of this preliminary budget before the harvest could be officially apportioned. In practice, this meant securing the approval of the brigade, itself subject to upper-level guidelines for team expenditures.

For the state, this budget served two purposes. First, once the budget was submitted and expenses itemized, the remaining grain could officially be designated surplus, thus legitimating the state's claim. Second, this report provided the authorities information necessary for rationally allocating the grain procurement quotas. Extra pressure could be applied to teams with increased output, and leniency given those with reduced harvests. This saved the state from having to resell grain to poor teams, which would otherwise have been overburdened by excessive sales and left grain-short. In general, the report provided the state with the necessary data to encourage most teams to sell this grain to the state because their expenses were already accounted for and there was still a surplus.[3] To describe this policy peasants said that the state let them "go hungry without starving them to death" (*chi bubao, e busi*).[4]

Each team submitted a final budget after the annual quotas were set, the preliminary budget reviewed and revised, and the sales quota finalized. This report recorded a team's official harvest allocation: grain used for each expense, including team members' basic grain rations and work-point grain. The state used these figures to update its record of the current year's distribution and to allow spot checks during the year to see that various teams were using their grain as prescribed in the official budget guidelines. The final budget also served as the basis for determining the next year's grain distribution. As a county work team member stated, "The annual rations are loosened or tightened depending on the county cadres' estimations of how much extra grain peasants should have stored from the preceding year's distribution."[5]

---

3. The idea was that the lower levels should sell to the state all grain left after expenses and guard against private withholding and sales (*xiaji gouchi gouyong shengxia laide yinggai maigei guojia fangzhi ziliu zimai*).
4. I 1/2680.
5. I 1/6680.

ON-SITE INSPECTION AND SUPERVISION

In practice, the state did not trust the production teams to accurately report their harvests. Reports were reinforced by a second layer of administrative controls: on-site inspections by higher officials during the estimation of the harvest and its delivery to state granaries. Again the state depended heavily on local cadres, this time those from brigade and commune, for effective regulation.

The Estimation of the Harvest.   Crop estimation was the only instance during the production and harvesting cycles when the state mobilized its cadres to inspect every one of its five million production teams. Approximately two weeks before the harvest, prior to teams submitting the harvest estimate, at least one upper-level cadre, usually a brigade cadre or a commune representative, would accompany each team leader to check the crop and to note the acreage and the output per *mu* to thwart the possibility of teams "hiding production" (*manchan*).[6]

The state did not bypass the brigade unless there was some question of collusion between the brigade and its teams or a team had unusually poor harvests. The state considered cadres above the brigade more dependable because they were usually not local people; therefore, they were less likely to be closely tied to those production teams they were inspecting.

To further ensure honesty, the state sometimes employed a divide-and-rule strategy similar to that used in allocating procurement targets; one team leader inspected another's crop.[7] The state hoped that out of self-interest team leaders would ensure that the teams they were sent to inspect made accurate reports. Obviously, the effects would be most acutely felt the closer the team leader was to the team he was inspecting. A team leader from the same brigade would have the most interest in seeing that neighboring teams sold at least their fair share because he would deal directly with this team in the quota-setting process. Cadres

6. See, for example, I 20/5380; I 29/13780; I 1/2680. Between commune and brigade was the *guanlichu*, the administrative arm of the commune. These cadres would check on the accuracy of the lower levels for the commune.
7. I 1/2680; I 21/8180. This strategy was sometimes used to inspect planting of crops. This process of using peers is also implemented in other rural settings to prevent corruption and collusion between local officials and individual peasants. See, for example, the description of bands of peasants following land consolidation officials assigned to draw lines fairly of new farms in Uttar Pradesh; Philip Oldenburg, "Middlemen."

and assisting team leaders were rotated during the inspection process to further reduce chances for collusion. An outside team leader had no assurance that if he lowered the estimate of another team's harvest, the favor would be returned. It was therefore in a team leader's interest to press for an accurate estimate of the other teams' crops.

The use of team leaders was a check not only on the accuracy of team reports but also on the brigade cadres, who were local peasants—sometimes relatives and certainly longtime associates, if not friends, of many of the team leaders. Brigade cadres were knowledgeable about local conditions and could accurately predict harvests. The question is how their personal relations with the various team leaders affected their enforcement of the state's policies, particularly because they also had economic and political ties with the teams.

Brigade cadres, the immediate superiors of team leaders, were directly responsible for ensuring that state policies were carried out. But unlike commune cadres, they were not on the state payroll. This is a crucial distinction. The wages and grain rations of brigade cadres came from the production teams in which they were registered; they were neither paid a fixed salary by the state nor given fixed grain rations, as were commune officials. These leaders were not exempt from collective labor; their only compensation for their administrative duties was supplementary work points and a small amount of cash. The economic interests of these cadres were directly linked to those they were supposed to supervise. In Chapter 6 I will consider how this and other factors affected the enforcement of state policies.

The Delivery of Grain.   The second instance of on-site inspections was during the delivery of grain to state granaries. However, state supervision of this process was much more selective than during crop estimation. Once the estimates were known, the state did not need to watch the harvesting and delivery process in every team. Instead, it mobilized special inspection teams, called "temporary work groups" (*linshi gongzuozu*), to oversee the process at the point of delivery.[8]

Usually organized at the county level with provincial supervision, a temporary "tax and procurement office" (*zhenggou bangongshi*) was

8. Unless otherwise noted, the information presented in the following section is based on descriptions provided by interviewees 1, 5, and 15, all county cadres involved with the procurement process.

set up annually to direct and oversee the collection of the harvest, including the timing of deliveries and transport by trucks and boats.[9] Led by the head of the county grain bureau (*liangshiju juzhang*), it directed the temporary work groups. A counterpart existed at the commune level headed by the commune grain management office (*liangguansuo*).[10]

The cadres who staffed these temporary offices and work groups were sent from various bureaus at the provincial, county, and municipal levels connected with the harvesting and collection process. The most important ones were the bureaus of grain, finance, taxation, and transportation. The bureaus of civil affairs, agriculture (a research and technical unit), and commerce were sometimes involved.[11] The tax and procurement office dispatched the representatives from the bureaus to different communes and sometimes brigades to oversee grain harvest and delivery. However, these agents seldom went to production teams.

If the harvest went well, work team members remained at the commune headquarters until deliveries were completed.[12] If the reports looked good and the commune authorities were trusted, they sometimes went back to their own units. The presence, or anticipated presence, of these cadres was deemed sufficient incentive for compliance. The work teams usually did not personally make policy changes or apply sanctions. Only if problems occurred would more stringent actions be initiated and controls tightened. The effectiveness of these inspection teams was predicated on the threatened, rather than the actual, enforcement of sanctions.

Overall, the effectiveness of routine control mechanisms was limited. The reporting system suffered from overaggregation of information. Harvest estimates, for example, which formed the basis of the procurement targets, were filtered through at least five levels of the bureaucracy before they arrived at the planning agencies. The reports passed, in turn, from the brigade to the commune, county, prefecture, and province. At each level the information collected lost precision; the higher up the hierarchy, the more all teams were assumed to be the same. As indicated

9. Trains did not come under the jurisdiction of this office; they were part of a different system.

10. As temporary ad hoc organizations, these offices existed for only a few months of the year around each harvest, usually between June or July to August and from November to December; the dates varied in different localities according to the harvesting schedule.

11. I 1/5680; I 15/12180.

12. I 1/5680.

earlier, statistics provided by production teams never went beyond the commune.[13]

Both the reporting and inspection systems depended on the team leaders' cooperation to accurately report information and the local brigade leaders' efficiency to accurately monitor the activity of team leaders during the on-site inspections. Inaccurate reports and collusion between lower-level cadres to overreport resulted in disaster during the Great Leap Forward. Sun Yefang admitted that in 1958 reports overestimated a 400-billion-*jin* harvest by 600 billion *jin*.[14] The inflated statistics lay at the root of the increased procurements that eventually led to famine.[15] Collusion also has the opposite effect; the state can be denied a larger share of the harvest through underreporting, as Chapter 6 will describe in detail.

NONROUTINE METHODS

To make the system of control more effective and to keep team leaders from becoming too complacent, the state's second line of defense consisted of surprise inspections and using outside work teams. For example, brigade or commune authorities would go unannounced to weigh a team's stored grain and check that the amounts corresponded to the final budget the team had submitted to the brigade. This would take place most often after the grain harvest and distribution, when teams weighed their remaining stocks on "granary cleaning" (*qingcang*) day.[16] This check would take place only if the brigade or the commune authorities suspected that a team was retaining too much grain; however, the consequences of this form of control were still relatively minor. If the amounts were in excess, the team had to sell the extra grain to the state. The team might remain suspect, but no other action would be

13. I 29/6680; I 29/13780.
14. Sun Yefang, "Jianqiang tongji gongzuo, gaige tongji benzhi" (Strengthen Statistical Work, Reform the System of Statistics), *Jingji guanli*, December 1981, no. 2, pp. II-3; "Gongchandangyuan yao jiang zhenhua" (Communist Party Members Should Speak the Truth), *RMRB* 13 June 1980:1, also describes the problems of false reporting during the Great Leap Forward.
15. Bernstein, "Stalinism, Famine."
16. I 1/6680; I 29/13780. There were other annual inspections by the grain bureau cadres, but those were inspections of storage procedures. In some areas they went to every team that had stored grain, but they were not specifically concerned with irregularities in the distribution process. I 29/23680; I 29/13780.

taken. The most stringent control, the state's most effective weapon, was using work teams (*gongzuozu*) staffed by outside cadres.

Work teams are by now a familiar feature of the Chinese political system. Much has been written about their role during land reform and various political campaigns. John Burns defines work teams as "cadres organized at one level of the government or party to go down temporarily to lower levels in order to investigate and report on conditions there, supervise the implementation of policy, and solve problems as they arise on the spot." [17] Burns, concerned with forms of participation and interest articulation, has focused attention on work teams primarily as channels of interest articulation and on their roles in political campaigns, such as the Four Cleans and the Cultural Revolution. [18] Another side of work teams—their role in the administration and regulation of economic policy—has received less attention, but it is equally, if not more, important for understanding routine grass-roots politics. Viewing work teams in this way does not ignore the distinction Burns makes between economically and politically oriented work teams, [19] but it warns that this distinction not be taken too literally. Often when political campaigns are carried out in the countryside, they in practice are aimed at economic problems. During the Maoist period many political campaigns were aimed at increasing production and grain sales.

The general pattern of state intervention seems most closely correlated to the amount of attention, either positive or negative, that a production team attracted to itself. [20] "Backward" (*luohou*) teams—poor, disaster-ridden, constantly needing relief, dependent on the state resale of grain, and, most important, unable to meet their state levies—were prime candidates for work team intervention. The objective of such interventions, as a former work team member explained, was to change the backward situation and improve production so the team could sell more grain to the state. [21] A team leader could fail to fulfill his grain sales quota, but if he continued for any length of time, the chances of the county or commune authorities sending work teams to investigate and intervene greatly increased. [22] Model teams, with relatively high produc-

17. John Burns notes that these work teams consist of groups of two or more cadres. "Peasant Interest," p. 192. My research found that work teams sent to a single production team sometimes consisted of only one person.

18. See Richard Baum, *Prelude;* Burns, "Chinese Peasant" and "Peasant Interest."

19. See, for example, Burns, "Peasant Interest."

20. A former cadre who spent most of his time out on investigations said that he went either to very rich or very poor teams. I 29/17680.

21. See, for example, I 1/16680.

22. I 1/2680.

tion, rich land, and high yields, likewise were targets of work team intervention. In those instances, the objective was to obtain even higher grain yields and bigger procurements.

The following discussion examines work teams as instruments of state regulation and intervention. I will focus on when, where, and how work teams intervened in production teams. To do this I have distinguished work teams on the basis of their ability to affect change within the unit to which they were assigned. Some were limited to close inspection and monitoring, without authority to intervene or make changes; I call these investigation work teams. Others had more far-reaching power and took charge of production and team affairs. They not only inspected and supervised but also decided the budget for apportioning the harvest;[23] these I term intervention work teams.[24]

INVESTIGATION WORK TEAMS

Full-time investigation work teams were made up of cadres from various bureaus concerned with agriculture. They included technical cadres, such as veterinarians and experts on agricultural machinery who routinely spent part of each year in the countryside inspecting production teams. These cadres, who were drawn from various bureaus for tours of duty, should not be confused with the regular work team staff; they were not the professional work team members that some counties employed full-time (see below). For example, a provincial agricultural bureau sent eight of its technical cadres for various lengths of time to investigate and report on conditions in the countryside. When they were not on inspections, they taught courses on their particular expertise in the county or the commune or returned to their offices in the provincial capital.[25]

The targets of these investigation work teams were usually the poorest production teams, often in areas that had suffered disasters. The process would begin with visits to successive levels of the administrative hierarchy, starting at the county and working down to the teams. The work

23. I 29/8680.
24. Burns distinguishes "investigation teams" (*diaocha dui*) from regular "work teams" (*gongzuo dui*). He states that investigation teams did not have the power to make on-the-spot policy or personnel changes. See his "Peasant Interest." I have chosen to depart from those terms because some groups that peasants called "work teams" did not have power to make changes, only to inspect.
25. I 29/8680.

teams would be briefed at each level on production, general economic conditions, household size, and estimated need for relief.[26]

When full-time investigation work teams went into the teams to oversee production, they stayed anywhere from a few weeks to a full year. If a work team were sent specifically to evaluate either the severity of a disaster or requests for relief, they stayed two to three months. In some areas they slept and ate in peasant homes; this allowed them constant presence in the team and provided the most comprehensive control, but in some instances this was not achieved. Some work team members stayed in the team during the day and returned to the brigade headquarters at night for their meals and sleep.[27]

If yearlong observation of a team were required, the inspection cadres sometimes were deployed in shifts, allowing each cadre or group of cadres to return to the city for at least part of the year; but at least one remained in the production team at all times to oversee the entire growing and harvesting work. A common pattern required that a group stay until one task of the agricultural cycle, such as planting or harvesting, was completed; then a new group relieved the first batch of cadres after a briefing on the production team's problems.[28]

Full-time investigation work teams primarily monitored policy implementation. When the work team was present, team cadres followed more closely regulations on cropping patterns, planting density, weeding, drying and weighing the crop, and dividing the harvested grain. These work team cadres kept and closely guarded their own record books of the team's affairs and were vigilant against attempts to withhold or hide grain.[29] In addition to monitoring policies, these technical cadres also provided expertise and technical assistance. If a team had been severely affected by natural disaster or was really poor, before

26. I 29/17680; I 29/13780.

27. One former inspection work team member in southwest China explained that the investigation work teams did not always live in the teams because the members were often higher-level county cadres who found the living conditions in the teams too harsh, particularly since they were sent mainly to the poorest areas in the province. Meals were the major problem. Each household that lodged a work team member was given an extra thirty *jin* of rice and nine *yuan* per month to feed the work team member. Because Chinese eat communal meals, the work team member's rations were cooked, served, and eaten together with those of the host family. Thus, the work team member often did not get a chance to consume the thirty *jin* of rice and other food rations supplied to the peasant household; instead, the host family gladly took larger helpings, and the work team member, being both polite and exemplary, often left the table hungry. These cadres thus preferred to return to the brigade headquarters at night and cook for themselves. I 15/12180.

28. This was the experience of both interviewees 29 and 15 (1979–80 interviews), who regularly did this type of work.

29. I 15/12180; I 29/8680.

tackling production problems they frequently requested relief grain to get the peasants back on their feet.

Investigation work teams depended on the cooperation of the local cadres, particularly brigade cadres and team leaders. This was especially true when an inspection team only stayed a few weeks or a few months. Inspection teams, as a result, had to be careful not to allow themselves to have the wool pulled over their eyes, or, as the Chinese say, to "get pulled into the water" (*laxia shui*), by local cadres.[30] Work team members had to be particularly careful not to get involved in factional disputes. Inspection cadres tried to counteract the possibility of biased information from team cadres by establishing good relations (*gao hao guanxi*) with trustworthy elements among the peasants. Work teams relied on those willing to provide accurate information on the village and details of the cadres' mistakes.[31]

The authority of inspection cadres was usually limited to giving advice; they did not change either personnel or production methods. They exerted their authority by holding meetings and making examples of bad elements, but that was the extent of their punitive activity. Their power lay in the reports they sent back to their superiors, at either the county or the province level; these sometimes resulted in the dispatch of other work teams to control production or change leadership.[32] For example, in 1975 a provincial inspection work team arrived at a county seat and found that county officials were forcing communes to pay their agricultural tax years in advance. Some were pressured into paying three years' worth of tax in one year, leaving production teams with little income. The work team members immediately reported this to the prefectural and provincial authorities, where appropriate action was taken.[33]

It is difficult to estimate the number of teams that actually underwent work team inspection because it varied by time and place. One former province-level cadre, who regularly participated in investigation work

30. I 14/211279.

31. Team activists were key elements in this process. If the work team sensed a split in the team, whether based on clan ties or just factionalism, then the work team would seek out the opposing side as the most likely candidates for speaking out. I 1/16680; I 1/12680; I 25/8480; I 1/3680; I 29/25680. According to a full-time work team member, after the beginning of the Cultural Revolution work teams became increasingly unwelcome. This, coupled with factionalism, made the job of work teams increasingly difficult. I 1/3680.

32. See I 15/12180.

33. The county secretary was reprimanded, but nothing serious happened to him because his mistake was merely to promote the interests of the state too vigorously. Cheating the state was usually treated as a more serious offense. I 29/17680; I 29/26680.

from the 1960s through the 1970s, estimated that in his north China province about 50 to 60 percent of the teams were inspected annually.[34] Another upper-level cadre, who inspected teams in a high-yield rice-growing region in southwestern China, estimated 80 percent. The discrepancies may be explained by looking at the time of these inspections. The cadre who estimated 80 percent said that rate referred to the period *prior* to the Cultural Revolution, before the mid-1960s.[35] A decrease in the frequency after the beginning of the Cultural Revolution was noted by the northern cadre, who estimated a 50- to 60-percent check; moreover, he prefaced his estimate by saying that during the Cultural Revolution (1966 to 1976) the inspections that took place were often only formalities. A county cadre from south China similarly described investigations in his area.[36]

Although it is impossible to know how accurate or representative these figures are, they support the general trend that emerges from other data. Interviews with team leaders and peasants reflect similar spottiness in the application of comprehensive control measures. Few ever had full-time investigation work teams watch their entire production process. Most production team leaders said that full-time inspection work teams seldom, if ever, came to their teams.

INTERVENTION WORK TEAMS

Intervention work teams took command of team affairs. They were the most effective but least used form of state control. Some were campaign-related; some were sent out as part of normal attempts to solve problems of production. To simplify the analysis I will use the familiar categories of campaign and noncampaign work teams.

Campaign Work Teams.   Campaign work teams were made up of cadres from various units, possibly from different areas. They were dispatched to carry out a specific policy or movement, such as the Four Cleans, Learn from Dazhai, Criticize Lin Biao and Confucius, or the Cleaning of Class Ranks. Except for Learn from Dazhai, most are thought of primarily as political campaigns.[37] But, as I suggested above,

34. I 29/13780.
35. I 15/12180.
36. I 19/3680.
37. Burns, for example, lists all except the Learn from Dazhai Campaign as political campaigns. See his "Peasant Interest," p. 220.

campaigns had multiple goals. Most, if not all, political campaigns assumed a heavy economic focus when carried out in the countryside. In the Four Cleans Campaign, for example, a sizable portion of the problems the teams were sent to resolve concerned grain production and distribution.[38] Work teams sought out corruption, speculation, and problems of work style, but in the final analysis they were sent to resolve economic problems that had adversely affected the amount of grain the state was getting from the team.[39] The following case illustrates this point.

During the later part of the campaign, in April 1966, a Four Cleans work team was sent to investigate a production team in Yunnan province. The production team had been delinquent in its taxes and grain sales and had requested resales of grain (fanxiao liang) as relief; it had suffered three bad harvests in a row. This example is particularly interesting because of what happened to the work team itself. The work team leader recommended sending relief grain and lowering the production team's estimated harvest figure; this would eventually lower its procurement quota. The relief was sent, but the work team leader and a number of his supporters were later criticized by county cadres and other work team members for being "too soft with the peasants."[40] The work team leader's alleged mistakes were sending relief and asking for reduced quotas instead of forcing the production team to increase production, pay its grain taxes, and meet its sales quotas. Clearly the county wanted more grain, and it expected this work team to succeed in its task.[41]

Similarly, in the late 1960s and into the 1970s many campaign work teams were sent to production teams that, affected by the chaos of the Cultural Revolution, had suffered reduced harvests or failed to pay agricultural tax or both. During the Cultural Revolution politics became an

38. There are a number of detailed accounts of Four Cleans work teams in the countryside. See Baum, *Prelude.*

39. I 25/8480; I 20/19380; I 20/5380; I 3/26380.

40. Because this incident took place just prior to the Cultural Revolution, there were a number of complicating factors, most notably splits within the work team itself. The "leftists" on the work team wanted to refuse the peasants relief grain and press for higher sales in spite of a poor harvest. The original work team leader was criticized and eventually replaced by a more leftist element. Interestingly, a few months after the work team had left the village and returned to the city, peasants from the village went to the city looking for the leftist work team leader who had refused to give them additional relief. They found him and forced him to return to the village for a struggle meeting. According to my interviewee, this practice of peasants seeking revenge on former Four Cleans work team members was not that uncommon in her area of southwestern China. I 20/5380; I 20/31280.

41. I 20/5380; I 20/31280.

even more potent weapon with which to attack certain types of economic problems. As I showed in Chapter 4, in the Campaign to Criticize Lin (Biao) and Confucius, some "capitalist roaders" were none other than those who did not want to build local grain reserves but wanted more grain distributed as rations.

In 1971–1972, as part of the One Strike Three Anti's Campaign, a work team was sent to a production team that had suffered a 20-percent drop in production in 1966 and had failed to pay its taxes from 1966 to 1968. The task of the work team was to put production in order and collect back taxes.[42] A similar work team was sent to Anhui during what was locally called a Socialist Education Campaign in 1970–1971. In this instance, the team accountant was also investigated for corruption and dismissed, but the payment of the team's back taxes seemed the major item on the work team's agenda. This production team, like that of the previous example, did not pay taxes from 1966 to 1968; instead, it had divided the extra grain among the team members.[43]

In another example, when the second Socialist Education Campaign was carried out in the early 1970s in an herb-growing region of southwestern China, work teams were sent when the peasants reportedly became "wild" and refused to listen. This was actually a case where the production team had refused to plant grain, preferring instead to cultivate herbs that brought a high cash income. The peasants earned large amounts of cash from growing herbs and purchased high-priced grain on the black market to pay their agricultural tax and meet their sales quota, but the state was not satisfied with this minimal amount.[44]

The following example from the Learn from Dazhai Campaign further illustrates the close link between the political and economic objectives of many campaigns.[45] Temporary work team members were sent to help the peasants learn from Dazhai.[46] As was so often the case, the lesson was to grow more grain. This particular production team had planted a crop of mandarin orange trees anticipating the big Hong Kong New Year's market for these plants. Although the sale of this popular item would have brought a large cash income for the team, un-

---

42. I 3/7480.
43. I 21/101800.
44. I 20/19380.
45. On Dazhai as a model, see Mitch Meisner, "In Agriculture" and "Dazhai."
46. The consensus of my interviewees was that people selected to serve on Learn from Dazhai work teams were people who had committed political mistakes—what the Chinese colloquially term *pigu hen heide* (people with black bottoms)—and that being sent to the countryside was a punishment or a sign of disfavor.

fortunately for the peasants, these sideline activities were considered capitalist. The work team ordered the peasants to uproot the orange trees, but the peasants refused. At that point the work team itself tried to pull up the trees. In this case, the peasants took violent action and beat the cadres.[47]

Noncampaign Work Teams. Aside from the ad hoc work teams described above, counties employed under their direct control a permanent work team force of cadres to inspect the countryside. These professional work team members were on the payroll of the brigade or commune, but they were paid, at least in part, by the state.[48] One such work team member explained that he was paid by both the state and the collective; he was considered "half a state cadre and half a local cadre." Half his pay came from the state as a set wage and grain tickets; half came in grain rations from his home team and cash from his brigade (but no work points). He generally spent one-fourth of his time in the county seat and about three-quarters in villages. After his selection for full-time work team duties he attended a short training course on general work style; the actual methods were left up to him to determine according to conditions in various teams. He was told to view his duties as "spitting out the weak and putting in the new."[49]

This force of permanent work team members provided a county with full-time troubleshooters and propagandists, who carried out campaigns and tackled production problems. As the state's specialized force, they handled the most difficult cases. Teams subject to this type of intervention were chronically overdrawn, needed relief grain, and relied on resales of grain (*fanxiao liang*)—generally in poor economic condition, owing taxes or making insufficient sales. For example, a full-time county work team was assigned in 1975 to correct the backward situation in a production team. This team came to the attention of the county because it owed the state over 10,000 *jin* of grain sales from 1973 to 1974 and had low grain production.

It took a work team member nearly two years to rectify the problems. He took charge of the production team and proceeded to improve its production, repay its debts, and rectify its leadership problems. After one year, production started to improve dramatically, and he began to

---

47. I 5/31780. Unfortunately, I lack the details of the final outcome of this incident.
48. This section, unless otherwise noted, is based on information from interviewee 1, who served on such a force for a number of years in Guangdong.
49. I 1/9680.

make up the team's past debts in grain sales. The debt was repaid in four payments of approximately 2,500 *jin* each, in addition to meeting the current year's grain sales quota. In 1975, the team sold a total of 18,000 *jin*; by 1976, it sold 30,000 *jin*.

How the team improved its economic situation reflects the power of work teams and the importance of upper-level assistance. At the same time, it reflects the positive side of work team intervention. The production increases were in part attributable to the work team member's ability to procure larger supplies of fertilizer. As a county work team member, he had privileged access to normally scarce chemical fertilizer. He also helped the team with irrigation. Thus, the work team member took control of production, but he also provided concrete assistance in necessary investments.

The work team member did not make any changes in leadership until nearly the end of his tenure in the team. Shortly after his arrival he told the production team leader to "stand aside" (*kaobianzhan*); he took away the leader's authority to direct production but did not actually dismiss him from his position. The work team member waited until he had carefully observed matters. That, he said, was common practice. When the work team member was about ready to leave, after consulting with his superiors at the county and with brigade and commune officials, he acted on his observations that the existing production team leader was in fact incapable of running production effectively, and he finally dismissed him. The work team member promoted the assistant production team leader to be the team leader.

This example illustrates the broader range of tasks and power of the intervention work teams in comparison with investigation work teams. The upper levels not only provided the technical input necessary to produce increased harvests but also gave the work team authority to make changes.[50]

PENALTIES AND SANCTIONS

What sanctions were used against deviant team cadres? Who carried them out? Sanctions against a cadre were applied by the work team, or more commonly they were left to the brigade and commune cadres. Again one sees the importance of local cadres in the control process. One should also understand that sanctions could be applied to any

50. I 1/6680.

peasant, although the discussion here has been limited primarily to team leaders.

A work team could institute at least four different sanctions once it intervened in a team's affairs. First, a team leader could be removed from office. In certain cases of corruption the offending cadre also had to repay the amount embezzled; in other cases the team leader was simply criticized and stripped of his office, as happened to the accountant in the earlier example. In most cases nothing more happened; the dismissed cadre simply returned to being a regular team member.

Second, a work team could demand that the team leader "stand aside," as in the example cited above. This was the most common sanction and one of the most feared. On the surface this might appear less severe, but in many respects this was more dreaded than removal from office; it effectively removed official power from a team cadre while not allowing him formally to leave office. During this period of uncertainty he would be under constant scrutiny. The suspect team leader would be the object of gossip while the work team gathered all the grievances peasants held against him.[51] If a cadre were immediately removed from office, at least he would be free of the psychological pressure and investigations and able to go about his work without continual suspicion. Both the first and second sanctions were applied in the above example where the work team member stayed two years.

Third, possibly the most severe sanction involved sending a cadre to "study class" (*xuexi ban*). This harmless-sounding phrase is a euphemism for keeping a cadre at commune headquarters to be "educated" on the error of his ways; here he was made to recognize, accept, and mend his mistakes and agree to follow policy correctly. While at study sessions, which could last a number of days, a team cadre (or peasant) was denied the opportunity to work and earn work points; worse, he was subjected to political and psychological pressures by brigade and commune authorities. For example, a team leader in north China during the early 1970s refused, with the support of his team members, to follow an upper-level directive to plant a new seed variety. As punishment he was sent to the commune headquarters to a study session where he was questioned and educated on his mistakes. The commune officials detained him at commune headquarters for three days to "think over" the correctness of the state's policies. He finally confessed his errors, but he was not allowed to resign his position. Instead, the commune officials

51. See, for example, I 3/26380.

forced him to return to his team to lead his team members to correct their mistakes. They were made to dig up the already sown seeds and plant the proper variety, provided by the upper levels.

This team leader was further subjected to the fourth sanction—criticism and public humiliation in a mass meeting of the brigade. This version of yet another type of punishment, struggle meetings, was commonly used during the Four Cleans and the Cultural Revolution.[52] In typical fashion the commune made an example of him to thwart similar behavior by other team leaders.[53]

THE LIMITS OF BUREAUCRATIC CONTROL

The most common forms of regulation were the least effective, while the most effective were the least used. The system of control was one of escalating interaction predicated on example and deterrence rather than on the comprehensive application of sanctions against each and every possible offender. Suspect or problem teams were selectively chosen as examples to illustrate the consequences of noncompliance with state policy. As a rule, state control was not based on surprise inspections and objective outside investigations. The bulk of regulation was through routine reports augmented with spot checks.

Because outside work teams were limited in use and selectively dispatched, only those teams that were models or had drawn adverse notice were subject to this close scrutiny and intervention by outsiders. As long as production teams appeared to follow state policy without attracting notice of the upper levels and appearing to stray from control, their team leaders were relatively free from upper-level intervention and sanctions. Team leaders who succeeded in escaping the notice of the upper levels were only subject to the routine periodic checks conducted by local cadres, whose interests and loyalties were closely tied to the teams they were assigned to police.

Thus, the system depended heavily on the cooperation of local cadres to effectively implement its more routine forms of control. The state tried to counteract the bias of local cadres by choosing outsiders, who were considered less likely to be swayed by personal ties and local pres-

52. For vivid descriptions of struggle meetings that took place in China's villages, see Anita Chan, Richard Madsen, and Jonathan Unger, *Chen Village,* and Richard Madsen, *Morality and Power.*
53. I 21/11280.

sures to bend the rules and more likely to enforce strictly and effectively the more stringent forms of control, to man the various work teams. But even these outside work teams were vulnerable to the plight and pleading of local peasants, which obstructed their objectivity in applying the state's policies. Regardless of who the cadre was, whether a local or an outsider, the exercise of authority was personalized, and the degree of enforcement was subject to individual cadre discretion. This personalization of authority formed the center of a clientelist system of politics.

CHAPTER 6

Evading Controls

Team Leader Strategies

Previous chapters have implied that the struggle over the harvest resulted from the need of production teams to retain more grain than was allowed under the state's apportionment policy. This chapter will present an accounting of these needs and consider the economic and political consequences of the strict budgeting process. The state created a context where the team leader faced conflicting demands for a limited good—the team harvest. The state's apportionment policy created a maximum surplus but left teams with insufficient funding to meet their expenses.

Team leaders were in a difficult position, but they were not without recourse. They had to accept the limitations imposed by the state, but they could learn to get around these limitations. Team leaders adopted a "rationality of evasion." Like bureaucrats in so many developing countries, team cadres were compelled to engage in technically corrupt practices. For China's rural cadres, much centered on the disposition of the harvest—hiding grain from the state, falsifying accounts, illegally using funds. This is a case where one must certainly look beyond greed or cultural predisposition as an explanation. The structural constraints imposed by the state left cadres little choice but to subvert the regulations. As Scott has pointed out in his study of corruption in developing countries, it is sometimes the direct result of too much regulation.[1] If

1. Scott, "Corruption."

this is the case, it is therefore not surprising that in China's centrally planned agriculture one would find such corrupt behavior in abundance—something that might be better called a "strategy of survival."

This chapter will detail how grain policy had the unintended consequences of forcing team leaders to engage in illegal actions to make ends meet and cultivate personal alliances that undermined the effectiveness of the state control system. It will also explain why brigade cadres, charged with guarding against the illegal retention of grain, "kept one eye closed" in supervising team leaders' implementation of grain policies.

THE TEAM LEADER'S DILEMMA

The team leader played the pivotal role in implementing the state's grain policy. As head of the collective unit of production, as the state's agent responsible for implementing its policies, and as director of the team, the team leader was a pivotal political actor. Each role, however, entailed different obligations regarding the division of the harvest.

Chapter 2 described the state's policy for the official apportionment of the harvest: the team's basic share consisted only of grain sufficient for seed, fodder, and the peasants' grain rations, and no more. The remainder was defined as the surplus. The following section describes the additional, frequently unavoidable, expenses—both requisitions by commune and brigade authorities and internal team expenses—for which the state failed to provide.

COMMUNE AND BRIGADE DEMANDS

Communes and brigades were units of administration, not units of agricultural production. They produced little grain of their own, aside from specialized production units under their control.[2] Communes, and particularly brigades, demanded that teams contribute toward their operating expenses, including funds for welfare, salaries of brigade personnel, and public construction projects. Team leaders felt pressure to supply the brigade and commune because they were their immediate overseers who decided how strictly to enforce state policies. Com-

---

2. There are a number of studies of team leaders, their backgrounds, and their selection. See, Michel Oksenberg, "Local Leaders," and Parish and Whyte, *Village and Family*, pp. 96–114.

pliance was especially important if a team leader wanted to remain in office and had political ambitions.[3]

After the mid-1960s the brigade played an increasing role in the appointment of team leaders.[4] Team elections were held, but brigade authorities were instrumental in selecting and approving the candidates. In some areas, the brigade simply appointed the team leader. In other areas, teams selected their own leaders from a list of names provided by the brigade, but the brigade decided on the team leader and assistant team leader from the winners.

When teams paid grain to the upper levels, it was referred to as grain "sent up" (*shang diao*). This consisted of grain to both the central government and the brigade and commune authorities. The agricultural tax and grain sales that teams delivered to the state were described in Chapters 2 and 3. The payments described here were made separately to the commune and brigade. The grain for these additional expenditures came out of the team's surplus, the same surplus that the state wanted to procure or have the teams keep as stable reserves.

OPERATING EXPENSES

Communes kept a small portion of the state-procured grain; but brigades depended almost entirely on contributions from their teams.[5] Team leaders had to pledge the amounts they would send up to the brigade, just as they pledged to meet the grain sales quotas. As early as 1965, some teams turned over 350–400 *jin* of grain to the brigade as "war preparedness grain." In addition, these same teams annually turned over at least 100 *jin* of grain to the brigade as general reserves (*zibei liang*) to fund meetings.[6] The amounts were figured in money, but

3. Previous studies have emphasized the election of team cadres. See, for example, Burns, "Elections." My interviewees stressed that prior to the Cultural Revolution they elected their leaders directly, but that practice changed. After the Cultural Revolution increasing numbers of team leaders were essentially appointed by the upper levels, although elections may still have been held. Whether directly appointed or not, all candidates and winners had to be approved by the upper levels. I 21/13180; I 21/8180; I 1/3680; I 10/9480.

4. Brigades and communes sometimes had the equivalent of a state farm (*nongchang*) or special production teams (*zhuanye dui*) that produced grain. See, for example, I 3/7480.

5. The commune's reserves usually consisted of a portion of the grain procurements that the county stored in the commune granaries. The counties could decide the amount of state grain left in the communes, but usually at least one-half of the procurements were kept at the county. I 29/24680; I 29/26680.

6. I 3/7480. Other interviews show that similar payments were made by teams in other areas. I 5/12579; I 29/24680.

the payments were based on the sale of grain or made in grain. This grain was sometimes considered an investment fund (*gongji jin*) to which teams contributed a lump sum. Some teams turned over a set percentage of their harvest to the brigade for welfare and investment. Of the 10 percent that some teams spent on welfare, only 3 percent remained within the team; the other 7 percent was sent to the brigade, which would then send approximately half to the commune.[7]

A portion of a team's surplus also paid for brigade administrative costs, such as the salary supplements for brigade cadres. As I explained in Chapter 5, unlike state cadres, who received both their cash wages and grain directly from the state, brigade cadres derived their income and food directly from their production teams. But teams also had to pay brigade cadres a cash supplement for their loss of work points due to administrative duties as well as pay part of the salary of peasants who worked in brigade-level enterprises. The amounts paid by the teams varied; at minimum, teams provided each member who worked in the collective factories with his basic grain ration. In one case, teams were responsible for one-half of the brigade enterprise workers' total income, including both grain *and* cash.[8] The bulk of profits from brigade-level enterprises, however, went to the brigade, not to the teams.

The practice of teams paying substantial sums for brigade expenses dates at least from the early 1960s. Documents of that period from Lianjiang county, Fujian, show that almost half of team payments for reserves, welfare, and administrative expenses went to the brigade. Only in the category of administrative expenses did teams consume as much as they paid to the brigade for similar expenditures (1.2 percent compared to 0.8 percent).[9] After 1979, when the commune system was criticized and disbanded in favor of the "responsibility system," the extent of brigade and commune demands were singled out as "burdens on the peasantry."[10]

Henan's Liuhe Production Brigade was cited as an example of this problem. This brigade had 146 brigade cadres, peasant teachers, and medical and industrial sideline production personnel, given a total of 537,100 work points. From the perspective of peasants in the produc-

7. That is, 3 of their 7 percent. I 4/27180.
8. See "Jianshao bu jianshao sheyuan fenpei" (Should We Reduce the Distribution to Peasants), *NFRB* 5 January 1979.
9. C. S. Chen, ed., *Rural People's Communes*, pp. 29–32.
10. See, for example, *FBIS* 26 August 1981, p. K1, and Song Dahen and Zhang Chunsheng, "Important Changes in the System of People's Communes," *Beijing Review* 19 July 1982, vol. 25, no. 29, p. 16. Also see *FBIS* 29 September 1981, p. K13.

tion teams, these were nonproductive work points because they did not directly contribute to producing the harvest. Yet these nonproductive work points forced those who engaged in agricultural labor to supply brigade personnel with 187,985 *jin* of grain.[11]

Public Works Projects (yiwu gong).   Peasants have long had to give public service to the state, beginning with corvée labor in imperial times. In post-1949 China, particularly after the mid-1960s, all peasants sixteen to sixty years of age (fifty-five in the case of women) were required to contribute a certain number of work days each year to the state. The number varied: in one locality it was sixty days for men and thirty days for women; some peasants were requisitioned for as long as a year.[12] The teams were responsible for the upkeep of the laborers—both their work points and their food (*huoshi fei*).[13] They were required to provide peasants sent for such work with sufficient grain or grain coupons for the duration of their public service. In addition, they were to be compensated with the highest number of work points for every day of public work.

Prior to the Cultural Revolution the state paid most labor expenditures for public works projects, such as irrigation or road building; teams sent only labor.[14] Around 1969 funding for many of these projects appears to have been decentralized; more burden was put directly onto the local levels. Projects were divided between those organized at the national or provincial level and those organized by the county, commune, or brigade. Only nationally and provincially organized projects continued to be funded, both in money and in grain, by the state; county, commune, and brigade projects suffered severe cutbacks in state funding. Once financing fell to the localities, production teams bore the brunt of the costs.[15]

11. *FBIS* 26 August 1981, p. K1. The article implies that this grain should rightly have been distributed as increased grain rations to the peasants working in the teams. The report also notes that in addition to the grain, each member contributed 32.95 *yuan* because each work point was calculated at 0.8 *yuan* per day, for a total of 42,968 *yuan*.

12. I 1/6680. Earlier studies of public service labor have few specific details on payment procedures. See, for example, James Edward Nickum, "A Collective Approach."

13. One team leader from the south said that in certain cases the teams could resist and claim there was no more grain in the team to pay for the water works projects; then the communes would be forced to provide more grain. I 1/6680. Such behavior, however, indicated a "backward element" and was therefore to be avoided.

14. The figure of sixty days was quite flexible and depended on the needs of the project. I 4/27180.

15. The state occasionally supplied some of these expenses. For example, in one northern province teams assigned to work on a *yiwu gong* project supplied sixty *jin* of grain per peasant; moreover, the team received money from the organizer of the public

Team expenditures for public works projects became one of the most costly demands made by the upper levels. One former team leader quickly identified these projects as the reason why many teams were poor.[16] Another said that thousands of labor days were lost; some of his people were away all year.[17] An official report on the burden of government-imposed public work found that the labor cost in one commune in Sichuan consumed 10 percent of its total labor input every year.[18]

In analyzing the costs, one must distinguish between the collective and the individuals. Both were affected; however, the individual peasants sent to work on public works projects suffered mainly because they were taken away from their families and private plots. They continued to receive their grain rations and the maximum number of work points. The production team as a collective bore the heavier burden. Because the value of the work point was determined by the total income of the team, the extra work points given to peasants sent on public service reduced the value of each work point, without producing any extra income for the team. This made the peasants called away for public service work, like those who worked in rural industry, "nonproductive personnel." But worse than the factory worker whose work points at least brought cash into the collective, public service workers made no immediate contribution to the team's annual income—in labor, grain, or cash. Instead, the high work points given to those sent out only lowered the average value of each individual work point for the team as a whole.

Water works projects constituted a major portion of these public service jobs; some of these projects were no doubt useful, but others were not. Again many team leaders complained that much grain was "wasted" when peasants were sent off to build irrigation works and other "basic agricultural construction" (*nongye jiben jianshe*) that did not benefit their teams directly.

Some of the most wasteful projects stem from the blind implementa-

---

works project, and the peasants received work points. I 1/6680. More research needs to be done, but from present data this seemed to be the exception rather than the rule after the mid-1960s.

16. Unfortunately, I do not know what precisely this meant in terms of actual costs to his team. I 2/211279; similar account in I 1/19680. Also see *FBIS* 29 September 1981, pp. K13–14.

17. See, for example, I 1/6680. The waste that resulted from the various construction projects under Learn from Dazhai has been confirmed in the Chinese press. See *FBIS* 26 August 1981, pp. K1–3.

18. Song and Zhang, "Important Changes," p. 16.

tion of policy in the heat of campaigns. In an extreme case, cadres under pressure to learn from Dazhai were forced to terrace a relatively flat piece of land. This wasted the team's effort; but worse, it meant that much of the team's farm machinery could no longer be used on the fields. The team not only paid the short-term costs of this "construction" but also bore the long-term costs as the use of their achievements in mechanization became impractical.[19]

In a 1977 example, a team was told to terrace a mountainside to plant crops. Both the team leader and the peasants opposed this; they knew felling the trees and clearing that particular area would cause erosion and the new fields would be washed away with one good rain. But because the team leader was ordered by the brigade secretary to follow higher-level directives, the task was undertaken. The brigade, perhaps because it too was aware of the folly of the project, tried to ease the situation by giving the team incentives to comply. The brigade offered extra grain as a positive incentive, along with the threat of a daily fine to ensure compliance. Peasants who refused to go were fined two *yuan* for each day they resisted. The project was completed, but the following year the fields were washed away by the runoff from the mountain, as the peasants had predicted.[20]

Since 1979 the state has publicly admitted the problems caused by the public service work and recognized the resentment it caused. It ruled labor requisition by communes and brigades unlawful without the consent of the teams themselves.[21] However, in the New 60 Articles the state makes clear that peasants still must pay some of the costs of rural construction. The units that benefit from the small-scale local projects are responsible for providing the costs. The state only provides for the medium and large projects.[22] In 1988, almost a decade into the reforms, peasants still have an annual public service quota.[23]

TEAM EXPENSES

At the same time that a team leader faced brigade and commune demands, he had pressing needs for grain within the production team itself. These internal team expenses varied, but they generally included production costs, social needs, and emergency funds.

19. I 29/8680; I 29/24680.
20. I 2/181279; I 2/3180.
21. See "New 60 Articles," pp. 110–111.
22. See Article 19, ibid., p. 106.
23. China Interviews, 1988.

Production Expenses.   Neither budgeted into the state's apportion-ment of the harvest nor taken into account in its definition of the surplus were routine production costs. These included funds for chemical fertil-izer, extra fodder, new equipment such as water pumps, and payment to those who worked for the collective, such as tractor drivers hired to plow or move crops. The investment fund (*gonggong jilei*) officially covered these production expenses, but it was frequently insufficient.

The paucity of the investment fund was particularly problematic dur-ing the Cultural Revolution, when the policy of "taking grain as the key link" forced an increasingly large percentage of a team's income to de-pend on the increasingly unprofitable sale of grain to the state, as shown in Chapter 3. During this period profitable sidelines and cash cropping were criticized, cut drastically, or in some cases completely halted.[24] As a result, some teams operated continually in the red; they had no in-come to distribute to their team members for years on end. Much in-come from grain sales went toward production expenses.

Such teams were caught in a vicious circle. They had to grow and sell grain to the state, but the income from grain sales was insufficient to cover production costs or allow a profit for further investments. To at-tain higher yields, teams had to make increasingly high investments in production inputs, particularly chemical fertilizer, but that required more funds. In the example of Gaocheng county, Hebei, which I cited earlier, production expenses increased from 35 percent to 46.7 percent of the total income during the period 1971–1977, when grain was grown almost exclusively and profitable sidelines discouraged. This county achieved high yields and made larger sales but was still poor. The county's total agricultural income from 1973 to 1976 increased to 12,550,000 *yuan*, but total investment climbed to 13,980,000 *yuan*, leaving the county over a million *yuan* in the red.[25]

Social Expenditures.   Aside from purely economic uses for grain, teams also needed grain for what can be called social expenditures. In the countryside, meals or gifts of food were common and effective meth-ods to cement useful personal relationships (*guanxi*). Such expenditures were seen as worthwhile investments for future favors. Upper-level offi-cials were customarily entertained and treated to dinner when they

24. The years 1971–1973 formed a particularly strict period for sideline industries in parts of north China. In fall 1973 regulations were sent to the lower levels, allowing some diversification of agriculture. Because my interviewee's team was in a mountainous, for-ested area, forestry became an income-producing option for the team, at that point. I 21/11280; I 21/22280.

25. "Gaochengxian zenyang gaibian," *RMRB* 8 July 1979:2.

came on inspection trips; tractor drivers were provided meals when they came to plow the fields.

The treatment of tractor drivers is particularly interesting because it illustrates the way food (grain) becomes a currency of exchange in the economy and bureaucracy during this period in China's history. Tractors were scarce and their services were in high demand. Most teams did not own large tractors but used the collective machines of the commune. During peak season all teams needed to have their fields plowed at the same time—a few days difference in plowing and planting could mean the difference between a fair and a good harvest. Often the tractor driver decided which team to serve first. One way to influence the schedule was by establishing a good personal relationship with the tractor driver. A key part of that strategy was to ensure that the driver was treated to a good meal when he came to the team.

Teams also used grain as gifts for gaining specific favors. In one case, the cadres in charge of a reservoir discovered that a team was using the runoff of the reservoir for irrigation. Inspectors threatened to restrict the team's access to the runoff but hinted that an understanding could be reached. During their stay they casually commented on the high quality of the team's rice. The team took the cue and quickly sent these cadres 200 to 300 *jin* of their best white rice. To be safe, the team also presented gifts totaling 1,000 to 2,000 *jin* of grain to the county cadres who were officially responsible for the reservoir, according to the status of each recipient.[26] Such gifts of grain, as a former team member explained, were common and well-accepted "means" (*shouduan*) of "going through the back door."[27] But teams were not provided any extra grain for such social and political purposes.

Emergency and Welfare Expenditures.   Finally, teams had to keep extra grain on hand for unforeseen expenses, including small loans to grain-short families and, perhaps more important, grain to meet the state tax levy and basic sales quota in the event of a lean harvest. Some teams were so poor in the late 1960s and 1970s that they depended on their reserves to meet their annual obligations to the state.[28]

26. I 14/122679.
27. The example just cited involved cadres at a May Seventh Cadre School. As cadres, they knew well the best means of getting things done. But using personal relations and "going through the back door" were also commonplace among peasants, as I shall describe in Chapter 7.
28. See, for example, "Quxiao 'bangmang tian' rushi bao chanliang'" (Get Rid of "Assistance Land," Report True Production), *RMRB* 24 February 1979: 2; and "Yaokao kexue chifan buneng yi laodazu weirong" (Make a Living According to Science, Don't Take Pride in Not Being an Expert), *RMRB* 16 January 1979: 2. Also see I 15/12180.

THE TEAM LEADER'S OPTIONS

Where did the team leader get the grain needed to meet the various demands placed on him? Team leaders who found themselves grain-short because of excessive sales quotas could apply for relief or resale of grain. But, as shown in Chapter 2, that was often a slow and complex process. Moreover, beginning in the Cultural Revolution team leaders were hesitant to ask the state for grain for fear of political reprisals and being labeled "backward elements" (*luohou fenzi*) who had failed to fulfill their tasks.

A team leader might also apply for loans from the collective loan association (*xinyongshe*). But by the late 1960s poor teams found it increasingly difficult, if not impossible, to borrow.[29] The state preferred to make loans to the more prosperous teams, which would more likely pay back the debt, not to poor teams, which were bad risks. In one example from the early 1970s, a poor team in north China tried unsuccessfully for almost three years to get a loan. The money was requested to build a concrete bridge; the team's old wooden bridge washed out at least two or three times a year. But as the team leader explained, "such loans were difficult to come by. One needed special *guanxi* with the brigade, which I didn't have."[30]

Moreover, if people needed grain, money was of limited use. The limited value of money also explains why a bad political stigma was attached to asking for relief grain (*fanxiao liang*). A distinction was made between requesting loans of money and loans of grain. If a team had to ask for a grain loan, it was more acceptable politically if it paid the loan back in grain; it was less acceptable to take aid in grain such as *fanxiao liang*, which required repayment only in money and contributed nothing to the state grain stores.[31]

The state, in short, provided team leaders with few simple solutions. Most team leaders were forced to solve their own problems; often they combined legal and illegal strategies.

LEGAL STRATEGIES

Team leaders left without extra grain to sell for cash and faced with production costs could borrow money from rich peasants, where over-

---

29. For example, based on I 3/15480 and I 21/23180, this was the case at least in some parts of Fujian and Anhui.
30. He was a sent-down youth. I 21/23180.
31. I 29/30680.

seas remittances were common. Such private loans were sometimes colloquially referred to as "high-interest loans" (*gaoli dai*) and officially
termed "taking out a loan for capital investment" (*jie touzi kuan*).[32] The
interest that a team leader offered to the lender in such circumstances
consisted of the right to purchase extra grain during the next harvest at
cheap state prices.[33] This privilege yielded considerable profit for the
peasant, particularly if he lived off overseas remittances and earned few
work points. The black market grain he would have otherwise had to
buy was substantially more expensive, at least three to four times the
state price. An industrious peasant who had obtained extra grain at the
low state price could also sell it for a handsome profit on the black
market.

If the team leader just needed extra grain, it was acceptable and possible to borrow from neighboring teams. The grain-short team leader
would approach a grain-surplus team leader with whom he had good
relations and try to borrow some reserves. Most borrowing occurred
during the traditionally lean months of May and June, the "green
sprouts" (*qinghuang bujie*) period, before the summer harvest was collected and after the preceding year's reserves had been depleted.[34]

Upper-level officials often knew of these loans and, in the case of borrowing to meet state levies, encouraged such transactions. Sometimes
the commune may have ordered one team to loan grain to another team,
but this did not seem common. For the most part, borrowing between
teams was done on a purely informal basis and depended on the personal relations of the team cadres involved.[35] The grain-rich team considered the prospects of repayment as well as the informal terms of "interest," which the borrowing team offered to sweeten the deal. The
interest was neither charged nor offered in money, but as in the case of
high-interest loans, the interest was provided in goods, usually rationed
or hard-to-procure items, including straw for sidelines, fuel, or fodder.[36]
Thus, in the political economy of the period, teams with grain had not
only security but also a favorable bargaining position for valuable
goods.

32. I 3/7480. This was in contrast to the low-interest loans available to teams through
the collective loan association.
33. See I 3/15480. The terms of the interest varied, but the extra grain option was
cited as a common policy if the borrower was the team. Private loans between individual
peasants were arranged on different terms, but grain sometimes figured into the deal.
34. See, for example, I 21/23180.
35. I 10/12480; also I 21/23180; I 15/12180.
36. I 15/12180.

Aside from these informal, but legal, options, team leaders were sometimes forced to adopt illegal strategies.

COVERT STRATEGIES

Previous studies have focused on the formal, overt channels of interest articulation and methods by which peasants affected policy formulation and implementation.[37] Descriptions exist of peasants' participation in direct resistance, work slowdowns, and protests to upper-level authorities, both through work teams and in elections.[38] Team leaders and peasants use these strategies to pursue their interests, but the question remains whether they are the most effective or the most common means by which interests are pursued.

Instances where peasants and team leaders resisted and took overt action appear limited to certain types of situations. Even then most action of this type is restricted to what Chinese call "soft opposition" (*ruan kang*).[39] Those who oppose a directive and want to appeal to upper-level authorities must proceed cautiously and follow certain unspoken rules so as to protect themselves from direct criticism or risk. For example, a team leader ordered to follow a new method of planting sweet potatoes knew that if he followed the directive wholeheartedly, the resulting harvest would be too small even to supply the team members with their basic rations. Nonetheless, he followed the directive. But, at the same time, he devised a way to plant an additional crop between the officially prescribed one.[40]

In this example, the team leader was well aware that his most effective strategy was to follow the directive, but only minimally. This would protect him politically but not preclude him from taking resistive action. A team leader could ill afford not to look both ways in managing production; he had to follow orders, but he also had to protect his team's interests, which in the above case was subsistence. An experienced and crafty leader carries out directives only to the extent that allows him to say he had followed orders. Then after he has imple-

37. Some earlier studies were impressed with the mass line style of leadership as a democratic form of participation. See Meisner, "Dazhai"; Blecher, "Leader-Mass Relations"; and Stavis, *People's Communes*.

38. For example, see John Burns, *Political Participation in Rural China*, on the various modes of interest articulation. Also see Butler, "Conflict and Decision Making," on the decision-making power of various levels in policy formulation and implementation.

39. See, for example, I 29/22680; I 29/30680; I 29/24680; I 29/1780.

40. I 29/22680.

mented a directive, he can legitimately go to a sympathetic upper-level cadre and show firm evidence—his experiences following the directives—that the new policy is bad. As one experienced cadre noted, "Nothing could be done until the evidence had been gathered; only then could the doubter 'open fire' (*kai pao*) and discredit his opposition; only then did he 'have anything that he could say' (*youhua keshuo*)."[41] Most team leaders would not dare do even this unless they had the support of an upper-level official, a patron, or what the Chinese often termed a "backstage boss" (*houtai ren*).

Use of the soft opposition strategy, however, was limited to certain types of issues. Team leaders could not wait patiently and gather evidence to protest against the state's grain policies. Action had to be taken immediately or the grain would be taken by the state. The rules and regulations for dividing the harvest were set and not open to discussion; the chances of receiving extra grain directly from the state in relief were minimal, at best. The only sure way to obtain extra grain was to retain more illegally. Illegal and covert action thus was often necessary to supplement the more overt and legitimate methods of interest articulation. Such indirect methods were the only viable means by which team leaders could fulfill their assigned grain obligations to the state, the collective, and the team.

The key to this strategy was to maintain the facade of compliance by exhibiting at all times correct "outward manifestation of attitude" (*biaoxian*). Outwardly, team leaders accepted state limitations; indirectly and covertly, they pursued their interests by subverting these same limitations. As heads of production units they had immediate access to the harvest and the potential to divert and hide part of the grain before the state could intervene, apportion, or extract it. Combining these two factors afforded team leaders the possibility of altering the basis of the procurement process, diverting grain, and using the surplus that the state wanted to extract or control. As long as noncompliance was not noticeable, a team leader through the covert methods could obtain a good portion of the needed grain.

Hiding Production (manchan).   The smaller the total harvest, the smaller the state levies. Hiding production was a common strategy to reduce the total amount of grain susceptible to state levies. Chinese econ-

41. See I 29/24180. The *houtai ren* were the more powerful cadres that lower-level cadres were loyal to and looked to for protection. They may be considered examples of the patrons I will discuss in the next section of this chapter.

omists have noted the widespread practice of underreporting in grain statistics.[42] For example, Hebei province reported 1978 grain output at 16.15 million tons when the actual output was 16.85 million tons, underreporting 0.7 million tons.[43] Anhui province, in 1979, only reported 16.1 million tons when output was 17.5 million tons.[44] These are examples of underreporting at the provincial level; underreporting also took place, perhaps more commonly, at the team level. This could be accomplished at different stages of the production and harvesting cycle.

While estimating the harvest, team leaders could try to hide some of the new fields, particularly those in the more remote areas or on hillsides. When upper-level cadres came to check a team's acreage and fields sown in grain, the team leader typically accompanied them to the fields; he tried to show them only selected areas. To measure each and every field is an immense and difficult task; upper-level cadres seldom had such diligence or stamina. The laziness or inefficiency of most inspecting cadres and the size of the task facilitated a team leader's ability to hide grain, but he could not hide all increases in production.

More likely a team leader would show the inspector a new field or two that had recently been put into collective production. The trick was to show only those new fields that the team leader had already reported. The logic was to show the inspector some new land and pay a bit more in levies, rather than have a suspicious inspector check all the team's area. Both the inspector and his superiors would more likely feel satisfied that they had done their jobs if at least some new fields and some increase in the harvest were reported. Meanwhile, the team leader, with some luck, was able to escape having all the team's new production discovered. The team might pay an additional 200 to 300 *jin* in taxes and sales, but it would have to pay much more if the full amount of reclamation had been reported.[45]

Regardless of the precise method, the key to the strategy was cementing good relations (*gao hao guanxi* or *la hao guanxi*) with the upper-level cadre doing the inspection. The team leader might appeal to his sympathies or take advantage of whatever personal ties of friendship or kinship (*ganqing*) the upper-level cadre had with the team. Customarily the team leader would bring the inspector back to the team for lunch; often a few small gifts were given.

42. See Sun, "Jiaqiang," *Jingji guanli*, pp. II 3–5.
43. Cited in Walker, "China's Grain Production." For original figures see Sun, "Jiaqiang," *Jingji guanli*, p. II 4.
44. See Walker, "China's Grain Production," pp. 226–227.
45. See, for example, I 21/13180. Here I refer to newly cultivated fields or reclaimed land that had passed the tax exemption period.

Hiding production also took place during and after the harvest.[46] But, as I indicated in Chapter 5, if a team leader wanted to hide production at this point, he had to keep in mind his own signed report of the expected harvest. He could not deviate too dramatically from his initial estimate. Nonetheless, even though the state sometimes stationed upper-level cadres to oversee the division of the harvest in suspect teams, it was possible to hide production as the grain was being harvested, dried, and brought into the granary. Grain could be delivered after dark, when the cadres had left the team for the night or while the cadres were not looking. This grain would, of course, be unrecorded in the official accounts. The official distribution would take place according to the official figures. The unreported grain would then be at the team leader's disposal.

The following example shows how such strategies work. In 1972, in Guangdong, a brigade sent a work team to investigate a production team suspected of underreporting. The production team leader tried to hide the team's real output by instructing his team members not to bring in all the grain from the fields but to leave a few baskets to be secretly brought into the granary after dark without the knowledge of the supervising cadres. The plan worked; the officials were fooled. But in this particular case, the strategy backfired for the team leader. The two peasants assigned the task of secretly bringing in the grain from the fields found the granary locked. They decided to take advantage of the situation and brought the baskets full of grain home. The team leader could take no immediate action; he could not officially impose sanctions on these peasants and report the "theft" to the brigade because this resulted from his own illegal action. There were no witnesses, and the team leader had no way of proving that the peasants actually took the grain to their houses.[47]

A more subtle method was to be purposely careless when harvesting the fields and leave them without carefully gleaning the fallen grain. The harvested grain would be dutifully brought onto the drying fields and weighed in the presence of brigade officials, if necessary. But, as a team leader explained, 1,000 to 2,000 *jin* of grain, or approximately 20 *jin* per *mu*, might remain in the fields. That much grain was left in the fields partly because the peasants were rushed, but perhaps, more important, they were not very concerned with such inefficiency because the grain

---

46. Butler, "Conflict and Decision Making," p. 54, presents similar accounts of hiding production.
47. I 2/211279.

"belonged to the state." The more they harvested, the more they had to turn over to the state.

The grain that remained in the fields either through carelessness or on purpose was not wasted. Once the official harvest had been completed and the "state grain" had been accounted for, peasants were very careful and thrifty about recovering this grain, much in the tradition of gleaning practiced in Europe and elsewhere. Animals were allowed to wander onto the drying ground or the harvested fields to feed. During the harvest, animals, both collective and private, officially were prohibited from being let loose in the drying areas, precisely to prevent this sort of free feeding. Yet it was difficult to prove or stop such action, particularly if the team leader nodded.[48]

Whatever the exact method of keeping back more grain, outwardly the team leader was following orders, harvesting the crops, and fulfilling state levies. But by surreptitiously reducing the total harvested and recorded, the team could legitimately receive lower levies while extra grain remained in the team, without appearing to resist the state's attempt to extract the surplus. If illegally retained stocks were later found, teams might claim that they were part of the grain that had been reported but not yet used.

Obviously this type of strategy had limitations. The amounts withheld from the state were necessarily small; large amounts could easily be detected by visual inspection and spot checks. If the amount of the team's stocks did not balance with the accounts (*shuzi bu xiangfu*), the guilty team would have to sell the extra grain to the state.[49]

Falsifying Accounts.   In addition to, and sometimes as a necessary correlate of, hiding production, team leaders engaged in falsification of accounts, that is, illegal use of legally retained funds (*nuoyong*).[50] Falsifying accounts was not so much to hide the total production from official knowledge as to hide *improper use* of legally retained grain. To do

48. I 21/11180. The parallels with the description in Scott, *Weapons of the Weak*, pp. 256–257, are striking. There he writes about the threshers in Malaysia who are paid according to piece rates, that is, the number of sacks harvested. To maximize their wages they only beat the sheaves two or three times instead of six or seven; this leaves about 10 to 20 percent of the grain, which members of their families will glean.

49. I 1/19680.

50. I 4/6380. The practice of *nuoyong* is not new. For an excellent account of the extent and the necessity of such practices by Qing bureaucrats, see Madeline Zelin, *The Magistrate's Tael*, particularly chap. 2. For studies of the problem for officials dealing with the Qing civilian granary system, see Jean Oi, "The Rationality of Corruption," and Wong and Will, eds., *Nourish the People*.

this, team cadres juggled the accounts and kept two sets of books. The
official set of books was used for inspections and submitted to the brigade; this set contained the figures that the county eventually used to
make the targets and guidelines for allocating the harvest. The figures
on the amounts actually distributed and their uses were kept in a set of
secret books, or perhaps just in the team cadres' head without formal
record.[51]

By juggling the accounts, a team leader could follow official guidelines for the distribution of the harvest but use the grain as he needed,
regardless of officially prescribed limits. For instance, if a team leader
wanted to increase grain rations, he could use grain legally retained for
seed or fodder. This illegal use of legally retained grain may explain why
the amounts of grain kept for fodder and seed increased so dramatically
during the Maoist period (see Chapter 3). The sharp increase reported
by Walker may simply have been local-level response to overly strict
grain ration limitations and local grain reserve regulations as harvests
were increasing and rations decreasing or stagnating.

If a team leader engaged in such strategies, he had to be careful and
stay within the official bounds of thirty to forty *jin* of grain per month
when he officially distributed the harvest, especially if upper-level officials were present. The extra amounts had to be given after the upper-
level cadres were gone. Most important, the team's cadres had to report
that only thirty to forty *jin* had been distributed. The extra distribution
could be falsely listed, if listed at all, as grain kept for seed or fodder or
reserves.[52] The team leader might also write it off as grain for the team's
utility fund (*jidong liang*), which did not require accounting in reports
to the brigade (*bu bei'an*).[53] At all times the team leader had to appear
to be following state directives on distribution of the harvest and therefore serving the state's interests. No discrepancies could exist in the accounts as to the amounts left for basic grain rations, seed, and fodder—
all had to agree with higher-level directives. Only beneath this cloak of
feigned compliance could he pursue his own and his team's interests.

The amount of grain the team leader could divert was still limited.
He had to be consistent in his accounts; large amounts would still be
subject to suspicion. The upper levels, including the commune and the

51. See, for example, I 15/12180. One of the first things work teams did when enter-
ing a team was to impound the team account books and check the actual stocks.

52. For reported cases of this, see, for example, "Renzhen luoshi zhengce zhuahao
shouyi fenpei" (Responsibly Implement Policies, Pay Close Attention to Distribution),
RMRB 12 December 1977:1.

53. I 29/27680.

county, had a relatively good idea of what production in each team should be, if only from past harvests and by comparing production with neighboring teams. Only so much grain could be retained illegitimately. Team leaders needed a legitimate explanation for extra grain remaining in the team.

Manipulating Policy.   Teams had few legitimate excuses to retain the surplus in the team. They were allowed to use a small portion of the surplus as a utility fund, the only extra grain they had free access to. The size of this fund was strictly limited, and overly large claims caused suspicion. The only other grain legitimately retained was the official team reserves (*chubei liang*). But, as detailed in Chapter 4, use of that grain was restricted. Especially after 1969, the state intended it for stable reserves, not to be touched except in emergencies and certainly not for routine expenses.

Regardless of the state's policy objectives, team leaders did use their official team reserves to their advantage.[54] The policy of local reserves, in practice, allowed the team leaders to survive the state's grain apportionment and procurement policies. Team leaders could appear to fulfill their obligations to the state by building local reserves and consequently sell less to the state; then by falsifying the team accounts, they could divert these reserves for unauthorized expenditures. Because most teams kept their grain in one granary, it was difficult to know exactly how much of what grain fund remained; all the grain would have to be carefully weighed, and the books carefully audited.[55] But, as suggested in Chapter 5, this was not a routine procedure. As long as the grain remained in the team, the team leader maintained the most immediate control over use.

Teams used reserves for various expenses, some more acceptable than others. The more politically acceptable diversion of reserves was funding public works projects, especially water works. When a provincial water control bureau chief was asked the purpose of team reserves, he immediately replied that it was to pay for peasants working on irrigation projects.[56] Less acceptable but no less common was the illegal use of reserves for individual loans and supplemental basic grain rations.

54. For an official condemnation of this practice, see "Bixu ba liangshi zhuajin," *RMRB* 5 November 1977:3.
55. In some areas the reserves were kept separately, and special seals were placed on the door of the granaries to keep track of each opening. When the seals were applied by upper-level cadres, it was much more difficult to divert grain from the stocks.
56. Personal conversation, May 1980, with a provincial cadre in China.

In the discussion of the local grain reserve policy in Chapter 4, I described a case in which teams in Anhui were required to reserve 20 percent of their harvest.[57] The teams had no choice but to reserve the grain at distribution time. However, once the grain was legitimately retained and a report made to the upper levels, individual team leaders usually used the grain as they needed. One team loaned out more than 80 or 90 percent of the reserves to grain-short households before the next harvest. Of 18,000 *jin* reserved after the harvest only 2,000 to 3,000 *jin* remained by the following harvest.[58]

In another example, a relatively rich production team increased its harvest from 1969 to 1972. During this same period its grain rations were decreased while grain sales quotas increased. The basic ration decreased from fifty *jin* per month in 1968 to only forty-five *jin* per month in 1969; at approximately the same time the "loyalty to Mao" grain sales were instituted as well as the "war preparedness" grain sales. To avoid selling large amounts of "loyalty to Mao" grain but still appear politically correct and keep more grain in the team, the team leader took advantage of the campaign to build local reserves, begun in 1969, and voluntarily reserved large amounts of grain. Accordingly, the team each year kept over 20,000 *jin* of reserves, in line with Mao's call to "store grain everywhere." But the team leader did not keep the reserves as a stable emergency stock. Instead, the reserves became the crucial source of grain to supplement the team members' reduced rations. In 1969 alone, the team leader loaned out over 14,000 *jin* to meet the grain deficiencies that existed in almost half of the team's households.[59] In other teams, reserves were similarly diverted to meet routine expenses. One team leader, for example, illegally sold all of his team's reserves at high prices on the black market—approximately 30 to 33 *yuan* per 100 *jin*, compared to approximately 9.8 *yuan* at state prices—to get needed cash to buy a water pump.[60]

These examples provide insights into how reserves existed during the Great Leap Forward, when most of China suffered shortages and famine. It is plausible that the newspaper accounts from the period claiming sizable reserves had an element of truth to them. Some of the most posi-

57. I 21/10180; I 21/11180. A directive stamped by the commune was sent down to the brigade concerning the requisite 20-percent reserve. This was a relatively poor area, but the team enjoyed a rich harvest that year.

58. I 21/11180.

59. I 10/4980.

60. I 3/15480.

tive stories are from 1961, the height of the food shortages.[61] Jincheng county, Shanxi province, claims to have sold 2,337,500 *jin* of grain to the state from 1955 to 1960. In the same six years the county reportedly also managed to reserve 388,700 *jin* of grain. In 1961 its brigades reported reserves of 198,500 *jin*, to which they added another 50,000 *jin* for a total of 248,500 *jin* (63.9 percent of the previous six years' total). Moreover, during the same period, its teams reserved 7,600 *jin* as members followed plans to restrict grain consumption.[62] Similarly positive reports boasted that some communes, brigades, and teams as well as individual households had so much extra grain that they sold their reserves to the state, in addition to fulfilling their regular procurement quotas. One brigade, confident of its food situation, sold 15,000 *jin* of its reserves in 1961 because teams under it also had reserved grain. A brigade in Fujian sold the state 31,000 *jin* of both brigade and team reserves, in addition to 10,000 *jin* of grain from individual household reserves.[63]

If these reserves existed, one must question how long they actually lasted as reserves. As the examples from the late 1960s and early 1970s illustrate, a distinction should be made between reported reserves and stable reserves. A local-level cadre could show his political loyalty by putting aside grain and reporting reserves, but once done he could use this grain for other purposes, whether to supplement team members'

61. Not only were reserves sizable, but the grain distribution figures also seem very high, particularly given the famine condition in most areas. For example, a 1962 article stated that between 1959 and 1962 grain distribution per capita in a brigade in Shandong was as follows: in 1959 and 1960, 500 *jin* of grain each year was distributed; in 1961, 496 *jin*; and in 1962, an estimated 600 *jin*. "Lingchenggongshe Dongguodadui jiti jingjide diaocha" (An Investigation of the Collective Economy of Dongguo Brigade, Lingcheng Commune), *Xinhua yuebao* 1962, no. 10. According to interviews with peasants from various areas in China, such distribution would be high even in good years.

62. "Liangnian jieyue chubei liangnian duo mai yuliang" (Two Years of Thrift and Reserves, Two Years of Increasing Sales of Surplus Grain), *RMRB* 28 October 1961:1. A county in Henan said that 71 percent of its teams had kept "*dingliu liang*," a local name for reserves. Originally the team wanted the state to sell it grain as a relief measure, but in the end it was able to reserve grain. "Zhenpingxian duidui jieyue yongliang" (Every Team Conserves on Grain in Zhenping County), *DGB* 20 November 1959. These and other reports of reserves during 1959 are plausible because the situation was not yet critical, but they are still very suspect. See "Xiuxian jihua yongliang xing zheng fengchi" (Xiu County's Planned Use of Grain Becomes Established Practice), *XNHB* 18 October 1959:2; and from Guizhou, "Chubei liang kechi liangnian" (Can Eat Reserved Grain for Two Years), *GZRB* 12 October 1959:2.

63. For the first example, see "Duo mai yiwan wuqian jin" (15,000 *jin* in Extra Sales), *RMRB* 13 December 1961:2. For the second example from Fujian, the 10,000 *jin* represented a collection from 69 percent of the households. "Qiaogang dadui ganbu dailing qunzhong duo shengchan duo mai yuliang" (Qiaogang Brigade Cadres Lead Masses to Increase Production and Sales of Surplus Grain), *XHSDX* 26 December 1961:2.

grain consumption or, in the case of less honest cadres, to engage in corruption and speculation.[64] During the Great Leap Forward, more than
any period, the state was the prisoner of inadequate information from
the lower levels. Reporting was emphasized; little effort was sustained
to conduct on-site investigations of the reserves or to check production.
The reserve program may, in fact, have allowed some areas to survive
the excesses of the "communist wind." Local-level cadres used the policy as an excuse to retain more grain in their units and to avoid larger
sales to the state.

The length of time that local reserves actually existed during the
Great Leap Forward, if they existed at all, is further called into question
by reports of peasants looting state granaries, such as occurred in Sichuan
in 1960 when collective reserves were centralized and put into special
warehouses for safekeeping. Reserves required heavy security, especially
as shortages became increasingly severe.[65] Local peasants sought unauthorized use, and grain-short peasants from nearby communities
sometimes attacked less well guarded collective granaries. In some instances, local peasants broke into their own local granaries.[66]

To what extent were the upper-level cadres, particularly the brigade
cadres, actually fooled by the various tactics of team leaders to hide production and illegally retain grain in the teams? The fact that such occurrences took place does not necessarily mean that the upper levels were
unaware. I shall show in the next section that key actors on each side
tacitly agreed as to how far to push the other. Upper-level cadres only
"kept one eye open" in regulating the state's grain policies.

COLLUSION AND THE
POLITICS OF PATRONAGE

Brigade cadres were local peasants who had intimate knowledge of
team activities. They knew, with relative accuracy, the size of each of
their team's harvest; they also had a fair idea of the various activities
of individual team leaders. The state's control system should have con-

64. It is not surprising that during the Four Cleans Campaign many abuses involving speculation, hoarding, and general corruption of grain were found to have occurred
throughout the famine years when possession of grain was the most valuable resource or
"currency" one could possess.

65. "Lixi gongshe an guiding tiliu chubei liang" (Lixi Commune According to Regulation Puts Aside Reserve Grain), HLB 23 February 1960:2.

66. Tung Chi-ping and Humphrey Evans, The Thought Revolution, pp. 120–121, recall an incident where peasants broke into their local granary in 1961 only to find it
empty, after having been told by their local cadres that it was full.

trolled more effectively the illegal activities of team leaders; its ineffec-
tiveness was due to a necessity of evasion operating at both the team and
the brigade levels. The necessity turned into a rationality of collusion,
which had both an economic and a political basis. This further shaped
the social basis of collusion that in special cases developed into clientelist relationships between brigade cadres and team leaders.

THE ECONOMIC RATIONALITY OF COLLUSION

I have shown that brigades, and to a more limited extent communes,
depended on the teams for a considerable portion of their expenses—
reserve fund, investment fund, personnel salaries, welfare costs, and
most costs of local agricultural investments and construction. This dependence on teams for funds affected their objectivity in regulating state
policies on dividing the harvest. If brigades forced their teams to sell
more surplus to the state, then less grain would be left in the team for
either the teams' or the brigades' own use. Brigades had an interest in
allowing teams some leeway to keep more than the legally allowed share
of the harvest; otherwise, they cut off a major source of their own
funding.

Individual brigade cadres also had reason to give teams some slack.
Because brigade cadres were classified as local, not state, cadres, they
had a personal interest in allowing, at least among their own teams,
both a security margin and an adequate reserve. Their basic grain rations and income were subject to the same basic considerations as those
of other team members. The harvest was limited; the more the state
took, the less was available for distribution and team use.

Farsighted brigade cadres also realized that if teams were allowed to
keep more grain for production expenses, the brigade would eventually
benefit through the teams' increased yields. Because brigade cadres were
local peasants and perhaps because they had been team leaders themselves, they knew well that the basic shares allowed under the state's
regulations were insufficient to meet the costs involved in successfully
managing a team, particularly if production was expected to improve
substantially. They knew that the ability of a team to procure and pay
for chemical fertilizer and machinery meant the difference between a
good harvest and a minimal-to-mediocre harvest.

The leeway that brigade cadres allowed depended in part on team
leaders' likely use of the extra retained grain. If a team had reserves and
then sold them to buy such items as a water pump or fertilizer, usually

the brigade cadres would look the other way. Brigades had to make sure teams sold their share, but they also had to be aware of forcing teams to sell so much that they would not have enough for future production.

Finally, if the teams were pushed to the limit and left with insufficient grain to loan to grain-short households, the brigade would eventually have to step in and provide the necessary welfare because it was the first rung on the relief ladder. If teams were unable to meet their expenses, eventually the team leaders would have no alternative but to apply for relief; this might tarnish the brigade's own political image.

Thus, an informal understanding developed between the brigade officials and the team leaders. Brigade cadres allowed team leaders certain breaks in estimating the harvest, keeping extra reserves, using these reserves, and enforcing higher-level policies—keeping one eye closed—in return for their cooperation in fulfilling the brigade's various demands for grain, free labor, and investment funds as well as in minimally satisfying the state's demands for grain. This was the economic basis of the relationship; brigade cadres were clearly the bureaucratic superiors, but they needed the cooperation of team leaders.

THE POLITICAL CONTEXT FOR COLLUSION

Another factor allowing a team leader to engage in evasion was the chaos that developed in the countryside during the Cultural Revolution. Tighter control is sometimes associated with the Cultural Revolution given the flood of directives from the upper levels, but the number of regulations issued does not necessarily correlate with tighter control. Various cadres at both upper and lower levels report that many directives were issued and team leaders were given numerous reports to fill out but few cadres were sent to see that the policies were implemented, much like at the time of the Great Leap Forward.[67] In other instances, general directives were given, but no detailed instructions were provided for implementing the policies; much commotion and talk but little action resulted. Consequently, team leaders were sometimes left with more autonomy than the piles of directives would indicate.

The factionalism that grew during the Cultural Revolution yielded

67. This section relies heavily on Interviewee 29 from north China, whose job was to check on policy implementation. His views were also echoed by other interviewees, for example, a county work team leader from Guangdong. I 1/3680; also I 4/7280.

conflicting directives and resulted in a less effective control system.[68] Because directives were sometimes contradictory, some were often only partially implemented, others not at all. During the height of the Cultural Revolution and into the 1970s, the factionalism in the leadership provided an umbrella for team cadres who did not want to follow certain directives. Depending on the fortunes of their supporters at the higher levels, lower-level cadres could with relative impunity ignore certain orders.[69] The teams that did not pay their agricultural tax during the worst of the Cultural Revolution upheaval constitute an extreme example of control breaking down.

The factionalism and the uncertainty of the Cultural Revolution were manifested in other more subtle and more common but nonetheless subversive effects on policy implementation. For example, the team leader cited earlier managed to circumvent both the legal limits on grain rations and the supervision of an outside work team when he surreptitiously distributed extra rations. The political climate of the period encouraged the work team and the local cadres to be less than vigilant. Statements from Beijing that stressed that peasants should be given their fair share provided them security and served to legitimate their inefficiency in implementing the harsh local distribution guidelines.

I should point out, however, that as in the case of team leaders who subvert regulations, the work team could not openly oppose instructions from its superiors. The members did not dare to resist openly a directive from the county first secretary; thus, they limited the official distribution to 30 to 40 *jin* of grain. But they quietly disagreed with the policy and showed their sympathies with the peasants. The work team allowed the teams to hide production and report lower crop harvests, informally leaving more grain in the teams. The teams then discreetly used this extra grain as they needed.[70]

The Cultural Revolution also saw a general undermining of the state's control system, which has always enforced compliance through the fear of sanctions. Although this was no doubt true in other periods,

68. For a discussion of various types and definitions of factionalism, see Nathan, "A Factionalism Model"; for a discussion of the factionalism at higher levels that eventually filtered down to the lower levels during the Cultural Revolution, see Lee, *Politics of the Chinese Cultural Revolution;* the prevalence of factionalism in Chinese politics, particularly in the last years of the Maoist era, is reviewed by Michel Oksenberg in "Economic Policy Making."
69. See, for example, I 29/24680; I 29/1780; I 29/24680.
70. I 1/19680.

with the onset of the Cultural Revolution there were even fewer guarantees that a cadre who deviated from the rules would be punished, particularly if he had protectors. Team leaders became harder to control; some became "local emperors"—a term used by peasants to refer to autocratic team leaders who abused their power.[71] This latitude, however, as I shall describe in Chapter 7, did not extend to the peasants; they remained under tight control.

THE TEAM LEADER AS CLIENT

The economic necessity of collusion coupled with the general political climate allowed all team leaders a degree of flexibility and understanding with their respective brigade leaders. The brigade had to view all teams with the same economic logic; all needed some leeway to produce the necessary grain and pay their expenses. Thus, to a certain degree all teams enjoyed some brigade largess. On one level, all teams were part of an informal patronage relationship, but not all teams were given equal consideration. On another level, overlaying these basic economic and political considerations, certain team leaders developed special relationships with their brigade cadres. These particularistic relationships determined the *extent* to which a team leader could maneuver within the economic and political context of Maoist China.

The special relationship that developed between brigade cadres and selected team leaders may be described as a patron-client tie—a dyadic relationship of exchange between two actors of unequal status.[72] A team leader cultivated a relationship with the brigade leader to receive special consideration in matters such as allocating quotas, granting loans, procuring scarce goods, generally acquiring extra resources, and, equally important, regulating policy. Successful cultivation of this relationship increased the team leader's power within the team and made his job easier. In return, the team leader enthusiastically carried out his patron's directives, fulfilled demands for grain and labor, showed support in political campaigns, presented gifts, and gave him "face."

71. The term was also applied to brigade-level cadres. For a detailed description of the power of brigade leaders, see Chan, Madsen, and Unger, *Chen Village;* also Madsen, *Morality and Power.*

72. For a concise summary of the various forms of patron-client ties and power relationships of exchange, see Landé, "The Dyadic Basis of Clientelism," and other articles in Schmidt et al., eds., *Friends, Followers, and Factions.* The present discussion is limited to clientelism between team and brigade leaders; I discuss clientelism within the team in Chapter 7.

As in traditional Chinese society, the object of such relationships was to establish connections (*guanxi*) and appeal to personal feelings of sympathy and friendship (*ganqing*) in return for favored treatment.[73] Because brigade leaders were likely to be long-time acquaintances or even relatives of many team leaders and team members, feelings of *ganqing* were easily reinforced. Whether the exchange relationship was the result of prior feelings of *ganqing*, existing in kinship or friendship, or whether the relationship was aimed at building *ganqing*, the team leader wanted to become a client of the brigade leader, who in turn allowed the team leader a degree of protection against the upper levels. Brigade cadres, particularly those with good connections at the higher levels, were capable of being protectors whom team leaders relied on in the factional struggles that developed after the Cultural Revolution. They could warn team leaders of impending investigations, particularly those by upper-level officials and outside work teams.

I have already cited a number of examples where team leaders used their connections (*guanxi*) and played on feelings of *ganqing* to facilitate their objectives. In Chapter 3 I mentioned the case of the team leader who was given a smaller quota because the brigade leader's daughter was in his team; the team leader had given her special consideration in the allocation of work assignments. Earlier in this chapter I described how team leaders tried to cultivate good relationships with the brigade cadres who came to estimate the crop; the brigade cadres were treated to lunch, given gifts, and generally made to feel that the team members and their leaders respected the upper levels and followed orders. The state tried to prevent these conflicts of interest by using higher-level cadres and outsiders less likely to be prejudiced by personal considerations. But even then, as my examples have shown, the state's control agents were still not free from personal bias.

Thus, the economic rationality of evasion necessitated by the state's grain policies extended to the brigade and fostered the development of patronage relationships between brigade and team officials based on particularistic economic, social, and political interests. This system of clientelist politics served as a channel of interest articulation and participation for those at the local level who had little or no input into the formal policy-making process. It provided team leaders with the necessary room to survive the conflicting demands for grain.

73. Morton Fried, *Fabric*, pp. 206–211, provides a good description of *ganqing* and its role in pre-1949 Chinese society. Its relevance for the analysis of contemporary Chinese peasant society is striking.

One should not conclude, however, that state policy lost completely in this situation. At the same time that patronage made authority more flexible, it also helped carry out policies that might otherwise have been unworkably harsh. The question of winners and losers in the struggle over the harvest is complex. I have shown that the grain illegally retained in the teams did not necessarily go toward the personal gain of the team cadres or the peasants. An accounting of the numerous expenses for which the team leaders needed to retain extra grain makes clear that in the end the grain may have financed agricultural construction or paid for brigade or commune expenses.

This chapter has shown that local actors can influence policy implementation, but it also reveals another of the state's many strategies to control the disposition of the surplus. The state was able to some extent to counteract stagnant procurements through such measures as decentralizing funding of public works projects; this indirectly forced teams to use at least a portion of the surplus, including team reserves.

CHAPTER 7

A Clientelist System

Collectivized Agriculture and Cadre Power

Some team leaders were clients to brigade and commune officials, but all team leaders had the potential to be patrons within their own production team. They could manipulate peasant income opportunities, welfare funds, and rationed commodities. This created the basis for a system of clientelist politics *within* the village. This chapter explores both the limits of team leader authority and peasant dependence to define the characteristics of socialist clientelism.

The Chinese terms for cultivating personal relationships are *guanxi* and *ganqing*. Both expressions may be roughly translated as having connections, or a personal relationship, with someone. But *guanxi* and *ganqing* are not equivalents; neither necessarily indicates a patron-client relationship. Having *guanxi* or *ganqing* with someone can represent either a horizontal or a vertical dyadic alliance. It can be a special system of exchange between persons of equal or unequal status; it can be clientelistic or nonclientelistic. *Guanxi* may be compared to the Russian *blat* or the Haitian *pratik*,[1] suggesting a somewhat casual and nonpermanent alliance. *Ganqing* more closely describes a clientelist relationship, but it can also refer to a strong horizontal dyadic alliance. These terms are of limited use in trying to define a clientelistic relationship because the terms *guanxi* and *ganqing* are applied indiscriminately by Chinese to all forms of personal ties; however, a subset of these relationships is clientelist in their definition here.

Clientelist politics in the Chinese countryside—as in other political

1. On *blat*, see Joseph S. Berliner, *Factory;* on *pratik*, see Sidney Mintz, "Pratik."

systems that exhibit strong clientelist patterns—are addenda to existing institutional arrangements that allow individuals to pursue private interests and to receive special consideration in distributing goods and rewards from those in positions of authority.[2] The degree to which peasants use this informal system varies, as does their dependence on those in positions of authority.

The use of personal relationships to pursue one's interests is so prevalent in China that it is "almost legal"; one's ability to use connections to go through the back door is a mark of status and intelligence. One respondent said, "A private seal [meaning personal connections] is better than a public stamp." It may be considered the "operational code" for how best to get things done in the countryside. As a former team leader summarized it, "People always talk about who has good relations [*guanxi*] with whom and therefore who should talk to whom about getting something done." Thus, in some cases use of patron-client relationships goes beyond being an addendum: it becomes the key to making the best of a hard life in China's countryside.[3]

In this as in other clientelist systems, those who control different resources command different degrees of power and derive different opportunities for benefiting from their positions of power.[4] Chinese peasants who sought to get ahead know well who holds what power. On a relative scale, the status of the team leader was low; the brigade leaders or commune leaders held much more power. But the team leader had the most direct impact on each peasant's well-being; he determined the reassignment or appropriation of private plots, assignment of better jobs, extra work points, an outside job, a contract labor job, or receipt of a loan from the extra grain or cash the team had managed to put aside.

TEAM LEADER
AUTHORITY AND RESOURCES

Production teams were led by a leadership committee made up of a team leader, assistant team leader, accountant, and granary manager.[5]

2. This discussion of clientelism as addenda follows Landé, "Introduction."
3. On the possibility of patron-client relations becoming a "central aspect of institutional patterns," see Eisenstadt and Roniger, "Patron-Client," p. 49. Walder, *Communist Neo-Traditionalism*, chap. 5, explicitly argues this was the case in Chinese factories.
4. One observant former resident of the countryside described this situation: "Cadres at different levels have unequal opportunities. Those at the mid-levels look for opportunities and take advantage of them; those at the lower levels who are friends of those in high positions 'go through the back door'; while those at the higher levels only have to wait for people to come and offer them opportunities." I 2/121879.
5. In some instances, because of the lack of qualified people, brigade accountants

Larger teams also included a work-point recorder (*jigongyuan*), financial officer (*caizhengyuan*), and cashier (*chuna*); in the smaller teams these tasks were handled by the accountant and team leader. Some teams also had a women's team head (*funü duizhang*) and a representative of the Poor and Lower-Middle Peasants Association. The most important team cadres were the team leader, the accountant, and, to a lesser degree, the granary manager.[6] The accountant controlled the finances and kept the books, while the granary manager was responsible for the team grain stocks, tools, and supplies. The team leader, however, usually stood out in this triumvirate as the first among equals. He was designated the "responsible person," the representative of the team in dealing with outsiders. Most important for the peasants, he directed production. As one peasant said, "If the team leader was lazy or inept, we would go hungry."[7]

All team officials were selected from within the team. No set criteria existed for office, but in practice in the pre-1978 period team leaders were predominantly party members.[8] Party membership was less important for the other team cadres, with the possible exception of the Poor and Lower-Middle Peasants Association representative. Although most team leaders were party members, their power stemmed not from party membership but from their office.

In contrast to urban areas, where the party and party members clearly played a distinct leadership role, in rural areas the party and party membership, aside from tenure in office, were relatively unimportant.[9] Neither the party nor party members, as distinct from team cadres, were identified as playing any significant role in the day-to-day

---

doubled as team accountants. In other instances, a team accountant in one team also served as the accountant in another team. For example, one team accountant also held the position in three other teams. I 21/131279.

6. The importance of the Poor and Lower-Middle Peasants Association seems to have varied. One interviewee stressed that the operation of the production team rested on the team leader and the accountant plus the head of the Poor and Lower-Middle Peasants Association—what he termed the "troika," literally the "three-legged horse" (*sanjiao ma*) of a team. In other teams, the Poor and Lower-Middle Peasants Association was much less important, often serving only as the watchdog organization against cadre corruption. I found that some teams deputized an old trusted peasant, often a Poor and Lower-Middle Peasants Association representative, to watch over the collection and distribution of the harvest. I 4/7280.

7. I 19/3680.

8. Parish and Whyte found that 70 percent of all team leaders were party members. Although I have no such precise figures, the general response of my interviewees that almost all team leaders were party members before 1979 suggests that the figure may have been even higher.

9. See, for example, Walder, *Communist Neo-Traditionalism*; also see Constance Squires Meaney, "Industrial Reform."

TABLE 14.   TEAM LEADER CONTROL OVER SOURCES OF
INCOME UNDER COLLECTIVIZATION

Collective Income	Private Income and Loans	Welfare
Distribution of officially allotted basic grain ration	Assignment of private plots	Distribution of state relief
Allocation of work points through assignment of work or work grade	Permission for private employment opportunities in urban and rural areas	Distribution of team relief
	Loan of collective tools and animals for use on private plots	Granting of money and grain loans

affairs of the team. In fact, there were seldom enough party members within a team to form a party branch; most were located at the brigade level.[10] When specifically asked about the party, interviewees answered that it was, of course, important—many team leaders and almost all brigade and commune leaders were members; and members who did not hold leadership positions could attend cadre meetings at the brigade. However, many summed up their assessments by saying that, on the whole, party members "were nothing special" (*meiyou shenme*). In fact, as one peasant put it, "they were often lazy, and we were not afraid to criticize them. They were no different from anyone else."[11]

Team leaders derive authority from their ability to influence the distribution of rewards in collective agriculture (see Table 14). The degree to which they can capitalize on their official positions varies, but unscrupulous team leaders have the potential and the power base to become "local emperors" (*tu huangdi*) in China's countryside. The team leaders' control over distributing these resources is similar to the "monopolization by the patrons of . . . access to the means of production, major markets and centers of the society."[12] Chinese peasants, like political actors in other societies where clientelist politics predominate,

10. A former cadre who taught in a party school said that at least three party members were needed to have a party branch (*dang zhibu*). I 12/11279. Also see Parish and Whyte, *Village and Family*, pp. 37–38. See "Role of Party Branch Committee Defined," *Dang de jiaoyu* (Party Education) 1 September 1985, no. 9, pp. 18–21, translated in *JPRS-CPS* 15 January 1986: 126–134, for details of party branch organization.
    11. I 19/3580.
    12. Eisenstadt and Roniger, "Patron-Client," p. 50.

have "a relatively low degree of autonomous access to the major resources needed to implement their goals and to the control, in broader settings, of their own resources." [13]

COLLECTIVE INCOME

After collectivization, participation in collective labor was the only means of obtaining grain outside the black market, where prices were high and supply uncertain. The amount of collective labor contributed by each peasant was measured by work points, calculated in cash value to cover the cost of rations, such as grain, oil, and vegetables distributed to a peasant household. Any excess cash value was paid in money.

Collectivization also meant that peasants no longer determined their own work schedules. Work was assigned by the team leader and rewarded with work points. Under a standard work-point system, collective labor was divided into various tasks of unequal work-point value and difficulty. Certain jobs worth few work points were both difficult and time-consuming—work that peasants termed "hard to chew [take]" like "pig bones." The peasant assigned these tasks expended much energy but received relatively small reward for his efforts. In contrast, another peasant could be assigned a prestige job, such as tractor driver, that not only paid high work points but also was physically less exhausting. Other jobs, such as collecting manure, offered high work points but were shunned because of the nature of the work. The ideal job assignment paid a maximum reward for a minimum effort.

The Dazhai work-point system was meant to avoid the inequalities created under the piece- and time-rates and to compensate for workers' physical inequalities. Under this system, different work-point values for each task were abandoned in favor of overall performance ratings for each peasant. Political attitude and class background became relevant in assigning work ratings and evaluating performance in order to minimize differences in physical ability. Poor work performance translated into manifestations of political problems.

Although the Dazhai system adjusted for differences in physical ability, it failed to account for differences among jobs. Peasants considered of similar work grade but not necessarily of similar physical ability received the same general work-point rating; those judged the "best" laborers received ten points for a day's work. However, the difficulties of

13. Ibid., p. 64.

the tasks assigned to the "best" laborers were not necessarily equal. There was still leeway for some to be assigned to more difficult or less popular tasks than others. One laborer with a ten rating could be a tractor driver, while another with a ten rating could be assigned to carry manure. As in the earlier standard work-point system, those assigned to the more difficult tasks had to expend more energy. In addition, under the Dazhai system, if a peasant failed to do one assigned task well, his overall work rating might be lowered for falling short of high work performance. Those assigned to relatively simple jobs could easily excel in their tasks and live up to their assigned rating; they could even demand promotion to a higher rating if they had not yet reached the ten level.

Some of the most sought-after jobs were nonagricultural in commune or brigade collective enterprises. For example, peasants sought to work in brigade-run electrical switch factories or commune-run plastic handbag factories as a step up the social and economic ladder; these jobs offered stable salaries, the highest work-point ratings, and better hours and working conditions. The workers were not exposed to the elements, did not have to wade knee-deep in mud or water, and generally did not expend as much physical effort. These jobs, however, were few. The 1979 figures, which reflect the post-1976 push toward economic diversification and sideline development, indicate that only 9.4 percent of the peasants worked in collective enterprises.[14] The percentage must have been considerably smaller in the late 1960s and early 1970s, when sideline industries were denounced as capitalist and most team activity was restricted to agricultural work.

The lack of sideline activity aggravated the additional problem of too much labor and not enough land in an area of high population density. There was simply not enough work to go around. In certain parts of Fujian and Shandong provinces, where labor was abundant and land scarce, at issue was not only the kind of work assigned but also the *amount* of work allocated.[15]

14. Of this 9.4 percent, 30 percent worked in agricultural enterprises, 51.82 percent in industrial collective enterprises, and 5.5 percent in transport. *Zhongguo baike nianjian 1980*, p. 355.

15. The frequency of this problem is hard to ascertain. Even within the same brigade some teams were short of labor while others suffered from the surplus described above. For example, in one brigade in Fujian province only five of nineteen teams were not land-short; in those five many peasants had migrated abroad. In labor-short teams peasants from labor-surplus areas were sometimes hired by various team members to "help" farm their assigned plots of land once the fields had been divided under the responsibility system. These "hired laborers" were paid three meals a day, cigarettes, and drink—all worth approximately one *yuan*.

Whether there was a labor surplus or not, the allocation of agricultural work and opportunities was the prerogative of individual team leaders in their roles as production managers. Each morning the team leader blew his whistle to signal the start of the workday; team members met under the village tree or at the village gate to be told their day's work assignment or to consult the assignment sheet posted by the team leader.

When there was a shortage of work in labor-surplus areas, additional allocation procedures were adopted. In some instances, lots were drawn; in other instances, the team leader assigned the right to work to specific households. Various objective criteria, such as the size of the household, the costs of distributed rations, and the amount of outside income, particularly remittances from overseas relatives, were used to determine the number of workdays or work points each household was allowed per month. In one team, an approximate limit was established so that each household could earn no more than fifty to sixty work points per month—an amount far from sufficient to cover basic costs.

Interviewees stressed that when extra work did exist, the team leader had discretion to allocate the jobs and the accompanying work points. A peasant from Fujian province reported that in his team, when sidelines were banned, the team leader's entire family—wife, two sons, two daughters, and a daughter-in-law—were always assigned work and thus received more work points than other families while one-third of the rest of the team had to search outside the collective for jobs. In some labor-surplus areas, women were seldom allowed to work in the fields, except during harvesting when all labor power was needed.[16] In brief, the team leader determined not only the peasant's work assignment but also the peasant's opportunity.

PRIVATE INCOME

In addition to being able to affect collective income, a team leader could affect a household's private income. Although the desirability of a team job was determined by its work-point value, another consideration was the amount of free time it left for sideline work. Peasants had to balance their need to work for the collective with the need for free time

16. In this example, the lack of work was directly attributed to the curtailment of the team's once lucrative sideline industries. Prior to "taking grain as the key link," the team did not have a problem of surplus labor.

to earn private income. The sales of goods produced on private plots or earnings from private sideline activities in the rural or urban areas provided peasants with private income.

Legal restrictions on peasant earnings from private sidelines have varied over the years. For instance, both the existence and size of private plots have been major issues of controversy. In the late 1960s, in some areas all private plots were abolished and put into collective production.[17] Regardless of the limits on private enterprise in different periods, the team leader always could directly or indirectly affect the income opportunities from private plots and private sidelines.

Private Plots. In some teams, private plots were allocated by the team leader; in others, they were allocated by lot. The assignment of plots was important because they were not of equal quality and desirability: distance from a peasant's home, fertility of the land, and access to water sources determined their value. An unlucky peasant who was assigned a plot far from home had to spend more time traveling; that cut into the time available for tending the crop. It was difficult, for example, to use an extra few minutes during lunch to weed or water—work that a team member with a closer plot could do easily without reducing his contribution to collective labor (and therefore his work points) or incurring the team leader's anger for missing work.

In some teams, private plots were reassigned annually; in others, only every few years; and in still others, never. In teams that reassigned private plots annually or every few years, a peasant family might spend time and resources to cultivate, weed, fertilize, and generally improve the land—only to have the team leader reappropriate that plot a year or two later; he could assign the plot to another family or make it part of the collective fields. The household from which the land was taken would be given another plot of equal size but not necessarily of equal quality.[18]

In addition, the team leader could indirectly affect the output of individual private plots by controlling access to collective tools and animals, such as oxen, that individual team members needed to plow their plots. First use of the team's few animals or tools was essential to a successful

17. *Zhongguo baike nianjian 1980*, p. 337.
18. The effect of such practice is evident in the need to reassure peasants and encourage them to invest in their fields after the responsibility system was adopted and individual households were given plots to contract. A 1984 directive guaranteed the use of contracted fields for a period of fifteen years without fear of appropriation. "Circular on Rural Work in 1984," *Beijing Review* 20 February 1984, p. 6.

crop because proper timing is so important in agricultural work. Use of the collective animals was facilitated for a family that was assigned the task of grazing the horses or oxen: the family not only received a few extra work points for this easy task, but it could also take advantage of its custody of the animals and use them on its private plot before collective work officially began for the day.

In certain parts of north China, private plots were not allotted on an individual basis. Instead, they were collectively farmed, and the harvest divided among the individual households. This solved the problem of the differences in plots, but peasants in such situations fully depended on the collective for this portion of their "private" income.

Private Sidelines.   A second way in which a team leader could affect a peasant's private income was controlling access to opportunities for outside employment—including sideline work and contract labor, and perhaps work in the city—that promised increased income. Transport work, for example, was and still is one of the most lucrative private sidelines. A peasant who owns a mule and a wagon can earn a sizable income by hauling goods privately for teams and individual peasants who must take large amounts of produce to market. A team leader from a particularly poor area in north central China reported that transport work yielded ten times the income earned by working in the fields— about seven or eight *yuan* per day. The same opportunities existed for those who had carpentry and masonry skills; these jobs produced high incomes, but they also cut into the collective labor time required of each team member. Peasants had to be excused from their collective work obligations by the team leader before they could take advantage of such opportunities.[19]

Peasants who wanted extra time for sideline work typically went to the team leader and asked for time off from their collective duties by saying that "they had [other] business" (*you shi*). Team leaders were well aware of the kind of business. They took the team's economic conditions, labor needs, and season into consideration when granting permission. In part of Fujian province, where there was a surplus of labor, team leaders had no choice but to let peasants work outside the collective agricultural system. The same was true during periods of severe food shortage, when some team leaders had to allow team members to go begging for food and find whatever income they could. Teams near

19. The actual authorization (*zhengming*) is issued by the brigade, but the team leader's permission is essential.

industrialized urban areas also tended to allow their adult males to work in lucrative jobs at the nearby factories.

Contract labor jobs in urban areas were particularly attractive because in some cases they afforded a temporary move to the city. When a company in an urban area announced that it needed a certain number of laborers, usually the local commune, brigade, or team cadres suggested people for the positions unless the job called for people with special expertise. The brigade leader and commune official played an important role in selecting the workers, but the recommendation of the team leader was usually a necessary precondition.

Regardless of the exact circumstances, in most cases the peasant who went outside to work was required to return during the busy season to help with the harvest. In instances where a peasant was allowed to spend a major portion of his time in outside employment, he had to compensate the team for loss of his labor.

The amount that teams received from a peasant's outside earnings varied. In one team, the amount of one *yuan* per day had to be turned over. In return, the team leader gave the peasant the maximum ten work points a day and his grain rations. In other cases, a set percentage was taken out. Peasants from a team in Guangdong province who went to Guangzhou (Canton) as temporary workers in 1974 were allowed to keep approximately 30 percent of their wages; 35 percent of the remaining wages went to their team and 35 percent to the brigade and the commune.

If a peasant tried to engage in outside labor without the team leader's approval, the latter had the power to withhold his grain rations. The peasant would then be forced to buy black-market grain, at considerably more expense than rationed grain. An extreme example, from 1970, involved a north China team composed of two surname groups and two nationalities, Han and Hui. The team leader was a Han, as was the majority of the team. Relations between the two groups were poor. Many Hui, instead of working in the team where the cash rewards were small, ignored their collective agricultural duties against the team leader's orders, plying their butchering skills to sell meat at the local markets. Fighting broke out when the Hui returned to the team and found that the Han team leader had cut off the grain rations of their families. The situation became so serious that the army had to be brought in to settle the disturbance. These circumstances were unusual; tensions were heightened by the ethnic factor and complicated because the team leader had molested the wife of one absent Hui peasant. The method of withholding grain rations, however, was commonly used by team leaders to exert control and ensure participation in collective labor.[20]

WELFARE FUNDS

If a peasant could not make ends meet through labor, theoretically he could obtain welfare from the team. The team's limited welfare funds were drawn either from its local grain reserve (*chubei liang*) or from the all-purpose utility fund (*jidong liang*). A team's reserves provided an unofficial margin of security that helped the team leader meet conflicting demands for grain, but it had to be used wisely. Even if there were no demands for extra grain from the brigade or the commune, the team leader still had to decide whether to use the reserves for collective expenses, such as purchasing new machinery, or for individual loans. Chapter 6 has already shown that team leaders operated with tight budgets and seldom had sufficient funds to satisfy all the conflicting demands for grain.

The power to allocate welfare and relief, like other team resources, was concentrated in the hands of the team leader. He issued all team loans; in the event of a severe disaster warranting state relief, he distributed any aid received from the upper levels. Those qualifying for the welfare status of "five guaranteed households" did not have to worry; their needs, including grain, were automatically provided. Where, however, a peasant's welfare status was questioned, the team leader gave the final approval, as he did for the more controversial status of "economically distressed household" (*kunnanhu*).

Both granting aid and borrowing were largely personal interactions between team leader and team member. The needy peasant would typically approach the team leader, tell him his problems, and ask for a loan. Sometimes this procedure was repeated several times before a loan was granted, if at all. Officially, the team leader needed higher approval before a loan could be granted; in practice, as the person charged with the management of production, the team leader controlled all the team's reserves and decided on their disposition. Loan applications never reached the higher levels for approval without the team leader's recommendation. A peasant might try to go around the team leader to the granary manager or the accountant, who in some teams was authorized

20. Butler, "Conflict and Decision Making," pp. 90–93, also mentions similar practices.

to grant small loans, but the chances for securing any substantial amount were slim without the team leader's approval.

During severe food shortages, favoritism on the part of the team leader could figure prominently in a peasant's ability to survive. In famine situations, such as the "three lean years" during the Great Leap Forward, the receipt of a loan or an extra scoop or two of grain could make the difference between life and death. For example, during the "three lean years," one team in north China lost half its working peasants (*laodong li*) to food shortages and related illnesses, such as edema. Before 1962 seventy peasants worked in the team; after 1962 there were only thirty-five. According to a former team member, those who survived the famine had stored extra grain, stolen grain, or been favored by team cadres. The team leader had given certain team members a little extra grain or invited them to eat with his family, which always seemed to have sufficient grain. As might be expected, the granary manager—who because of his position had direct access to grain—also suffered little during the grain shortage. Perhaps equally important, as my interviewee termed it, "he and the team leader wore the same pants" (*chuan yitiao kuzi*)—that is, they were on very good terms and provided each other with special favors. Other friends of the granary manager also fared relatively well during the famine.[21]

In addition, team leaders could practice more subtle forms of discrimination in distributing rationed goods. Manipulation in such cases could involve both the amount and the *quality* of the goods distributed. A team leader could show his displeasure by giving certain peasants level scoops of inferior-quality grain rather than rounded scoops of higher-quality grain. (Grain was often distributed by the granary manager or the accountant, but during harvest time the team leader personally took charge in some teams.) The unfortunate recipient could not say he had been cheated because he had received the minimum amount specified under the official guidelines.

PEASANT DEPENDENCE AND CADRE POWER

Although peasants were tied to their production teams, the nature of their dependence differs from that of clients in other developing countries. In collective agriculture, all peasants in China enjoyed a cer-

21. In this team, conditions were particularly severe because cadres at all levels, from the team to the commune, had engaged in overreporting. As a result, 80 percent of the harvest was sold to the state in 1960.

tain security level or subsistence guarantee, sometimes termed "the iron rice bowl." Official guidelines state that each peasant was to receive a monthly minimum amount of grain as a basic ration (*jiben kouliang*), independent of work points. If grain were available, a peasant who stayed in the team and within the law would rarely be denied grain or left to starve. This minimum security is one of the greatest accomplishments of the People's Republic, a most important distinction of clientelism as it exists in China.[22] Chinese peasants pursued clientelist politics not so much out of fear for their subsistence but in order to live *above* the subsistence level.

The degree of dependence on the leaders also varied. Peasants with outside sources of income sufficient to buy black-market grain (for instance, through overseas remittances), or those with other means of obtaining grain, could afford to be more independent of the team leader's allocation of work and private plots.[23] Team members such as sent-down youth, whom the state supplied for a time with grain ration coupons, extra grain, and money, probably had the greatest degree of independence from the team leader. A former team leader from north China recalled that the sent-down youths on his team were extremely lax about participating in collective labor. Because he held no power over their well-being, he had difficulty disciplining them. Given their independent sources of food and income, they were indifferent about their private plots.[24]

Moreover, as in other patron-client systems, the relationship between peasants and team leaders was not a simple one-sided dependency: team leaders also depended on team members. In the socialist Chinese context, the dependence of the team leader on the team members assumes a particular importance because the position of the former rested on the cooperation of the latter in producing a successful harvest. If a team leader failed to meet production and sales quotas and thus did not fulfill

22. Although peasants have the right to this minimum subsistence, there is not always sufficient grain to ensure these levels; Wan Li admits that 150 million people had been grain-short for many years. Here I want to stress that of the grain available in a village each peasant is given a minimum share.

23. From 1960 to 1966 in Guangdong, for example, those getting overseas remittances were given special coupons for extra rationed goods; however, this is something of a special case. Areas where overseas remittances play an important role have been largely limited to Guangdong and Fujian provinces.

24. Sent-down youths were some of the worst offenders of overdrawing and tended to become permanently "overdrawn households." Part of the problem may have been due to sent-down youths not receiving the same number of work points as local peasants doing the same work; the other part was the unwillingness or inability of sent-down youths to work. For the most comprehensive treatment of sent-down youths, see Thomas Bernstein, *Up to the Mountains.*

his official duties, he was subject to sanctions by his superiors at the brigade and commune levels. As I described in Chapter 5, he ultimately may be removed from office.

Former team leaders explained that although a team leader could use his position to further his own interests and practice favoritism, he always had to be alert to the possibility that he might alienate the majority of his team members to the point where they would no longer obey his orders. He had to maintain a certain degree of fairness.[25] For example, during the famine years of the late 1950s, a team leader could give extra grain to his relatives and favored peasants, but he also had to make sure that the ablest peasants received enough food to continue working. The team leader's need to ensure production and to satisfy the state thus prevented a despotic exercise of his power.

Similarly, political considerations constrained a team leader's power. Relationships were entered into with great care after the Socialist Education Campaign and the start of the Cultural Revolution in the mid-1960s, when peasants were "struggled against" and criticized for associating with those who had either "bad" class backgrounds or a history of political mistakes. A politically wise team leader would rarely grant a former rich or upper-middle-class peasant a loan when there were needy families with "better" class backgrounds.[26] In some cases, particularly during politically charged periods, those with bad class backgrounds were openly discriminated against. For example, a man labeled a "rightist" and "historical antirevolutionary" consistently received poor treatment from his team leader. He had great difficulty getting loans and received lower work-point ratings for his labor; other team members were afraid to befriend him.[27]

The application of punishment was also influenced by political considerations. Team leaders as well as work teams hesitated to apply harsh punishment when the offenders were peasants of "good class back-

25. I would like to thank James Scott for pointing out the similarity to Riker's idea of minimal winning coalitions. William H. Riker, *The Theory of Political Coalitions.* In this case it is to keep enough support to maintain production but not so much that rewards are too diluted.

26. Those with power, however, were not always afraid of taking on clients of bad class backgrounds who provided sufficient economic benefits. In one case, the son of a Nationalist agent became the client (godson) of a brigade secretary. It may be significant that a higher-level cadre—a brigade secretary, not a team cadre—took this sent-down youth as a client.

27. Parish and Whyte, *Village and Family,* pp. 98–100, show that those with bad class backgrounds are at a distinct disadvantage in obtaining leadership positions. Moreover, those related to persons with bad class backgrounds were also routine targets in every campaign.

ground"—that is, poor peasants. As one work team member stated, they would have to do a lot of explaining if a poor peasant were punished, whereas no questions were asked if formerly rich peasants were dragged out and beaten.[28]

A team leader was thus not an independent patron with sole authority over the basis of his power—the allocation of resources and income opportunities. The power of a traditional patron, such as a landlord, is based on personal ownership of the wealth or property used for patronage; by contrast, a team leader's power, granted to him by the state, derives from his position in the administrative hierarchy. A team leader himself depends on others—both the state and his team members—for his power. In this sense, socialist clientelism is one of the more unstable varieties of patron-client relationships.

The team leader can best be described as both a patron and a client, similar to Powell's "political broker."[29] A team leader, as a part of the hierarchical commune system, is a patron to his team but also a client of the brigade cadres. As I described in Chapter 6, he depends on the brigade for his office, his right to distribute the goods available within the team, and thus ultimately for his power. If the upper levels decide to reduce agricultural inputs, cut the team budget, demand higher grain sales, and lower grain rations, the team leader, as a subordinate, has no choice but to carry out such directives.[30]

Still, limits placed on a team leader's power by the higher-level officials and his relative lack of power in the overall commune system do not necessarily affect his power *within* his team. Power within this bureaucratic system is not a zero-sum game.

PEASANT STRATEGIES

All peasants paid attention to their team leaders, but not all peasants employed personal relations in the same way or for the same purpose. Some sought to use personal connections to maximize their opportuni-

28. Team leaders and work team members reported that those with the not-so-good backgrounds were the most cooperative and the least troublesome. They were the easiest to control because they knew that they were the first to be criticized in the event of a campaign and therefore always walked a thin line. The poor peasants, on the other hand, were often the biggest troublemakers; they knew they were "red" and therefore to a certain degree above reprimand.

29. Powell, "Peasant Society."

30. Christopher Clapham notes the conflicting role of brokers as agents of the center and spokesmen for the locales. See his "Clientelism and the State," p. 10.

ties, others only to secure their minimum due. Some merely obeyed, careful not to offend the team leader, and only *occasionally tried* to use connections (*gao guanxi,* or *la guanxi*) with the team leader when they needed a special favor. Others obeyed, careful not to offend the team leader, and *constantly tried* to use connections with the team leader to maneuver themselves into the best jobs and receive special favors. And a few *succeeded,* through the use of personal connections, in attaining favored status as a client of the team leader and were routinely assured of preferential treatment.

The system is fluid. As in other clientelist systems, the behavior and treatment of people shift; they are not always clear. In many instances, it is a matter of the degree to which favored treatment is accorded. However, certain patterns of behavior differentiate those who employ personal relations in the Chinese clientelist context.

CLIENTS

A client is most likely to be assigned the best job, the best private plot, the greatest opportunity for contract or temporary jobs in the urban areas; generally the client receives favored treatment.[31] Rather than having to ingratiate himself actively with the team leader each time he wants a favor, a client relies on an established, long-term understanding of exchange with the team leader. Favors need not be immediately repaid. The balance sheet may stretch over many years; there are "long-range credit and obligations."[32] The long-term nature of the relationship is particularly common if the same person remains team leader for many years or repeatedly returns to power after short intervals out of office. Because there is no set term, a team leader may be in office for twenty years or for only a few months.

As in all patron-client relationships, the value of the goods or favors exchanged is not always comparable or even measurable. The relationship is based on loyalty and trust: in the long run, each must honor the mutual obligations of being patron and client. The patron is obliged to give his client favored treatment; in return, the patron has certain expectations regarding the benefits he will receive.

In the Chinese context, one of the most important benefits for a team leader was respect and the support that entailed. The client was charac-

---

31. It is not assumed that all clients are accorded equal treatment. As Landé, "Introduction," p. xxiv, states, there is favoritism within the clientele.
32. Eisenstadt and Roniger, "Patron-Client," p. 50.

teristically the team leader's most enthusiastic supporter and helper. He could be counted on to praise the patron's leadership and to encourage others to do likewise. He was the first to carry out orders and made sure others did the same. He was the team leader's additional eyes and ears and looked out for the team leader's position. If a political meeting were called, he was the first to speak out in favor of the team leader's position and to encourage others to follow suit. If the team leader had not made his stand public, the client would voice an opinion that he thought the team leader wanted to hear and promote.

Various students of peasant politics have noted that to be spoken well of is of the utmost importance in a village setting.[33] In China, such support is essential because cadres were subjected to investigation in the many and varied political rectification campaigns. When a work team came to investigate a team leader, they proceeded to solicit opinions from team members; then a team leader could turn to his client for help. Team leaders were notorious for trying to bias investigations by placing work teams in the homes of supporters and steering them toward people trusted to praise their performance. In situations where everyone was expected to criticize the team leader, a client would do so, but he would make only the most minimal and insignificant accusations, giving as little damaging information as possible.

Team leaders also benefited from clients privately and materially. Clients routinely provided their patrons with preferential access to rationed or scarce goods that they happened to control. Clerks in the local cooperative store, for instance, alerted their patrons to the arrival of a new shipment of particularly well-made or scarce items and perhaps made them a generous deal—whether a little extra pork or a little extra cloth.[34] In some cases, the items were given as outright gifts. Dinner invitations were also extended, particularly on special occasions, such as when a pig was slaughtered. If the team leader did not accept the invitation, then a prime piece of pork was taken to his house.[35] In short, these peasants, like all clients, tried to make themselves "useful and likable" to their patrons.[36]

33. Scott, *Moral Economy* and *Weapons of the Weak;* George Foster, "Peasant Society"; Parish and Whyte, *Village and Family.*
34. Peasants have a saying: "What peasants need three dollars to buy, cadres can get for one dollar." The meaning is, of course, that position and personal relations make a difference in pursuing one's interests.
35. When team leaders take advantage of their positions in these ways, peasants term it *zhan xiao pianyi* (loosely translated, "taking small advantages").
36. Landé, "Introduction," p. xxiii.

NONCLIENTS

The majority of peasants were not clients, but their behavior was nonetheless affected by the importance of the clientelist system. Nonclients also tried to establish good relations and secure special favors, but the relationship was unstable. Some of these peasants might have given the team leader valuable gifts in private and enthusiastic support in public, but the expectations and understanding of the exchange were qualitatively different. Favors were exchanged on a more precise and instrumental basis, one for one—what Eisenstadt and Roniger would classify as "specific exchange" rather than "generalized exchange."[37] This type of exchange, along with the general phenomenon of "going through the back door," may be likened to the "grease for the administrative wheels" described by Scott.[38] A peasant might have given a chicken or special help to the team leader but with a *specific* favor in mind; the expectation is definite, and the return fairly immediate. Nonclients who persist in using gifts and sycophantic behavior may eventually become clients, but it is difficult to predict. Considerations such as kin ties or good class background seemed to incline team leaders more toward some peasants than others.[39]

Opportunities to cultivate good relations did not always present themselves. Poor peasants who possessed few goods or lacked special skills had few chances to secure favors from the team leader through private gift giving. They could not easily cultivate good relations with the team leader, for example, by inviting him to dinner—especially if there were barely enough for themselves. If, however, the team leader expected to be invited to dinner or given a piece of pork whenever a family slaughtered a pig, then even nonclients usually followed suit.

Such limited manifestations of respect may not have been sufficient to remain on the good side of a team leader. Peasants who had few gifts to give could adopt defensive strategies to protect themselves and their families from discrimination by the team leader and to ensure their minimum due of available goods and opportunities. As a general rule, if one cannot *gao guanxi* or be a client, one should at least aim at

37. Eisenstadt and Roniger, "Patron-Client."
38. Scott, "Corruption."
39. The relationship between kinship and the prevalence of the patron-client system is complex. The data for China are still sketchy. My findings suggest that clanism translates into clientelist behavior most often when two or perhaps three strong surname groups exist within the same team rather than one or many surname groups. But kinship is just one of the many factors that influence whether someone will become a client.

not offending those in power; thus one must show the team leader proper respect, give him "face" and at least minimal compliance, exhibit proper political attitudes (*biaoxian*), and most important, not speak out publicly against him.

Saying the wrong thing—especially in public, and particularly against a team leader—had potentially serious consequences. A person may be labeled politically unreliable, unpatriotic, revisionist, or anti-Mao—to name only a few dreaded designations. If a team leader wanted to discriminate against a team member in distributing economic goods and opportunities, such a designation provided a perfect excuse. People sometimes attacked one another for past political mistakes, bad class background, or reportedly unpatriotic comments, when, in fact, the real reason for the attacks stemmed from longtime personal or economic feuds and vendettas. Political labels and ideology can be used to disguise patronage politics, a common practice during the Cultural Revolution.

In one case, a team member was singled out and punished for reportedly criticizing a 1974 local grain reserve policy that ordered teams in a particular area to keep 20 percent of the harvest from distribution to the peasants. The accused peasant was used as an example: he was not allowed to work on his private plot and was ostracized by the other peasants. This attack actually stemmed from a personal economic feud with another team member, not from his political statements. His accuser was the person with whom he shared a large house; they had argued over the ownership of some chickens and pigs that both families raised in their common courtyard.

Many peasants are unwilling to voice their opinions in political meetings and generally avoid political activity if they can. But peasants were sometimes coerced or in some instances—after the start of the Cultural Revolution—paid to go to meetings. In one area, peasants were given eight work points—when ten was a maximum in many teams for a day's work—and sometimes free food as an incentive for attending political meetings. In another instance, peasants had work points deducted when they failed to attend. Both former team leaders and peasants reported that peasants disliked attending meetings, seldom spoke, and definitely would not express their true feelings in formal settings, even if called upon to speak. Most important, they would not speak out against their leaders.

A former team leader described most meetings, particularly political ones, as a time when peasants talked among themselves, slept, or knitted; they seldom actively listened or responded as he discussed, explained, or read the latest directives from the upper levels. When he was in front of the peasants wearing his "team leader's hat"—acting in his official capacity—the peasants generally did not share their opinions on policies he was formally presenting, particularly if upper-level officials were present. But they were not without reactions: when he took off his "official hat" and talked among them privately and informally as a neighbor, "off the record," he was barraged with their opinions. He said "it was like being two people."

Peasants were sometimes quite active in meetings that directly affected their economic well-being, such as those that determined work points and work ratings or decided the year-end distribution.[40] These meetings often turned into shouting matches as peasants fought with each other over payment for their collective labor. But even in these economic meetings, peasants tended to watch what they said. In politically charged periods, such as the Cultural Revolution, too much open concern for one's work points, grain rations, and income could result in charges of being a "capitalist roader." Advocating the distribution of more harvest as rations, rather than selling more to the state or keeping reserves, resulted in political attacks during the early 1970s.

When peasants did speak up at political meetings, participation seems to have been more a necessary response than a spontaneous remark. A good example is the criticism sessions held during campaigns. When a person was under investigation and the outcome was relatively clear, peasants—even those following a defensive strategy—felt obliged to speak up. If a response was called for by the leadership or the work team conducting the meeting, politically astute peasants followed the cues of the activists by speaking out, harshly or leniently, about the person under investigation. The "activists" (*jiji fenzi*) in a team usually consisted of young, ambitious people who were not afraid to speak

40. During such discussions peasants complained and asked for higher rations, but in the end the team cadres decided the actual amounts. Team cadres had a monopoly on information needed to make such decisions. They knew in advance how much they had to keep for expenses, to sell to the state, and to distribute to the peasants. There was participation in these routine business meetings, but it was controlled participation: the agenda of issues and outcomes was never much in doubt. In some cases, a decision may have been a foregone conclusion, but the team leaders nonetheless presented it for collective discussion and approval, as a necessary courtesy. The purpose of most collective team meetings was to educate, explain, and convince the peasants of the correctness of decisions that leaders had already made, rather than to allow peasants actually to formulate policy. Slight adjustments in a decision might be made, but the main policy was usually not changed.

out—frequently the so-called "backbone elements" (*gugan fenzi*) who had good class backgrounds and nothing to hide. Work teams sought out these people for information on problems in the team; they met prior to criticism meetings—for instance, to prepare "black materials" (*hei ziliao*) used to incriminate the person under investigation and to decide who would raise what points during the public meeting. The agenda was set, and each person's part was rehearsed. At the mass meeting, they would proceed as planned, present the evidence, make the accusations, and then try to arouse others in the audience to follow their lead.

Fear of offending those in positions of authority who determine their immediate well-being is most apparent in a reluctance and even resistance to using the formal channels provided by the government for interest articulation and protection against bad team leadership. Peasants have the option to appeal to higher-level authorities against their team leaders. In some cases, special work teams are sent to investigate and remove ineffective or corrupt team leaders. Peasants as well as former members of work teams repeatedly reported that although work teams supported a team member's charge against a team leader and removed him from office, most peasants hesitated to speak out against the team leader. Their concern was that he would some day come back to power and make life miserable in minor but nonetheless significant ways; the Chinese call this giving someone "small shoes to wear" (*chuan xiao xiezi*).

It was not uncommon for a team leader to rise and fall several times in his career, particularly if he was basically successful in organizing production. For example, over a period of eight years—from 1963 through 1970—one team had four changes in leadership. The peasant who was team leader fell in 1963, came back in 1965, fell again in 1967, and then came back to power once more in 1970.

In short, the economic dependence of team members undermined the effectiveness of the formal channels of interest articulation, which previous studies have described.[41] The team leader may have been in the same socioeconomic class as his team members, may have received relatively small official compensation for his services, and may have been under the thumb of the upper-level cadres, but that did little to change the fact

---

41. See Meisner, "Dazhai"; Blecher, "Leader-Mass Relations"; Stavis, *People's Communes;* and Burns, "Elections" and "Chinese Peasant."

that he held tremendous power over peasants within the production team.[42] Whether passive or active, both public and private political behavior of peasants consisted of calculated responses in keeping with the general strategy of maintaining good relations with the team leader who was in immediate control of their economic well-being. Peasants pursued their interests through the discreet, informal, and personal channels of a clientelist system of politics.

SOCIALIST CLIENTELISM

The pervasiveness of personal ties, informal influence, and personal authority makes one wonder about the nature of the changes wrought by the communist revolution. One might be tempted to conclude that collectivization and the new power structure are but thin veneers that shield traditional types of behavior. There are, for example, striking similarities with Morton Fried's descriptions of the pre-1949 Chinese countryside, where personal relationships (*ganqing*) formed the "fabric of Chinese society."[43] It would be a mistake, however, to think that the fabric is the same. Personal relationships still constitute the fabric of Chinese society, but the new cloth has a significantly different weave and color.

Under collectivized agriculture, peasants have fewer opportunities to cultivate the multipatron networks described by Fried. Separate ties are not established with local officials, landlords, rice merchants, middlemen, and various peddlers. Under Maoist socialism, sale and procurement of essential goods and services are funneled through a single, state-approved local official, the team leader, or the state cooperative store. Authority is concentrated in the hands of a local political official on whom the peasants economically and politically depend. In collective agriculture, clientelism is comparable to authority relations in feudal or traditional premarket agrarian settings; that is, peasants are almost totally dependent on a single elite. However, peasant dependence and elite power in a socialist system are significantly different.

---

42. My view differs from previous studies, such as Parish and Whyte's work that questions the power and rewards of team leadership. They recognize the potential for power and the concentration of resources in the hands of team leaders, but in the final analysis they conclude that "rewards of office barely compensate for the costs of extra hours of work and criticism from villagers below and government above." Parish and Whyte, *Village and Family,* p. 114.

43. Fried, *Fabric,* provides the classic description of the peasants' need to cultivate good relations in their daily lives.

First, the local leaders and the peasants who directly depend on them often have the same socioeconomic background. Patrons and clients may all be, and frequently are, poor peasants. As in Djilas's "new class," power and (unequal) opportunities in a socialist clientelist system are based on *position* within the communist bureaucracy.[44] Local patrons derive their power from their position to allocate essential goods and services rather than from private ownership of the bases of patronage. Comparisons may be drawn between socialist patrons and the party bureaucrats described by Powell who become "political brokers" through the distribution of party-controlled goods.[45] An essential difference, however, is that in the Chinese socialist case only one party and its agents control access to all essential goods—including food, work, and income opportunities, not just public goods such as road building or schools.

Second, even though under socialism peasants depend on their political leaders for a wide range of goods, their position is much more secure than that of Scott's traditional peasants. Under collectivization, peasants are guaranteed a minimum subsistence through the distribution of the basic grain ration, regardless of their physical abilities. Consequently, they do not need to pursue clientelist politics in order to safeguard their subsistence. But peasants do pursue clientelist politics as a means of getting ahead and receiving special consideration in the distribution of the rewards available in a system that theoretically prohibits unequal access to goods and resources. Clientelist strategies are *interest-maximizing* rather than risk-minimizing.[46]

Introducing markets into a traditional agrarian setting has been seen as disruptive to patron-client relations, causing landlords to extract more surplus for sale from the peasants.[47] It has also been argued that markets provide increased opportunities for peasants to develop exchange relationships with elites other than their landlords and can thus strengthen their positions.[48] Opportunities are even greater for peasants if there are competitive electoral politics in which potential patrons vie for support.[49] It is unlikely that Chinese peasants will ever find them-

44. Milovan Djilas, *The New Class.*
45. Powell, "Peasant Society."
46. In this sense, my analysis is closer to Popkin's view of clientelism. See Popkin, *The Rational Peasant*, pp. 72–82.
47. Scott, *Moral Economy;* Scott and Kerkvliet, "Traditional Rural Patrons"; Wolf, *Peasant Wars;* Moore, *Social Origins.*
48. Popkin, *The Rational Peasant.*
49. Scott, "Patron-Client Politics" and "Corruption."

selves in a situation of competitive electoral politics, but since 1978 sweeping economic reforms have given markets an increasingly important role. The system of collectivized agriculture has been dismantled; peasants now contract for and work individual plots of land. Team leaders no longer have the power to determine peasant income through the assignment of work, nor do they have the power to apportion the grain harvest. In fact, peasants are no longer required to participate in collective labor. Rationing still exists; but grain can be purchased, if at higher prices, on the free market, where peasants, after meeting their quotas, can sell their surplus.

What impact have the sweeping reforms of the 1980s had on peasant-state relations and village politics? I consider this question in the remaining chapters of this book.

CHAPTER 8

A New State Strategy

Prices, Contracts, and Free Markets

Just two years after the death of Mao Zedong, the December 1978 Third Plenum of the Eleventh Party Congress opened the door to a new era of rural development. In rapid succession the government reopened markets, raised state procurement prices for agricultural goods, diversified the rural economy away from its singular emphasis on grain production, and replaced the collective system of agricultural production with the household responsibility system.[1] In 1985 it abolished the system of unified procurement in favor of contract purchases. Thus, within less than a decade after Mao's death, the party dismantled the defining structural features of collectivized agriculture described in this book and laid the foundation for a new stage in peasant-state relations.

The return to household farming signaled the state's decision to change the terms of the struggle over the harvest. Most important, it pointed toward the state's decision to allow the peasants, for the first time since collectivization, to define the surplus. Peasants are now allowed to consume as much as their own family harvests can provide. No longer do they depend on the team for their basic food supply. Work points, grain rationing, and state-set limits on consumption are relics of the past.[2]

1. The details of the responsibility system have been examined elsewhere. See Kathleen Hartford, "Socialist Agriculture Is Dead; Long Live Socialist Agriculture." For an overview of the economic problems that led to the reforms as well as the reforms themselves, see Carl Riskin, *China's Political Economy.*
2. Grain rationing technically still exists in that each person is allowed to procure a limited amount of grain at state prices. But for those peasants who grow grain, the system

The responsibility system has nullified the collective's legitimate claim to the harvest. Each household now owns its individual harvest. It turns over a set amount of the harvest to the state in taxes and sales, and then it is free to dispose of the remainder as it pleases, including selling it on the free market. The collective no longer stands between the peasant and his harvest; no longer is it allowed to retain grain for fodder, seed, rations, or local grain reserves. The collective receives only the grain that the state provides, that peasants might voluntarily contribute to the village, or that it can squeeze from the peasants through illegal surcharges.[3]

The state has further facilitated the peasants' ability to define the surplus by changing the procurement system itself. It has reduced its procurement quotas and allowed peasants more leeway in deciding how much to sell to the state. Concerning a village's grain harvest, Scott and Tilly may have been right in stressing that "what is taken out" may not be as important as "what is left" in determining peasant political action.[4] But the disappointing performance of Chinese agriculture during the Maoist period made the leadership aware that what is taken out and what peasants are allowed to consume are important in determining peasant enthusiasm toward production.

Not only have the reforms left more grain in the village, but they also have for the first time since the 1950s allowed peasants free access to that grain. The reforms nullified the local grain reserve system, put stricter limits on the amount of funds that villages had to expend on the "public works," and simply allowed peasants unrestricted access to larger portions of the harvest.

The state is still a competing claimant for the harvest, but the terms are more favorable to the peasants. The agricultural tax remains as inevitable as ever, but it is decreasing relative to the increasing size of the harvests. In 1983 it was only 4.1 percent of the total grain output; after tax remissions and reductions the actual rate was only 3 percent, the lowest in the PRC's history—21 percent of the tax levied in 1952.[5] In

---

for all intents and purposes is defunct. There are no limits on the amount that they can keep. Those who do not grow grain are, however, still limited by the rationing system, but now large supplies exist on the open market, if at higher prices.

3. This lack of access to the income from agricultural production is at the root of the demise of collectives that engage only in farming. Collectives that have other sources of income, such as rural industry, are quite strong and able to continue to redistribute substantial amounts of income to their members. See Oi, "The Chinese Village, Inc."

4. See Chapter 2.

5. "Dui gaige," *NYJJWT* 1985, no. 4, p. 36.

poor areas that do not meet minimal levels of production and distribution the agricultural tax has been reduced and in some cases eliminated.[6] Perhaps more important, the state pays peasants more for the grain that it does procure. The reforms dramatically shifted the state strategy from one based on administrative measures to economic incentives, using both procurement price increases and increased production of consumer goods to secure the grain surplus.

Few would question that these reforms have restructured the relationships between the state and the peasantry and between the peasants and their local cadres. The question is precisely *how*. In this chapter I will consider the impact of these changes on peasant-state relations; in the next chapter I will examine how these changes have affected village politics.

PROCUREMENT PRICE INCREASES

The state not only needed the peasants to produce more, but it also needed to induce them to sell more of what they produced. To achieve this, the state had to pay the peasants more for their grain. For the first time in over a decade, in 1979 the state increased procurement prices, paying on average 20 percent more for basic procurements and increasing the bonus for overquota procurements by 50 percent.[7] The increase in basic procurement prices alone accounted for a 44-percent rise in the value of collective sales to the state between 1979 and 1981.[8]

Peasant incomes increased substantially. The average increase in rural per capita income, adjusted for inflation, was 11.4 percent per year between 1978 and 1981, compared to only about 0.5 percent per year between 1957 and 1977.[9] The increases have continued each year. From 1980 to 1984 peasant average annual income increased from 191.5 to 355.3 *yuan*, with an annual growth rate of 16.8 percent.[10] Average rural

6. "Caizhengbu jueding bing guiding shishi banfa jinyibu jianqing nongcun shuishou fudan" (The Ministry of Finance Decides and Stipulates Procedures to Further Decrease the Rural Tax Burden), *RMRB* 2 October 1979:1.

7. "Guowuyuan tigao shibazhong zhuyao nongchanpin shougou jiage" (The State Council Increases the Price of Eighteen Major Agricultural Products), *RMRB* 25 October 1979:1. In some areas, to provide further incentives to grain producers, township governments have started paying them an additional subsidy of twenty cents per kilogram of grain sold to the state. Xue Muqiao, "Rural Industry Advances Amidst Problems," *Beijing Review* 16 December 1985, vol. 28, no. 50, p. 19.

8. Lee Travers, "Getting Rich," p. 114.

9. Ibid., pp. 111–112.

10. "PRC State Statistical Bureau Survey Shows Peasants' Improved Lot," *China Daily* 28 September 1985:1, in *JPRS-CPS-85-110* 28 October 1985:39.

income reached 400 *yuan* by late 1985. Adjusted for inflation, the overall rate of income increase from 1980 to 1985 was 14 percent per year.[11] Equally, if not more, important, in contrast to earlier periods, this increase in sales and income did not come at the expense of consumption. Basic grain rations, which had fallen by 1 percent from 1957 to 1977, rose by 5 percent in 1979 while average grain consumption rose by 3.6 percent and average fine grain (rice and wheat) consumption rose by 13.8 percent.[12]

To further spur production and sales to the state, the government reintroduced the system of negotiated sales (*yigou*) to compete with the newly opened free markets. Under this arrangement, the state pays a high negotiated price for the overquota purchase of grain. The price is pegged to the market price of grain—in that sense it is "negotiated." A version of these sales existed in certain areas before 1964, but it was abolished during the Cultural Revolution and did not become widespread until 1979, when peasants were allowed to sell their extra grain on the open market after paying their taxes and satisfying the basic quota sales.[13]

The government uses these negotiated sales to regulate the market flow of grain, in much the same way as the traditional Qing state used the *pingdiao* system of selling grain from its system of local civilian granaries to bring down its market price.[14] The contemporary state's policy, called *tun tu*, to "swallow and spit up," buys and sells grain as the market demands.[15] Money for negotiated purchases is issued from the central government to counties, which make purchases through their grain stations.[16]

When the system first began in a grain-rich part of Guangdong in 1979, the state instituted a profit-sharing plan for granary cadres to ensure that those cadres exerted maximum effort in buying up the peasants' surplus grain, which might otherwise be sold on the newly legal-

11. Tian Jiyun, "On the Present Economic Situation and Restructuring the Economy," *Beijing Review* 10 February 1986, vol. 29, nos. 6 and 7, p. VI.

12. *Nongcun gongzuo shouce* (Handbook of Rural Work), pp. 317, 320.

13. I 5/10380; I 29/13780; I 29/24680. I also found that they existed in 1970 in southwestern China where the price was 18 *yuan* per 100 *jin*. I 15/12180. According to Maxwell and Nolan, "The Procurement of Grain," p. 305, it was reinstituted in the early 1970s.

14. For a discussion of the Qing practice of *pingdiao*, see Wong and Will, eds., *Nourish the People*.

15. "Jiaqiang lingdao zuohao liangshi gongzuo." (Strengthen Leadership and Improve Grain Work), *RMRB* 26 November 1979:1.

16. I 5/10380.

ized grain market. Of the profits made from the sale of this grain, 70 percent went to the national government, the county grain bureau (*xian liangshiju*) kept 10 to 20 percent, while the commune grain station (*liangguansuo*) kept 10 percent. Within each level of the granary system, the cadres could decide among themselves who would get how much. In Guangdong, this incentive system had a tremendous impact on the earnings of granary workers. Salaries almost doubled. The average monthly base salary for a granary cadre at the commune level was between forty and sixty *yuan*. The head of such a commune grain station, for example, was paid fifty-two *yuan* per month; the bonus that one such granary head earned from negotiated sales ranged from forty to eighty *yuan* extra per month.

Granary cadres thus eagerly solicited grain sales from local peasants. Like other types of sales, all grades of grain were accepted. Prices varied; for example, during one period, the granaries purchased the grain from the peasants at approximately twice the lowest state price (*paijia*).[17] The combination of high prices and granary cadre initiative resulted in an increase of negotiated sales from just over 0.2 million metric tons in 1977 to 3.25 million metric tons in 1978 to 8.6 million metric tons in 1980.[18]

INCREASING PEASANT CONSUMPTION

At the same time that the state provided direct cash incentives to the peasants to produce and sell more grain, it also shifted gears and provided more consumer goods so that the peasants would have something to do with the extra money they were receiving. This was an essential reconfiguration of the economy because resistance to state procurements during the Maoist period was not due simply to low prices. Rationing and extreme scarcity of consumer goods, along with the severe curtailing of sideline enterprises, had left consumers with little to purchase. From 1978 to 1983, the gross value of light industrial output increased by 56.1 percent while heavy industry increased by only 14.8 percent.[19] Production of most consumer items increased by at least 100 percent (see Table 15).

Significantly, the consumption of these commodities increased most

17. I 5/10380; I 5/4380.
18. Travers, "Getting Rich," p. 115.
19. Robert Michael Field, "Changes," p. 752.

TABLE 15.   CONSUMER GOODS PRODUCTION,
SELECTED YEARS, 1952–1983

Item	1952	1957	1965	1978	1983	% Change, 1978–1983
Cloth[a]	3,830	50,500	62,800	110,300	148,800	35
Sewing machines[b]	660	2,780	12,380	48,650	1,087,000	123
Bicycles[b]	0.080	0.806	1.838	8.540	27.580	223
Televisions[b]	—	—	0.004	0.517	6.840	1,222

SOURCE: *Zhongguo tongji nianjian 1984*, p. 6.
[a]Million *mi*.
[b]Millions.

rapidly in rural areas. Figures on per capita retail sales of consumer goods for 1978–1981, adjusted for inflation, show that rural spending increased by 57 percent from 1978 to 1981 (from 61.6 to 97.0 *yuan*). If one includes free market purchases, the increase is 122 percent (to 136.9 *yuan*).[20] By 1987,

> over 50 percent of the purchasing power of society as a whole is in the hands of the peasants and over 60 percent of the total retail prices of commodities in society is derived from sales to the rural areas. At the same time, over 60 percent of the money supply in society as a whole is also in the hands of the peasants.[21]

This trend is further evident in the increased number and type of consumer goods owned by peasant households. The number of luxury items such as radios and watches increased as did the possession of woolen, silk, and satin clothing while consumption of common cotton cloth declined (see Tables 16 and 17).

As I indicated earlier, peasant consumption of fine grains, as opposed to the cheaper coarse grains, has increased along with incomes. Wheat flour and rice accounted for 78.4 percent of peasant grain consumption in 1984, compared with 63.4 percent in 1980. Consumption of cooking oil, meat, eggs, poultry, and aquatic products was up by at least 40 percent of the amounts consumed on average between 1980 and 1984. The

20. Travers, "Getting Rich," pp. 126–127; also Field, "Changes."
21. "Study on Rural Economic Structural Reform," *Jingji yanjiu* 20 January 1987, no. 1, pp. 2–16, translated in *JPRS-CEA-87-033* 16 April 1987:31.

TABLE 16. PEASANT POSSESSION OF CONSUMER
GOODS, 1978, 1979, AND 1983

Item	1978	1979	1983	% Change 1978–1983
	(average per 100 rural households)			
Bicycles	30.7	36	63.4	106.5
Sewing Machines	19.8	23	38.1	92.5
Radios	17.4	26	56.8	226.0
Clocks	—	55	—	—
Watches	27.4	28	91.4	233.5
Televisions	—	—	4.0	—

SOURCES: 1979, *Nongcun gongzuo shouce,* p. 319; 1978 and 1983, *Zhongguo tongji nianjian 1984,* p. 14.

TABLE 17. INCREASES IN PEASANT CLOTHING
PURCHASES, SELECTED CATEGORIES, 1979

Type	Amount	Change from Previous Year	
		Absolute Amount	*Percentage*
Woolen goods[a]	17.00	10.00	142.9
Silk and satin[a]	15.00	9.00	150.0
Synthetic fiber[b]	2.18	0.94	75.8
Wool and woolen sweaters and pants[c]	7.00	3.00	75.0
Cotton[d]	0.89	0.10	12.7
Cotton cloth[b]	15.60	−1.30	−7.7
Rubber (plastic) shoes[e]	0.44	0.12	37.5

SOURCE: *Nongcun gongzuo shouce,* p. 320.
[a] *Chi*/100 persons.
[b] *Chi*/person.
[c] *Jin*/100 persons.
[d] *Jin*/person.
[e] Pair/person.

overall level of consumption shows an increase of 9.1 percent annually between 1981 and 1984.[22]

PROCUREMENT PROBLEMS, 1979–1985

The state's efforts to increase production and procurements succeeded to an unprecedented degree (see Table 18). Grain production increased by 27 percent between 1978 and 1983, with bumper harvests in 1982 and 1983; this was followed by a record harvest in 1984 of 800 billion *jin*.[23] The 1985 harvest, smaller than that of 1984, is still the third largest harvest since 1949.[24] Most important, for the first time peasants were eager to sell grain to the state. Procurements for each of the five years since 1979 have topped 100 billion *jin* despite a drop in production in 1980 and 1981. In 1983 alone total state grain procurements increased by 50.2 billion *jin*.[25] In 1983 the net state purchase equaled 83.5 percent of the increased output.[26]

Ironically, the reforms succeeded so well that by 1983 peasants were selling more grain to the state than it wanted or had the capacity to store. For the first time the supply of commercial grain (*shangpin liang*) outstripped state demand.[27] The annual increase in grain consumption has been less than 25 billion *jin*. From 1982 to 1984, grain output increased by more than 150 billion *jin*, averaging an increase of 50 billion *jin* annually.[28] I should note that in absolute terms China does not have too much grain.[29] The problem is that peasants do not diversify the use of this grain for feed and sidelines but sell it to the state as unprocessed food grain.

22. "PRC State Statistical Bureau Survey Shows Peasants' Improved Lot," *China Daily* 28 September 1985:1, in *JPRS-CPS-85-110* 28 October 1985:39.
23. Kenneth Walker, "Chinese Agriculture," pp. 789–791.
24. Wang Dacheng, "No Relaxation in Grain Production," *Beijing Review* 9 December 1985, vol. 28, no. 49, p. 4; also see Lin Wusun, "1985, 1986, and Beyond," *Beijing Review* 6 January 1986, vol. 29, no. 1, p. 4.
25. "Fengshouzhinian hua mailiang" (Talk About Selling Grain in a Year of Abundant Harvest), *ZGJJJB* 1984, no. 4, p. 27.
26. Development Institute, "A Memorandum on the Foodgrain Issue," p. 5.
27. In 1983 there was already a surplus of 3,700 million *jin* of commercial grain; by 1984 the surplus increased to over 4,000 million *jin* or about 17 percent of the grain supply. Wu Shuo, "Dangqian liangshi shangpin de qushi, wenti he duice" (Trends, Problems, and Policies of the Current Grain Commoditization), *NYJJWT* 1985, no. 2, pp. 6–10.
28. Development Institute, "Memorandum," p. 2.
29. The Chinese press emphasizes that the record grain production of 800 billion *jin* is not too much grain and warns that grain production efforts cannot be relaxed. See, for example, "We Must Certainly Not Relax Grain Production: Third Comment on Readjusting the Rural Production Mix," *ZGNMB* 30 January 1985:1, translated in *JPRS-CRA* 6 March 1985:4–5; and "Across the Board," *Liaowang* 21 January 1985, no. 4, pp. 18–19, translated in *JPRS-CRA* 6 March 1985, pp. 8–12.

TABLE 18.   GRAIN PRODUCTION AND PROCUREMENTS,
1976–1986

Year	Total Production	Gross Procurement	Net Procurement	Procurement as % of Harvest	
				Gross	Net
1976	286.305	58.250	40.720	20.3	14.2
1977	282.725	56.615	37.560	20.0	13.3
1978	304.765	61.740	42.710	20.3	14.0
1979	332.115	71.985	51.700	21.7	15.6
1980	320.555	72.995	47.970	22.8	15.0
1981	325.020	78.505	48.775	24.2	15.0
1982	354.500	91.860	59.110	25.9	16.7
1983	387.275	119.855	85.270	30.9	22.0
1984	407.305	141.690	94.605	34.8	23.2
1985	379.108	115.640	58.320	30.5	15.4
1986	391.512	134.600	100.107	34.4	25.6

SOURCE: *Zhongguo tongji nianjian 1987*, p. 570.
NOTE: Measured in millions of unhusked tons. Grain year is April of current year to March of the following year. Net procurement is total procurement minus resales to the countryside.

Bountiful harvests and the peasants' new eagerness to sell to the state resulted in soaring procurement costs and overloading storage facilities. Peasants soon found it difficult to sell their harvests as overburdened granaries curtailed procurements. These problems would spur the eventual abolition of the system of unified procurements, created for a situation of grain scarcity, not surplus.

THE INCREASING COST OF GRAIN
PROCUREMENTS

By 1985 state officials voiced increasing concern over the costs of state grain procurements.[30] The old system of unified procurement had been useful and the costs justified because it guaranteed a certain level

30. "Jiji wentuo di gaohao jiage tixi de gaige" (Enthusiastically and Safely Do Well the Reform of the Price System), *NMRB* 9 January 1985:2. Statistics on this problem are presented in "Fengshouzhinian," *ZGJJJB* 1984, no. 4, pp. 26–28, and in Zhang, *Nongchan*. The best work in English on the costs of subsidies is by Nicholas Lardy. The following paragraphs draw heavily on his efforts. See his *Agriculture*, particularly chapter 5, and his "Consumption."

of grain supply to the state, but it also entailed certain obligations. Unified procurements locked the state into a requirement to buy as much grain as the peasants had to sell. As sales dramatically increased, the costs of unified procurements became prohibitive.

The state has long subsidized the price of rationed cereal foods and edible oils by keeping the consumer price artificially low. The disparity between the state procurement costs and the retail price of grain became substantial beginning in 1966. In the early days of unified purchase and sale, the state was able to meet the costs of procurement, processing, storage, transport, and other expenses related to the supply of grain to the nonagricultural population. A decrease in profits became noticeable in 1961–1962, when procurement prices rose by almost one-third while consumer prices remained unchanged; but the state still broke even.[31] Retail prices for rationed cereal products increased in January 1965, but, as the Chinese themselves now admit, the increase was too small.[32] The 15-percent increase in procurement prices in 1966 negated the retail price increase, and losses continued to mount:

> Between 1974 and 1978 the cumulative losses were 20.8 billion *yuan* or in excess of 4 billion *yuan* per year. Subsidies for cereals and oil for urban and non-agricultural residents approached 2 percent of national income.[33]

The 1979 decision to increase prices to spur production and sales cost the state dearly. Basic agricultural procurement prices were raised by 17.1 percent, at a cost of 7.99 billion *yuan*. Overquota procurement costs for 1979 increased from 1.6 billion to 3.6 billion *yuan*.[34] The impact of the price rise was magnified by increases in the size of procurements. For the years from 1950 to 1979, annual grain procurements were under 100 billion *jin*. However, as indicated above for each of the years from 1979 to 1984, procurements have consistently topped that figure. In 1983, for example, total state grain procurements including quota, overquota, and negotiated sales were double that amount (197.6 billion *jin*).[35]

Lardy has calculated that the costs to the state in the form of subsidies for cereal products jumped to more than 6.8 billion *yuan* in 1979,

---

31. Lardy, *Agriculture*, p. 193.
32. See Zhang, *Nongchan*, p. 13.
33. Lardy, *Agriculture*, p. 193.
34. The average price increase for cereal crops purchased as basic procurement was 20.9 percent; when overquota purchases of grain are added, the percentage increases to 30.5 percent. Zhang, *Nongchan*, pp. 6, 14–15.
35. "Fengshouzhinian," *ZGJJJB* 1984, no. 4, p. 26.

10.3 billion in 1980, and 12.9 billion in 1981.[36] In 1979 the losses incurred by the state on the purchase and resale of rationed cereals amounted to 0.15 *yuan* per kilo (0.075 *yuan* per *jin*), approximately 45 percent of the average state sales price for grain.[37] By 1981 the losses were 0.2 *yuan* per kilo (0.1 *yuan* per *jin*) of cereal.[38]

Moreover, given the price structure, it was possible for speculators to buy grain from the state at a low rationed price and then sell it back to the state at higher procurement prices. The state has tried to prevent such practices by selling negotiated-price grain in husked form that peasants cannot resell to state granaries.[39]

LACK OF STORAGE FACILITIES

The system of unified procurement obligated the state to accept unlimited amounts of grain. By 1983 the huge increases totally overwhelmed state storage facilities. Until 1983 the national storage ratio was 1.78 units of storage capacity for every unit of procured grain; by 1983, however, the capacity had dropped to only 0.7 units of capacity for every unit of procured grain.[40] In some places grain production was reportedly double storage capacity:[41]

> In 1983 state grain inventory increased 37% compared to 1982. By the end of December 1984 state inventory had exceeded warehouse capacity by 150%, leading to a large amount of grain being stored in the open air.[42]

The government had to adopt various ad hoc solutions to deal with the problem. Grain was put in hurriedly converted structures. When the

36. Lardy, *Agriculture,* p. 196.
37. Lardy, "Consumption," p. 854.
38. Lardy, *Agriculture,* p. 196. The costs of this subsidy may have stabilized. An article written in 1984 states that for every *jin* of rationed grain sold, the government subsidy is approximately 1 *jiao* (or 0.1 *yuan*). It further reports that the state has adopted a plan to try to recoup some of these losses. As of April 1984 grain produced under the state plan can be sold outside the rationing system at a *"pingzhuanyi jia"* price. This price would be equal to the basic procurement price plus management costs plus a reasonable profit for the state (this amount is not stated). For each *jin* of grain sold at this price, one to two *fen* would be turned over to state revenues (*zhongyang caizheng*) to make up the money the central government has to spend on overquota procurements. "Fengshouzhinian," *ZGJJJB* 1984, no. 4, p. 28.
39. "Fengshouzhinian," *ZGJJJB* 1984, no. 4, p. 28.
40. Ibid., p. 26.
41. "Rich Peasants Still Have Worries," *China Daily* 4 December 1983:4. Also see "Investigation of Difficulties in Selling Grain Reported," *NYJJWT* August 1983, no. 8, pp. 52–54, translated in *JPRS-CRA* 12 January 1984:43–48.
42. Development Institute, "Memorandum," p. 3.

makeshift warehouses were filled, the grain was simply left outside.[43] Finally, in 1982–1983, the state was forced to return to a "people's storage" system (*mindai chu*) similar to one used in the 1950s when the system of unified procurement began. The state signs contracts with peasants for the purchase of their grain but leaves the grain with the peasants until state granaries have space. Peasants receive 50 to 75 percent of payment in advance for the sale while they are storing the grain for the state.[44]

People's storage has allowed local granaries to accept more grain, but it has also presented the state with extra costs. According to one estimate, the state pays an additional fifteen *yuan* for each 10,000 *jin* of grain stored.[45] Grain-specialized households receive fifty *yuan* for every 10,000 *jin* of grain they keep.[46] This may still be a bargain compared to building more state storehouses, but recent reports suggest that the system is unreliable and vulnerable to corruption.

Some peasants have signed contracts to store grain for the state and accepted the storage fee, but they either did not actually have any grain to store or sold their grain to a third party. In 1984, for example, nineteen granaries in one county had contracted with 15,420 households to store 120.57 million *jin* of grain, for a fee of 15.472 million *yuan*. An investigation revealed that in six townships false reporting, illegally selling state grain, and other various misappropriations (*nuoyong*) amounted to 8.26 million *jin* of grain. The state lost over 1 million *yuan*.[47]

How is this possible? One reason is the relative ease with which a peasant can get a contract for storing grain. Peasants simply go to their local granary and offer to sell or store grain for the state. The granary signs a contract with the peasant for the storage of an agreed amount of

43. For example, Shanxi provincial storehouses have been accumulating larger and larger stocks of grain since 1979. Because of poor conditions in the makeshift granaries, which the province was forced to use, 20 million *jin* of corn was lost to insects. *Nongye xiandaihua yanjiu* (Research on Agricultural Modernization) 1985, no. 2, pp. 24–26.

44. "Yuncheng Linfen diqu duofang kuoda kurong duo shouchu liangshi" (Yuncheng, Linfen Prefecture in Every Way Expands Its Storage Capacity and Increases Its Collection and Storage of Grain), *ZGNMB* 6 September 1984:1. For further details see Jean C. Oi, "Peasant Grain Marketing."

45. "Mindai guochu liguo limin" (People's Storage [of grain] for the State, Benefits the State and the People), *SXNM* 14 December 1984:1.

46. This figure is based on examples from Hubei and Shandong. "Dangyangxian caiqu santiao cuoshi baohu zhongliang jijixing" (Dangyang County Adopts Three Measures to Maintain Enthusiasm for Grain Cultivation), *NCGZTX* 1984, no. 11, pp. 14–15; and "Shandong duofang waqian jiejue chuliang wenti" (Shandong Adopts Many Methods to Clear Space to Solve the Grain Storage Problem), *ZGNMB* 16 October 1984:1.

47. "Xinminxian 'Mindai guochu' zhong wenti yanzhong" (Severe Problems in People's Storage [of grain] for the State in Xinmin County), *JJCK* 22 May 1985:2.

grain. The state then pays the peasant for that grain and its storage. The granary, however, does not always inspect the grain or even check to see that it exists before the contract is signed, particularly during periods when it is deluged by peasants wanting to sell grain.

Another, and perhaps more important, reason why such bogus contracts can get through the system is that those engaged in fraud include local village cadres and granary officials, people responsible for approving and monitoring the storage contracts. In one case, granary cadres who colluded with township and village officials and peasants defrauded the state of 30,000 *yuan* by claiming to have stored 200,000 *jin* of grain. A granary accountant cheated the state out of 1,500 *yuan* by claiming to have stored 10,000 *jin* of grain.[48]

ABUSES AT STATE GRANARIES

The problem of too much grain not only afflicted the state but also caused problems for peasants. Shortly after the responsibility system was instituted, peasants faced a situation known as "difficulty selling grain" (*mailiangnan*). For the first time in post-1949 China, instead of scheming to hide grain or buy more grain from the state, peasants and cadres were using their connections to sell grain to the state.[49] The change in the grain situation is well described by a former peasant from Anhui: "It used to be the case of having to go through the back door to buy grain, but starting about 1980 it was necessary to go through the back door to *sell* grain."[50] Peasants in grain-surplus areas have had few alternatives but to wait to sell their grain. Some were lucky and managed to sell their grain after waiting only one day and night in front of the granary; others waited a month, and some waited two or three months.[51]

Not all peasants suffered equally from the glut in grain. Those who could afford to wait out the market made much bigger profits. Many grain farmers, however, found themselves unable to afford this strategy. The less well-off peasants, barely solvent and needing money from the

48. Ibid.
49. For press accounts see, for example, "Zai shougou liangshizhong kaihoumen shouhuilu Qingduizi liangku Li Dewen deng shou chufen" (Qingduizi Granary's Li Dewen and Others Receive Punishment for Opening the Backdoor and Taking Bribes During Procurement), *RMRB* 16 March 1985:5.
50. Hong Kong Interview 13/8/7.
51. See, for example, "Mailiang ji" (Notes on Selling Grain), *ZGNMB* 12 January 1984:2; and "Women zheli mailiangnan" (Selling Grain Is Difficult Here), *GDNMB* 18 August 1984:3.

sale of their current harvest to buy seed and fertilizer for the next season's crop, were the hardest hit. For them, waiting meant going into
debt.[52] Few peasants owned the necessary carts or tractors to transport
and sell their grain to another granary.

In theory, unified procurement guarantees the seller a set price regardless of the dearth or surplus of grain on the market. In practice, during the period of dramatically increased grain production, peasants not
only had difficulty selling their grain, but they were not even assured of
receiving the state-guaranteed price. Granary cadres engaged in corruption reminiscent of practices in pre-1949 China, when scales and prices
were often arbitrarily determined by local officials and clerks.[53]

When peasants sell grain, each batch is graded and priced accordingly. The granary cadres have final say. If a granary cadre says that a
peasant's grain is of poor quality, the peasant receives a lower price.
Some cadres arbitrarily lowered their evaluation of a peasant's grain and
paid a lower price, a practice that has become known as "*yaji yajia*" (to
suppress grade and suppress price).[54] Peasants desperate to sell their
grain had either to accept an obviously unfair price or forfeit the opportunity to sell to the state.[55]

The corruption not only involved pricing but also acceptance. In
some areas, a peasant needed a special relationship with granary cadres
before they accepted any grain for sale. One article describes the plight
of three peasants who had their grain turned down by the state grain
station, supposedly because of poor quality. Some men standing nearby
offered to buy the peasants' grain; they paid the peasants a low price of
0.16 *yuan* per *jin*. Because these buyers had the proper connections
with the granary cadres, they then immediately sold the grain to the
state at 0.21 *yuan* per *jin*. The peasants summed up their bad experience by saying that "what is being procured [sold] is not wheat, but

52. Hong Kong Interview 13/8/7.
53. On corrupt practices of Qing granary officials see Zelin, *Magistrate's Tael*, and
Ch'u T'ung-tsu, *Local Government*.
54. This practice is not limited to grain. A particularly interesting case of extortion by
cadres from purchasing stations involves peasants waiting in line to sell cotton. The cadres
approached the peasants and offered to buy their cotton and save them the trouble of
waiting. The catch was that the price they were offering was significantly lower than the
official state purchase price. When the peasants hesitated, the cadres retorted that if they
refused to sell their cotton to them then, they were still going to lose when they got inside
the purchasing station. The cadres said that they were the ones who weighed and graded
the cotton. "Sanhexian yixie mianhua shougouzhan qiaozha maimianren" (Some Cotton
Procurement Stations in Sanhe County Extort Cotton Sellers), *RMRB* 16 March 1985:5.
55. See, for example, "Weifa luanji liangzhan beizhengdun" (Granary Is Rectified for
Illegal and Arbitrary Transactions), *ZGNMB* 14 July 1983:3; and "Fengshou fengshou
xishang tianyou" (Abundant Harvest, Abundant Harvest, There Is Delight and Increased
Anxiety), *ZGNMB* 12 January 1984:2.

TABLE 19. CHANGES IN MARCH GRAIN PRICES IN 206
MARKETS, 1977–1981

Grain	1977	1978	% Change	1979	% Change	1980	% Change	1981	% Change
Rice	.500	.475	−5.0	.404	−15.0	.379	−6.2	.370	−2.4
Wheat	.430	.404	−6.1	.327	−19.1	.297	−9.2	.297	0.0
Corn	.342	.325	−5.0	.234	−28.0	.198	−15.4	.181	−8.6

SOURCE: Zhang Ruhai, *Nongchanpin jiage wenti yanjiu*, p. 190.

face" (*shougoude shi mianzi, bushi maizi*); in other words, what counts is who you are, that is, connections.[56]

Why did peasants not avoid this grief and take advantage of the newly legalized grain markets? In the midst of the huge surplus of grain, the free market offered little relief for grain-rich peasants.[57] Of the market for grain 80 percent is supplied by the state grain ration system.[58] The demand for food grain will only shrink as diets improve and secondary food products, such as vegetables, fish, and meat, become more abundant. As Table 19 shows, grain prices declined steadily from 1977 to 1981. In 1984 in the midst of the surplus, grain prices on the free market dropped 12.5 percent nationwide in 1984 (see Table 19). During that time, the market price of grain was lower than the state overquota prices.[59]

STATE RESPONSE TO
PROCUREMENT PROBLEMS

The government quickly took measures to try to resolve the difficulties of sale. As early as 1980 it issued a directive that all granaries continue to buy as much grain as peasants wanted to sell. Similar directives continued to be issued in spite of the fact that local granaries were

56. "Jiyou mailiangnan buyao zai diaonan" (It Is Already Difficult to Sell Grain, Do Not Make Things More Difficult), *ZGNMB* 2 September 1984:2. "Caodun Sanliu liangdian gouliang zuofeng buzheng sunguo kengnong" (The Work Style of Caodun's and Sanliu's Grain Shops Is Not Correct, Harming the State and Cheating the Peasants), *ZGNMB* 9 October 1984:1, presents another clear case of granary cadre corruption where connections and not quality determined what grain was accepted for purchase.

57. Until 1984 the peasants could not officially sell their grain legally on the free market until the state had officially finished its quota procurements. *ZGNMB* 19 June 1984:1. As of 1988 the free grain markets were still closed during the procurement period.

58. Wu Shuo, "Dangqian liangshi shangpin de qushi wenti he duice," *NYJJWT* 1985, no. 2, p. 7.

59. Development Institute, "Memorandum," pp. 4–5.

overflowing with grain.[60] Unfortunately, the state's directives had limited success. Some granaries heeded them and adopted various ad hoc measures to accommodate the grain; others did not. In spite of the people's storage policy and other state efforts to buy more grain and reduce the surplus, "difficulties in selling grain" continued into 1984; they were serious enough that Premier Zhao Ziyang addressed the problem in his major speech at the beginning of 1985.[61]

The state also tried to take other measures, some indirect, to reduce the total amount of grain coming into state storehouses.[62] For example, teams in grain-surplus areas were no longer required to sell even the minimum grain quota to the state. Peasants only had to pay their agricultural tax in grain; they could meet the compulsory sales quota with money.[63] Later it did not even want the agricultural tax in kind. The state decided that most peasants should pay the agricultural tax in money (*zhezheng daiqian*) rather than in grain.[64] In stark contrast to policies of the Cultural Revolution period, peasants may now need special permission from provincial or municipal authorities to pay in grain.[65] In 1984 the State Council ruled that "poor areas" (*pinkun diqu*)

60. Directives were issued at various times and places. See, for example, "Guowuyuan Fuzongli Tian Jiyun tichu yao renzhen jiejue 'mailiangnan' wenti" (State Council Vice Premier Tian Jiyun Puts Forth the Need to Earnestly Resolve the 'Difficulty Selling Grain' Problem), *GDNMB* 3 November 1983:1; "Liangshi gongzuo de yige da gaige" (A Major Reform in Grain Work), *ZGNMB* 6 February 1983:1; "Yao jiji chaogou he yigou nongmin daixiao de liangyou" (Enthusiastically procure overquota sales and negotiated sales of the grain and oil that the peasants are waiting to sell), *ZGNMB* 25 August 1983:2; and "Jiangsusheng fangkai liangyou yigou yixiao zhengce" (Jiangsu Province Relaxes Its Policy on the Negotiated Procurement and Sale of Grain and Oil), *RMRB* 18 June 1980:1.

61. See, for example, "Jiyou," *ZGNMB* 2 September 1984:2; and "Fengshou," *ZGNMB* 12 January 1984:2. For Zhao's speech, see "Fangkai nongchanpin jiage cujin nongcun chanye jiegou de tiaozheng" (Relax Agricultural Products' Prices and Promote the Readjustment of the Rural Production Structure), *RMRB* 31 January 1985:1.

62. In Guangdong, a "grain-money payment" system (*liangqian jianshou*) was instituted, which allowed peasants to meet their grain sales quota to the state partly in cash and partly in money. In 1984 this resulted in a 3.5-percent provincial drop in the number of acres planted in grain. "Guangdongsheng shixing liangshi jihua shougou" (Guangdong Province Implements Planned Procurement of Grain), *NMRB* 30 January 1985:1.

63. In one area the state allowed peasants to fulfill their basic grain sales quota in money, at a rate of 10 *yuan* per 100 *jin* of unhusked rice. Hong Kong Interview 22/7/29.

64. "Fengshouzhinian," *ZGJJJB* 1984, no. 4, p. 28.

65. "Nongye shui you zheng shiwu weizhu gaiwei zhezheng daijin" (The Agricultural Tax Changes from Payment Primarily in Kind to Conversion in Money), *NMRB* 24 May 1985:1; and "Nongye shui you zhengliang gaiwei zhezheng daijin de jige wenti" (A Few Problems in the Change from Payment in Kind to Payment in Money for the Agricultural Tax), *NMRB* 25 May 1985:1. The rate at which the tax is to be figured is based on the amount of grain that the peasant household owed under the original system. The conversion rate is the same *dao sanqi* system used for figuring grain sales. Of the amount of grain owed as tax, 70 percent is calculated at the overquota price while the remaining 30 percent is figured at the basic procurement price. The total worth of this grain is the peas-

no longer needed to abide by the system of unified procurements and forced quota sales but could adopt a free sales system (*ziyou gouxiao*).[66]

But it was too late for such measures. A dramatic turnaround had already occurred in both the peasants' and the state's relationships to the harvest. On the one hand, the state no longer worried about the peasants not selling enough grain, as had been the case throughout the Maoist era. The peasants, on the other hand, no longer wanted to sell less grain; they wanted to sell as much as possible. Consequently, the largess of the state in declaring that certain areas no longer had to sell grain did not help those grain-rich peasants who could not sell their grain and were short of funds. The peasants wanted to sell more grain and be paid for their sales.

The state was caught in a difficult position. Under the terms of the unified procurement system it was committed to buy the surplus. The system of unified procurement guaranteed a minimum supply of grain for the state, but it had no mechanism to limit the amount of grain produced or purchased. If the state stopped buying grain, the peasants might indiscriminately reduce output; the state did not want that. It constantly worried that peasant enthusiasm would become overly depressed and grain production turn too sharply downward.[67] There were already signs that peasants, unable to sell their grain, were drastically reducing production.[68]

Thus, by the end of 1984 the state faced an increasingly unattractive, unworkable system of procurement desperately in need of reform, not so much because it was not serving the interests of the peasants but because it was becoming too much of a liability. The system was conceived

---

ant's current agricultural tax due. To take account of price variation for different crops, the conversion rate is pegged to the price of the major cereal crop of an area.

66. For a very detailed account of some recent proposals calling for the total revamping of the agricultural tax system, including using new base figures, see "Dui gaige," *NYJJWT* 1985, no. 4, pp. 36–38, 59. None of these changes seems to have been adopted except the change of payment from tax in kind to money. Sun Yefang earlier had also called for reform in the tax system, proposing that the state increase the direct agricultural tax; this proposal, however, was dismissed by the government. See Lardy, *Agriculture*, pp. 218–219.

67. See, for example, "Jue buneng fangsong liangshi shengchan" (We Must Never Slacken in Our Grain Production), *NMRB* 30 January 1985:1, which was published almost the same time as Zhao Ziyang's speech that urged diversifying the economy and limiting grain production.

68. After the "difficulty of sale" experienced by peasants, in one area there was a 41-percent decrease in grain sold to the state. Li Pinghan, "Yiliang diqu diaozheng chanye jiegou buying zai jianshao liangshi mianji shang zuowenzhang" (In Areas Suited to Grain Production When Adjusting the Structure of Production, Do Not Willfully Misinterpret the Policy to Reduce Grain Acreage), *Nongcun caiwu kuaiji* 1985, no. 6, pp. 48–50.

in a situation of grain shortage, but in the early 1980s the state faced a grain surplus. The state needed to limit the amount of grain being produced or at least limit the amount it would be responsible for buying at guaranteed prices; but it also needed to be guaranteed a stable grain supply.

CONTRACT PROCUREMENTS

The state's solution was to return to what Lardy terms price planning, a method not used since the early 1960s.[69] The state would limit the amount it would buy, restructure procurement prices, and use binding contracts to ensure sufficient purchases.[70]

The state began the reform process by announcing a reversal of the procurement price structure. Previously, peasants received a lower basic procurement price for the bulk of their sales (see Chapter 3). Beginning in 1985 peasants received a higher overquota price for 70 percent of their sale and the low basic procurement price for the remaining 30 percent; hence the term *dao sanqi* evolved, that is, "reversal of the three-seven ratio," the old policy whereby 70 percent of sales were paid at the low basic procurement price. Different areas may use different ratios for different types of grain. In any one area the actual ratio for overquota and quota sales of a single crop may be higher or lower than 7:3. The exact ratio is determined by the market and demand in each locality for individual cereal crops.[71] This requires the state spend more per *jin* of grain procured, but it now has more control over what is produced and the amount it will have to buy in local areas.

To keep the treasury solvent and eliminate the obligation to purchase all surplus grain at now higher guaranteed prices, the government simultaneously announced limits on the amount of grain the state would buy. The target set for 1985, for instance, represented a 19–24 percent decrease in procurements from 1983.[72] Once the announced target is met, the peasants must sell their surplus on the open market. The state, in a complete about-face from the Maoist period, hoped that the peas-

69. See Lardy, *Agriculture,* chap. 2, for a discussion of the state's various experiments with price planning.
70. "Fangkai," *RMRB* 31 January 1985:1.
71. For details, see Oi, "Peasant Grain Marketing."
72. Out of a total production of 774.5 billion *jin* of grain 197.6 billion *jin* was purchased in 1983. "Liangshi fangkai quanpan jiehuo" (Let Grain [Production] Go, All Knots Will Be Untied), *Liaowang Zhoukan* 1985, no. 4, p. 19; "Fengshozhinian," *ZGJJJB* 1984, no. 4, p. 26.

ants would plant remaining acreage in other crops, knowing there was a limit on the amount the state would procure.[73]

The limit absolved the state of its responsibility to buy all grain grown, but it still faced a difficult problem: how to ensure a sufficient supply of grain while moving the agricultural economy toward commodity production.[74] Sensitive to the possibility that peasants would overreact to the limits, the state announced, along with the limits on procurement, its provision of a minimum guaranteed price for all grain grown. If the market price dropped below the basic state procurement price, the state would protect the peasant by buying his surplus grain at the basic procurement price.[75] The problem with such a safety net was that it could work at cross-purposes with the state's goal of wanting to limit procurements and encourage peasants to ignore the state's advice to limit grain production. The state, it seems, was willing to take that risk to ensure sufficient production. It was concerned that the limits might cause peasants to stop producing grain altogether.

With the price changes and limits in place, the state took the final step and announced the abolition of the unified procurement system and the adoption of a grain contract procurement system (*hetong dinggou*).[76] The new system took effect on 1 April 1985, the beginning of the grain year. Each contract is drawn with the national procurement limit in mind and incorporates the new overquota/basic quota procurement price ratios described above.[77] Each contract specifies the type of grain

73. See, for example, articles in *NMRB* 22 February 1985:2. On the limitation on cotton production see "Zhi nan er jin jiji tiaozheng" (Press Forward in the Face of Difficulties; Enthusiastically Carry Out Adjustments), *JJCK* 11 April 1985:2.

74. See, for example, "Buyao yin 'mailiangnan' jiu xianzhi liangshi shengchan" (Do Not Restrict the Production of Grain Because 'It Is Hard to Sell'), *JJRB* 18 March 1985:1; "Zhuyi kefu fangsong liangshi shengchan miaotou" (Pay Attention and Overcome the Tendency to Relax Grain Production), *RMRB* 14 March 1985:1; and "Quebao liangshi shengchan wenbu zengzhang" (Ensure the Steady Increase of Grain Production), *SXNM* 12 April 1985:1.

75. For example, "Quxiao liangshi tonggou zhihou" (After the Abolition of the Unified Procurement System), *NMRB* 30 January 1985:2.

76. The changes were announced by the State Council in "Guanyu jinyibu huoyue nongcun jingji de shixiang zhengce" (Ten Policies for Further Enlivening the Rural Economy), commonly referred to as "1985 Document No. 1." This document is printed in a number of sources; see, for example, *JJRB* 25 March 1985:1. For a discussion of the elite decision-making process surrounding this policy see Alistair Johnston, "Policy Process."

77. The contracts cover the procurement of rice, wheat, and corn, as well as soybeans (*dadou*) from the six designated primary production regions (*zhuchanqu*): Liaoning, Jilin, Heilongjiang, Nei Menggu, Anhui, and Henan. Together this equals about 80 percent of the grain crops the state procured in 1983 and 1984. The remaining 20 percent of grains that the state used to procure, the peasants must now sell on the open market. "Quxiao,"

the peasant will grow, including the seed strain, the quality, the quantity, the price the peasant will receive, and the date and place of delivery.

As an added incentive, each contract also specifies the special consideration (*youhui*) a peasant will receive, such as the amount of fertilizer and insecticide the state will provide, at the low state price, for selling to the state.[78] This is an important incentive. As I will discuss in detail in Chapter 9, beginning in 1984 some areas abolished the rationing system for such agricultural inputs as chemical fertilizer, making peasants buy them on the free market. Peasants might get a higher price for grain on the free market, but the savings from the lower-priced and sometimes scarce agricultural inputs made it worthwhile to continue selling to the state.[79]

To reassure peasants that the terms of the contract will be honored, contracts (particularly the larger ones) are to be notarized.[80] In case of harvest shortfalls caused by natural disaster, appropriate reductions in the sale can be negotiated with the authorities.[81] If, on the other hand, the state cannot accept the peasant's grain on the agreed delivery date, it must pay the peasant interest on the money owed and pay for storage until it can accept the grain.[82]

NEW LIMITS ON INCENTIVE

The changes in state procurements had far-reaching implications for both peasants and cadres. The lure of higher prices, so attractive after

---

NMRB 30 January 1985:2. If cereal crops other than those listed are the major staple crop of an area, similar contracts also can apply. "Shenme shi liangshi hetong dinggou" (What Is a Grain Production Contract), *NMRB* 30 March 1985:2. A similar contracting system exists for oil crops, including cotton, rapeseed, *humazi*, peanuts, sesame, and yellow mustard seed. See "Zansheng quxiao liangshi tonggou" (Our Province Abolishes Unified Grain Procurements), *SXNM* 12 February 1985:1.

78. "Jiu liangshi hetong dinggou gongzuo shengliangshiju fuze tongzhi da jizhe wen" (Comrades in Charge of the Provincial Grain Bureau Answer Questions on Contract Grain Procurements), *ZJRB* 31 March 1985:2.

79. For details see ibid.; also see "Quzhou shiwanduo nonghu fangxin zhongliang" (More Than Ten Thousand Quzhou Peasant Households Plant Grain with Minds at Ease), *NMRB* 22 March 1985:2.

80. "Liangfang qianding liangshi dinggou hetong shixing gongzheng" (Both Sides Sign the Grain Procurement Contract, Implement Notarization), *NMRB* 18 April 1985:1.

81. "Shenme shi," *NMRB* 30 March 1985:2. Guangdong has retained its earlier policy of letting peasants meet their grain responsibilities to the state in cash or grain.

82. "Liangmian hetong dinggou banfa zhongzhong" (Various Methods for Contract Grain and Cotton Procurements), *NCGZTX* 1985, no. 5, pp. 38–39.

the initial price increases in 1979, vanished. The new price structure guaranteed higher prices for a larger portion of the contracted sale but only for the amount of the contracted sale. No longer could the peasant count on the higher overquota prices for all his surplus grain. If the state did keep its word, it would only pay the lower basic quota price. Therefore, the total income from a rich harvest would be lower. According to a report written by a research group under the State Council, the price changes and the limits on procurements resulted in at least a 10-percent decrease in the amount of income peasants received selling their increased output.[83]

Consequently, in those areas where the procurement limit was lower than proven production potential, peasant incomes could suffer. In one area the amount of grain sold to the state was almost one-quarter less than in the previous year.[84] Some peasants have been able to make up lost income by planting cash crops for the market, but not all have the knowledge or the resources to diversify production. Some have simply ignored the state's instructions and planted their past acreage in grain, hoping that the state will buy their grain, even if at lower prices.[85] Some local cadres, caught between the state and the peasants and without the ability or the willingness to help peasants diversify, have been criticized publicly for failing to carry out instructions to limit grain and cotton production and illicitly helping peasants circumvent state policies.[86]

Overall the response was a drop in production. The 1985 harvest decreased by 25 million tons. More worrisome for the state, some peasants failed to fulfill their state contracts. This then led the more conservative elements within the leadership, such as Chen Yun, to renew calls not to let grain production decline.[87] Although there has been no retreat from the contract system, by summer 1986, when the government expe-

83. Development Institute, "Memorandum," p. 6.
84. "Xian bang nongmin ding 'panzi' hou yu nongmin ding hetong" (Find Clients for Peasants First, Then Help Them Make Contracts), NMRB 15 March 1985:1.
85. See, for example, "Liangshi shengchan rengshi fazhan qushi" (Grain Production Is Still the Trend of Development), JJCK 2 April 1985:2. For a case involving cotton, see "Woguo mianhua yi chan dayu xiao qie wu mangmu kuoda zhongzhi mianji" (Our Cotton Production Already Surpasses Sales, Do Not Blindly Expand the Cultivated Acreage), JJCK 25 April 1985:1.
86. See "Zhi nan," JJCK 11 April 1985:2; and "Woguo," JJCK 25 April 1985:1.
87. Chen said, "Feeding and clothing a billion people constitutes one of China's major political as well as economic challenges, for grain shortages will lead to social disorder. We cannot afford to underestimate this matter" (p. 61). Chen Yun, "Speech at the National Conference of Party Delegates (23 September 1985)," Hongqi 1 October 1985, no. 19, pp. 35–37, translated in JPRS-CRF-85-024 12 December 1985:60–64.

rienced problems fulfilling its contracts, there was renewed stress on the "responsibility and obligation" of peasants to sell grain.[88]

Why has the contracting system been less than successful? Clearly, the system has some inherent flaws. Even after the 1979 procurement price increases, grain production was still less profitable than farming cash crops.[89] The price scissors has reappeared; the increases in procurement prices have been insufficient to deal with the rising costs of inputs and agricultural machinery.[90] Reports in 1988 indicated that the state is going to raise the procurement price of grain, but it is unclear by how much this will rectify the current scissors problem for the peasants. The details of the increase are not yet available.[91] To compensate, the state had already begun to give grain-specialized households extra subsidies, such as expanded access to lower-priced production inputs. To induce rural households to stay in grain farming, the government has also decreed that rural enterprises, the most prosperous sectors in the rural economy, must directly support agricultural production under what is called the "industry supplementing agriculture" programs (see Chapter 9). Moreover, provinces, prefectures, counties, and townships must now allocate a portion of their surplus revenues and increased taxes on township enterprises to support agricultural production, especially grain.[92]

In addition to structural defects, problems have arisen due to bad faith on both sides. In some instances, the state failed to live up to its promises to supply the low-priced fertilizer and other agricultural inputs.[93] In other cases, peasants simply reneged on their side of the bargain

88. See, for example, the front-page editorial of *Jingji ribao* 10 June 1986:1, which stated that the new procurement system was not only an economic contract but also a responsibility to the state. It made clear that the quotas had to be fulfilled. "Jishi jingji hetong youshi guojia renwu" (This Is Both an Economic Contract and a Responsibility to the State).

89. For a discussion of this problem in Dahe Commune, Hebei, see Butler, "Price Scissors." For a more general discussion of this problem, see Development Institute, "Memorandum"; also see "Xiaogandiqu liangshi xingshi diaocha" (Investigation of the Grain Situation in Xiaogan Prefecture), *RMRB* 2 June 1986:2.

90. See Butler, "Price Scissors"; Development Institute, "Memorandum"; "Xiaogandiqu," *RMRB* 2 June 1986:2; and "Nadao qiqianwan shiqu yiyisan" (Take In 70 Million, Lose 1.3 Billion), *NMRB* 12 May 1988:1.

91. "China Reimposes Price Controls on Key Items," *Boston Globe* 20 January 1988:3; also see articles in *RMRB* 19 January 1988.

92. Pig raising and vegetable cultivation on the outskirts of large and medium-sized cities are also supported by these funds. Tian Jiyun, "On Present Economic Situation," *Beijing Review* 10 February 1986, vol. 29, nos. 6 and 7, pp. xi–xii.

93. China Interviews, 1986.

when they found more lucrative markets for their grain.[94] The contract system has also fallen short of expectations because of the problems in the local cadres' implementation of the program.

PROBLEMS OF IMPLEMENTATION

How are the contracts negotiated? Who is involved in the negotiations? Most important, what is the role of local cadres? What is the role of the individual peasant households? One cannot assume that the return to household farming and the addition of contracts has fundamentally altered political relationships. Increased reliance on price and market incentives does not necessarily undermine older patterns of administrative control. Much of the political process may remain the same, although the administrative form has changed.

On one level, the grain contract system has opened the door to a new era of peasant-state relations and finally resolved the struggle over the harvest between the state and the peasantry. But in China, as elsewhere, policies do not always bring expected outcomes. Merilee Grindle has argued that the content of a policy is not always as important as the *context* in which the policy is implemented.[95]

The contract system was instituted to enliven the circulation of grain in the economy, promote the diversified use of grain (*liangshi zhuanhua*), and rationally adjust agricultural production. The idea is to have peasants decide what to plant based on price and sales targets and contracts.[96] But when the policy was implemented, there was considerable debate over the role of the peasant. Authorities have said that peasants are "confused" and uncertain about how much to contract;[97] thus, they require help in making these decisions. Some even directly question the right of peasants to participate in the contracting process. Debate exists about whether peasant households should take part at all in direct negotiations with the state for their contracts or whether representatives should be appointed.

94. The reasons for this change are somewhat unclear. In part, the newly emerging demand for the grain seems spurred by the increase in food-processing industries that must now procure at least a part of their needed raw materials on the open market.
95. Grindle, "Policy Content," pp. 3–39.
96. See, for example, "Shenme shi," *NMRB* 30 March 1985:2.
97. "Dongtingcun shi zenyang jianding liangmian dinggou hetong de?" (How Did Dongting Village Determine Its Grain and Cotton Contracts?), *NMRB* 6 May 1985:2; also see "Liangmian," *NCGZTX* 1985, no. 5, pp. 38–39.

Theoretically, the rightful principals involved in the contracting process should be the local grain departments (*liangshi bumen*) and the peasant households. In practice, some grain departments have been allowed to sign contracts with "representatives of the grain farmers" (*liangnong daibiao*), cooperative economic groups (*hezuo jingji zuzhi*), or state farms (*guoying nongchang*), rather than negotiate with individual peasant households. Contracts negotiated with collective representatives are then divided among individual peasant producers. The contract provided each peasant producer is a detailed and specified enumeration of obligations and benefits.[98] Each peasant's contract becomes valid when he stamps and approves it.[99]

Those who argue for direct negotiations with individual peasant households have inadvertently pinpointed weaknesses in the contract process and show how the system can be abused. They stress the need for direct negotiations because they would ensure that the two parties have the opportunity to know each other and communicate their interests and needs. The grain bureau could directly disseminate information and techniques, and no third parties need enter the negotiations. They further point out that if one went through the administrative and governmental organs at the local levels, the buyer and seller would have no direct contact; information would have to filter through third parties, causing delays and possibly distortions. Most important, using "representatives" would more likely introduce a coercive dimension to the contract process. In the end, what may look like a "contract" might still be in reality an administrative order, and the entire contracting system would lose its meaning.[100]

Unfortunately, such criticisms were correct. The grain contracts hold little meaning as voluntary market agreements between the peasant and the state. Grain contracts are less than open business agreements whose terms are negotiated directly by the individual peasant and the state. In reality, contracts differ little from the old procurement system; the process for determining the quota for each village is almost identical to the

98. The contract the peasant receives is sometimes referred to as a *qingdan* (clear list). During the Qing dynasty, *qingdan* were enumerated lists, specifying in detail items that were only generally discussed in the main text. Such lists were often appended to memorials. The use of this term in the present context of contracts fits with the traditional usage. It is a detailed examination of a larger, more general document, in this case, the collective contract.

99. "Jiu liangshi," *ZJRB* 31 March 1985:2.

100. Xu Dejun and Men Gaoyu, "Shixing liangshi hetong dinggou xuyao jiejue jige wenti" (Several Problems to Be Solved in Implementing Contract Grain Procurements), *NCGZTX* 1985, no. 4, pp. 33–34.

one I described in Chapter 3; only the titles of the officials involved have changed.[101]

In some areas cadres led by the party organization and governmental bodies at each level have been organized into work teams and sent to villages to oversee the new system.[102] Like the production teams before, each village is allotted a certain procurement target that must be met. This "recommended figure" (*jianyi shu*) is supposed to be based on the county's and the township's estimate of an area's ability to adjust and diversify production. Some areas take a survey of the previous year's grain production conditions in each township, village, and household. The villages (cadres) discuss these recommendations and work out the division of the target, which in turn is sent to individual households, who then sign individual contracts directly with the grain bureau.[103]

The village government, which now must act something like a general contractor, takes the recommended target sent from the township and subcontracts specific quotas to individual peasant households. The total of the individual peasant contracts has to tally generally with the targets sent down from the upper levels, just as the total sales by the different teams had to tally with the brigade's overall target. How large a contract each peasant should get is determined by official evaluation of a peasant's past performance and future potential. The precise method varies.

In one area, cadres used statistics from the past three years to help peasants decide on an appropriate contract amount.[104] In Sichuan, officials took 1984 grain sales as the base year. Those who could diversify

101. Interview with a grain bureau official, China Interviews, 1988.

102. See, for example, "Heilongjiangsheng dapi ganbu xiaxiang zhidao chungeng" (Large Number of Cadres in Heilongjiang Province Go to the Countryside to Supervise Spring Planting), *JJRB* 4 April 1985:1; and "Liangmian," *NCGZTX* 1985, no. 5, pp. 38–39.

103. According to published reports, the township economic management station (*jingguanzhan*) is directly responsible for the contracts while the township government supervises and notarizes the transaction. The township grain station (*liangguansuo*) and economic management station also have a contract. The grain bureau pays the station 0.15 *yuan* in handling fees for each household contract: ibid. On the basis of my research in 1988 I found that the agricultural tax is listed as part of the grain contract that each household receives. This tax can now be paid in money, but in most cases it is still paid in grain. The finance bureau, not the tax bureau, is the government office that is responsible for the collection of the agricultural tax and from which the levies are issued; China Interviews, 1988.

104. "Zunzhong qunzhong yiyuan luoshi dinggou hetong Longyou nongmin jizao anpaihao nongzuowu buju" (Respect the Masses' Wishes, Implement Contract Procurement, Longyou Peasants Plan Crop Mix Way in Advance), *ZJRB* 17 March 1985:1.

sold less; those who did not diversify sold the same amount as in 1984; those who had surplus grain could sell more; those who planted less than five *fen* of land did not need to sell any grain.[105] It is unclear what happens if a peasant wants to sell more or less than the cadres think appropriate.

Elsewhere, county, district, and township governments organized work teams to carefully examine available current statistics and village account books before peasants were allowed to make contracts. The township cadres added these contract pledges and tried to achieve an overall balance between the peasants' desired sales and the recommended target.[106] In Hunan a meeting of the village (production) group heads (*cunmin zuzhang huiyi*) was called to discuss the planned procurement target that had been sent down by the township government to the village.[107] A proposed target was given to each production group, according to its production conditions. Each production group then called a meeting of its household heads (*huzhu hui*) to announce the proposed targets; each household pledged the type of crop and the amount it would sell. The village contracts had to tally with the proposed target for the group (*zu*), but, like teams in the past, households could decide among themselves who would sell how much.[108]

What appears to be a straightforward voluntary business arrangement is open to cadre manipulation. The spirit of the contract system has been undercut by the "commandism" and particularism still practiced by those charged with implementing the program. Some local cadres have not even attempted to implement the negotiation spirit of the reforms; they simply continue to use the old quota system. As in the past, they merely tell the peasants how much they must sell to the state. Some even use the notification slip, informing each household of the quota it owes the state, as the peasant's contract.[109] Some cadres dis-

105. "Liangmian," NCGZTX 1985, no. 5, pp. 38–39.

106. Ibid.

107. The (production) group (*zu*) is the division below the village; this has different names in different areas.

108. In Zhejiang, a similar type of meeting was called of the household heads to help them decide on the amount they would contract to sell. The village cadres, including the team accountant, reviewed each household's production situation before the contracts were signed. "Liangmian," NCGZTX 1985, no. 5, pp. 38–39.

109. See, for example, "Henan yixie diqu wei luoshi dinggou cuoshi jingyi shougou tongzhidan daiti qianding hetong" (Some Areas in Henan in Order to Implement Contract Procurement Have Used Procurement Notices in Place of Signed Contracts), NMRB 12 February 1985:1; and "Zhonggong Weifangshi weinongcun gongzuo weiyuanhui, Yao ba tong nongmin qianding dinggou hetong dangdai yijian dashi laizhua" (Treat the Signing of Procurement Contracts with Peasants as an Important Matter), NCGZTX 1985, no. 4, p. 37.

tribute the contract procurement target equally according to acreage or population, without consulting with the peasants.[110] This, in fact, was the *norm* in villages I studied in 1988. Peasants are handed their grain contract by village officials, who simply divide the total village quota by the number of *mu* of land in the village and multiply that figure by the amount of land a household has contracted to farm.[111]

AN UNCERTAIN PEASANT-STATE RELATIONSHIP

The post-1978 Chinese state has adopted a more traditional role in the disposition of the harvest and relies more on market and price mechanisms to secure its needed grain. The division of the harvest is no longer the major issue of conflict between state and peasant. Meeting the state's procurement quotas is no longer the major burden it once was, although peasants still lose money either in high production costs or in buying grain on the free market to meet the mandatory quota. Basic procurement no longer cuts into peasant subsistence, thanks to increases in production, the state's decision to allow peasants to decide what is surplus, and, most important, its decision to allow peasants autonomy over the increasing amounts of grain being retained in the village.

At the same time that the state exhibits new confidence and adopts market-oriented strategies, there is a certain ambivalence over how far it should step back and to what degree the reforms should be allowed to go forward. The way contracts are being implemented underscores this ambivalence. The form has changed, but the procurement process remains essentially the same. The village no longer has the right to the fruits of a peasant's labor, but it still has the power to decide the minimal amount a peasant must sell to the state. The harvest is now the property of the household, but procurement targets still must be met, albeit now through the use of the so-called contracts. The state mediated the struggle over the harvest and gave peasants more power to decide how much they can keep, but it did not free them from the authority of village officials.

Whether procurements will disappear completely as an issue between the state and peasant seems to depend largely on the state's perceptions

110. See, for example, "Miaoshangxiang shishi qiushi luoshi xiaomai dinggou renwu" (Miaoshang Township, Seeking Truth from Facts, Implements the Wheat Quota), *SXNM* 12 April 1985:1.

111. China Interviews, 1988.

of the sufficiency of grain output. Some have suggested that not every peasant household needs to produce or sell grain. Considerations of efficiency of scale and the increasing number of peasants who no longer farm have produced a debate about who should get the grain contracts. Should they be distributed evenly or be concentrated in the hands of the grain-specialized households? Is giving special consideration to grain-specialized units the only way to promote the diversification of the economy?[112] The state's quick reversion to the position that grain contracts are an obligation of all peasant households indicates its continued insecurity and makes it unlikely that peasants will be completely free of their burden any time soon.

112. "Shixing liangshi," *NCGZTX* 1985, no. 4, pp. 33–34.

CHAPTER 9

The Evolution of a Clientelist System

The Household Economy and Cadre Power

The state decision to adopt the household responsibility system and abandon collective agricultural production ushered in a new stage in the rural economy, allowing peasants a generally higher standard of living and an altered way of life. Peasants are now free from the confines of the collective and the dictates of the team leader. Now the possibility of more income options and diverse rural employment opportunities exists. Peasants may become specialized households within the agricultural sector, or they may leave agriculture entirely and engage in sidelines, work in factories, and participate in the free market.

To achieve this new stage, the millions of production teams and brigades had to undergo an intense and often drawn-out process of decollectivization, almost as complicated as the original land reform.[1] Conflicts over dividing collective property were as fierce and emotional as those over dividing the landlords' property.[2] Each item of collective property—land, tools, boats, fish nets, tractors, even entire factories—had to be contracted out or, in the case of equipment, sold. The questions were many: Who received which items? At what price? And who would get the contracts for running enterprises, orchards, fishponds, and farming the most desirable parcels of farmland?

Dividing the land held center stage. The issue was not primarily *how*

---

1. In some places it took over a month to complete the process; in a few it took even longer and required outside assistance.
2. For a vivid description of these problems in the original land reform, see William Hinton, *Fanshen*.

much each family received but who got the rights to farm *which piece* of land.[3] Fertility, proximity to water supplies, homes, and roads were all key considerations. Team cadres used different methods, some more equitable than others, but all left cadres open to charges of favoritism. The process usually began with cadres drawing maps dividing the collective land into parcels of varying size and quality. The more authoritarian cadres would then simply distribute the land with minimal discussion. Others more concerned with equity would divide all the land into good and not-so-good parcels; each household would then be assigned some parcels of the good land and some of the poorer land. But there was always room for debate about the precise quality of a particular piece of land. To avoid these problems, some teams simply drew lots. In theory, that should have removed any question of fairness because it was all a matter of luck; however, in practice, some peasants still accused cadres of rigging the process.[4]

Equally heated arguments ensued over the disposition of equipment, particularly lucrative transport items, such as boats and tractors, and draft animals. Some teams or brigades kept ownership and merely leased the equipment to individual households, or to groups of households in the case of large equipment such as tractors. One brigade, for example, originally had only three tractors for six teams; it kept ownership but contracted use of the tractors to individuals, who were then required to pay rent, fifty *yuan* each year, to the brigade.[5] Other teams and brigades simply sold all their equipment to the highest bidder. Some argued that wealth should not decide property distribution.

Allocating the few draft animals in a team presented particularly complex problems. In those cases where there were few draft animals and many buyers or would-be renters, the animals either became the property of a group of households or were contracted out to a group of households and remained collective property. In either case, each household would try to make maximum use of their time with the ani-

---

3. The official guidelines called for land to be distributed equitably based on population and/or labor power.

4. How many of these allegations are true I have no way of knowing, but complaints of cadre mismanagement and corruption abound. My data do not allow me to make any statements about the extent of cadre corruption. As in earlier sections, my purpose is to point to those areas where cadres had discretion over the disposition of those resources that affect the ability of peasants under the reforms to prosper.

5. Hong Kong Interview 12/8/2. The rental rates peasants pay vary in different areas. In one brigade the rate for a large tractor to plow and rake the soil was ten *yuan* per *mu* of land; in another, the cost was eight *yuan* per hour plus food for the driver. Peasants with small hand-held tractors were making two *yuan* per hour during the busy season.

mal. Unlike the tractors, which could rotate from plot to plot without rest, the one draft animal that was shared and rotated from household to household soon became exhausted; some were so overworked that they died.

The collective enterprises posed a somewhat different problem. They were not sold but leased to individuals or a group of individuals. There was less general competition for these items because the rents due the collective were usually substantial and few regular peasants were confident in their abilities to undertake such a major venture. These enterprises usually went to former factory managers or in many cases to the team cadres. A second category of enterprises—team fish ponds, orchards, or forest land—was more in the realm of general peasant expertise and therefore more in demand. Here again cadres seem to have had the advantage, getting the contracts to these very lucrative rights.

When all property had finally been divided, the production team as a collective entity was dead. It officially still owned all the land and most of the property, but the team cadres no longer directed production or divided the harvest. Offices stood empty, the team became obsolete as a level of administration, and eventually it was abolished in most places. The team cadres, who had held so much power over the peasants' lives, had their power usurped by the household responsibility system, which made each household the unit of production and accounting. For the most part, team leaders had to exit the historical stage—no longer the key political actors in the Chinese countryside through whom the peasant dealt with the state, no longer the gatekeepers who determined the peasants' livelihood both inside and outside the collective. But the story does not end there.

The post-1978 reforms robbed team leaders of most of their power, leaving them, either as team leaders or as newly designated village small group leaders, with few duties. Not surprisingly, some cadres resisted these reforms, feeling betrayed by the state for taking their power away and resentful that peasants no longer listened to them.[6] But the fact that they initially opposed the reforms does not mean that they did not then develop strategies to deal with the new political wind or that they sat idly by as their power was being reformed out of existence. The power

6. On resistance to reforms and the negative feeling of cadres see, for example, Richard Latham, "Comprehensive Socialist Reform" and "The Implications of Rural Reform"; Helen Fung-har Siu, "Collective Economy"; and David Zweig, "Opposition." On the decline of the collective also see Hartford, "Socialist Agriculture"; Vivienne Shue, "The Fate of the Commune"; and Andrew Watson, "New Structures."

of these cadres did not just end. Because of their positions and the prevalent clientelist politics in the Maoist period, those who had been cadres may have lost their offices but not necessarily their power.

The clientelist nature of politics manifested itself in the decollectivization process and allowed the team cadres and their friends and relatives the upper hand in getting the best land, the most desirable equipment, and the most lucrative contracts at the most favorable terms. For example, when it became clear to cadres that the collective property was to be divided among individual households, those who realized the profit involved in transport work were quick to take advantage of their position. Some cadres arranged to purchase for themselves or their friends and relatives collective tractors before most peasants even knew of the opportunity; others secured either the tractors at an artificially low price or the contract for their use at favorable rates.[7] Most important, in China's new economic context, former team cadres were quick to contract the lucrative collective enterprises. Moreover, it was not unusual for these former team cadres, particularly the team leaders, to end up in one capacity or another in the new village governments. Consequently, many of these cadres set themselves up to take maximum advantage of the opportunities the new system had to offer. As soon as they saw which way the wind was blowing, they quickly made the most of the situation.

Furthermore, in considering cadre power and village politics during the post-1978 period, one should not limit the discussion to the team. One must look beyond the demise of the teams and their leaders' loss of formal power to the situation peasants faced after decollectivization. The reforms made the village, not the team, the intersection of state and society. One must examine the resources of these village cadres just as one did the team leaders. One must examine the relationship of peasants with the new village (former brigade) officials, now the lowest-level administrators, with whom the peasants would have routine contact. One must ask whether the reemergence of markets and the reforms in agriculture, sweeping as they were, altered the dependency relationship of peasants and the clientelist nature of politics.

Those who have written on the evolution of clientelist systems suggest that market reforms or the development of a modern economy does not necessarily mean the demise of clientelist politics. For example,

7. See, for example, "Baichi pingguo qiyou cili" (Eating Apples Without Paying Is Outrageous), *SXNM* 3 September 1983:1.

Judith Chubb, who has studied the situation in Italy, found that in spite of all the trappings of a modern market economy, as long as local officials can continue to influence the distribution of scarce and valued resources and opportunities, they have an effective power base.[8] Controlling bureaucratic procedures, granting licenses, issuing permits, and partially enforcing regulations are a few of these resources. There is evidence that this is also the case in China.

In this chapter I will show that breaking up the collective and opening the markets have resulted in change but not destruction of local cadre power. The reforms changed but did not destroy the clientelist politics that existed in the Maoist period. The reforms only freed the peasants from the power that team leaders held and undermined the position of the team leader as the peasants' all-important patron. Several questions must be asked: Not just what power have cadres lost, but what power have cadres kept? What power have they acquired at the newly established village level? What are the new bases of power? And who has that power?[9] This can be done by examining the role of local government and how local cadres can affect the well-being of peasants.

THE NEW ROLE OF VILLAGE GOVERNMENT

The reforms abolished the production team as the lowest level of administration, but peasants must still go through the bureaucracy for important inputs, opportunities, and services. In fact, the reforms have created an even greater need for peasants, who have been thrust into the unfamiliar and increasingly complex market environment—where they must procure inputs, find market outlets, and arrange transport—to seek help. Peasants also need help in deciding what to produce and in some cases how to produce the most profitable crops. Specialized households must apply for licenses and permits, seek enforcement of legal rights that exist on paper, and avoid various surcharges and fees.[10] Those whom they seek help from are more often than not the local cadres, both those who were the team leaders and, most important, the new village (former brigade) leaders.

8. See Chubb, *Patronage, Power, and Poverty.*
9. Few studies have taken this approach. A notable exception is Thomas Bernstein, "Reforming China's Agriculture."
10. "Nongmin congshi geti shangye kunnan chongchong" (Peasants Who Want to Engage in Private Business Are Surrounded by Numerous Difficulties), *ZGNMB* 15 April 1984:1.

TABLE 20.   CADRE CONTROL OVER SOURCES OF
PEASANT INCOME AFTER DECOLLECTIVIZATION

Agricultural Inputs	Market and Sales Opportunities	Salaried Job Opportunities
Distribution of rationed and low-priced inputs —chemical fertilizer —motor fuel	Permission to grow choice of crop	Recommendation for nonagricultural jobs —state factories —collective enterprises in urban and rural areas
Access to scarce non-rationed inputs (farm equipment) —draft animals —tractors	Access to market information and technical expertise	Granting of authorizations (*zhengming*)
Allocation of collective resources for contract (*chengbao*) —land —factories —equipment	Access to sales contracts —state —collective —private	

The reforms, rather than eliminating the role of village government, have created new and in many ways more demanding tasks for basic-level government, which in the new context is the *cun* (village). Village cadres now oversee a wide range of commercial transactions and local enterprises and make sure that their village prospers in the new market environment. They must strive to diversify the economy, develop commodity production, and find markets for these goods.[11] These tasks of village government may be divided into three sets of functions: procurement of inexpensive agricultural inputs, location of markets, and access to nonagricultural jobs (see Table 20). The following sections will show how cadres play a key role in allocating these major resources on which peasant livelihood currently depends.

11. Ai Zhiguo, "Party Shifts Consolidation to Countryside," *Beijing Review* 30 December 1985, vol. 28, no. 52, p. 5; also "Zhuanhua xiaoshou you zhuoluo zhongzhi jihua you genju Baimiaozixiang nongmin zhashi beigeng" (Specialized Sales Have Been Set Up, the Cropping Plan Has a Foundation, the Peasants of Baimiaozi Township Are Preparing for Ploughing in a Down-to-Earth Manner), *NMRB* 7 February 1985:1; "Budeng zhibiao kan shichang, zixiaershang ding jihua Shuangyushuxiang jiajia huhu 'yinianzao zhidao'" (Shuangyushu Township Does Not Wait for the Quota but Looks to the Market, Making Plans from the Bottom Up, Every Household Makes Plan a Year in Advance), *NMRB* 7 February 1985:1; and "Shenlixian ganbu zijue wei fazhan jingji fuwu" (Shenli County's Cadres Voluntarily Help to Develop the Economy), *NMRB* 19 April 1985:1.

THE VILLAGE AS LANDLORD AND
FRANCHISING COMPANY

Although individual households have become the basic unit of production, the means of production—especially land—remain collectively owned. The task of village government is overseeing the allocation and the management of contracts to individuals or groups of peasant households who work this property. Under the initial terms of the responsibility system, village cadres, mostly team cadres with some brigade supervision, were instructed to evaluate and divide the collective property, as I described at the beginning of the chapter. As the reforms proceeded, the village cadres took over completely from the team leaders, and now they oversee these properties and contracts. During the course of the reforms, the issues have changed and the work of cadres has in many ways become more difficult.

The conflict over land, for example, central in the decollectivization process, has taken on a different character. No longer is it just a question of equitable distribution. The state is pushing the local levels to achieve maximum efficiency; increasingly it condones concentrating land holdings and developing large specialized households to fulfill the state's grain contracts.[12] Specialization is thus equated with efficiency, enabling local governments to merge the many scattered plots that resulted when land was initially divided.[13] Some Chinese economists go so far as to argue that this is the only way to achieve rural economic diversification.[14]

The government actively encourages such specialization. It has given various types of special-status households, such as the *zhuanyehu* (specialized household),[15] privileged access to larger amounts of state-priced

12. Alternatively, some peasants enter into voluntary cooperative farming (*lianhu lianpian, jizhong gengzhong*). They jointly farm adjacent plots of land or jointly contract a large piece of land. In a county outside Tianjin, 2,368 peasants formed 582 small groups to farm 21,585 *mu* of land. "Tudi xiang zhongtian nengshou jizhongde yixie banfa" (Several Ways of Concentrating Landholdings into the Hands of Farm Experts), *NCGZTX* 1984, no. 8, pp. 14–15.

13. Zhongyang Guangdongsheng Kaipingxian Gongchenqu Weiyuanhui, "Heli tiaozheng tudi youli jizhong lianpian" (Properly Adjust Landholdings, Profitably Concentrate Plots), *NCGZTX* 1984, no. 12, pp. 32–34.

14. "Shixing liangshi," *NCGZTX* 1985, no. 4, pp. 33–34.

15. *Zhuanyehu* are peasant households that produce one item, for example, a cash crop, grain, or livestock, often under contract with collective or state companies. Within the category of *zhuanyehu* are *zhongdianhu*, "key point households," that were singled out for special assistance. Beginning in 1984 this last designation seemed to go out of use; they became known simply as *zhuanyehu*. There are also *kejihu* (scientific households) that use the latest agricultural techniques and equipment. "Moba kejihu biancheng guanxihu" (Don't Turn Scientific-Specialized Households into Connection Households), *ZGNMB* 24 April 1983:3.

inputs including chemical fertilizer, animal feed, and loans for enterprise expansion.[16] Moreover, it has linked access to particular inputs to different types of commodity production. Specialized households engaged in secondary food production, for example, are provided with grain ration coupons so that they will be free to concentrate on their specialty production. Those who raise geese are given ration coupons to buy state-priced grain, freeing them from having to grow their own. Grain-specialized households are provided bonuses of such inputs as low-priced high-quality fertilizer.

This concentrated land holding has not been a major problem in areas where sidelines and enterprises have developed rapidly. In those areas there is a surplus of land, as a significant proportion of the population has moved away from agricultural production to nonagricultural enterprises and sidelines. Where sideline enterprises are booming, some peasants have wanted to dispose of, or at least decrease, the land they originally contracted. A survey of one county in Jiangsu found that 1,266 of 1,475 households wanted to reduce the amount of land they contracted—nearly 11 percent of the land under contract. Only eighty-one households requested more land, and those extra land requests totaled only 116 *mu*.[17]

Not surprisingly, in such areas one finds a few households contracting to farm all of a village's arable land.[18] A 1984 survey outside Beijing found that 11 percent of the labor power in a village in two brigades, where sidelines were developing rapidly, contracted to farm 94 percent of its land.[19] In 1985, in a village in Liaoning, eighteen households contracted to farm 5,000 *mu* of land; one household alone contracted 600 *mu*. In 1988, in a village outside Tianjin, nine peasants farmed the village's 5,000 *mu*.[20] Such large grain-specialized households might bring to mind the managerial farmers in late imperial China.[21] In the contem-

16. Hong Kong Interviews 19/9/31 and 7/6/7.

17. Jiangsusheng Jintanxian Nonggongbu, "Xin wenti yu xin cuoshi" (New Problems and New Measures), NCGZTX 1984, no. 11, p. 30.

18. In one case four women contracted all of the village's land. "Sige 'Mu Guiying' chengbao yicun tian" (Four "Mu Guiying's" Contract to Farm All of the Village Land), SXNM 20 November 1984:2. In another case one household contracted all 167 *mu* of the village land. "Linhai zhongliang dahu Zhou Zhenghua chengbao quancun yibaibashiqi mu liangtian" (Linhai's Large Grain-Specialized Household Zhou Zhenghua Contracts to Farm All 187 *Mu* of the Village Land), ZJRB 29 March 1985:2. Also see "Xiqianliucun 31 hu nongmin chengbao quancun gengdi" (Thirty-one Households in Xiqianliu Village Contract to Farm All of the Village Land), ZGNMB 6 December 1984:1, where only 31 of 220 households (14 percent) had contracted any of the village's 571 *mu* of land.

19. "Tudi jizhong zai gedi" (Concentration of Landholdings in Various Areas), NCGZTX 1984, no. 12, p. 33.

20. China Interviews, 1985 and 1988.

21. See Philip C. C. Huang, The Peasant Economy, chap. 4.

porary case, the grain-specialized households farm the land themselves, although they may hire laborers, mostly other peasants from the village, during the busy season to help them work the fields.[22] But there is a difference: the land remains the property of the collective, and the specialized household that runs the farm must pay the village an annual fee and the state its tax.[23]

In response, some local village and township governments have had to set up "land contracting companies" (*tudi zhuanbao gongsi*). These companies take over farmland returned to the collective by peasants who no longer wish to cultivate it. Peasants who return their land to the village pay their assigned monthly share of the collective public welfare fund (*gongyi jin*);[24] in return, they are allowed to buy a set amount of grain rations at the state price. The company then contracts the land to a third party, known as "expert cultivators" (*zhongtian nengshou*). These cultivators work the land, receiving both a parity price (*pingjia*) for their crop and a subsidy from the company. The head of the village government manages the land-contracting company and supervises its execution of the contracts.[25]

Some areas even welcome outsiders to contract farmland and run it as a family farm (*jiating nongchang*). Under these still experimental arrangements, a peasant, regardless of native region, may contract land from state agricultural research stations. The contract binds the peasant to turn over a specific amount of grain based on an agreed minimum yield. Any surplus is the peasant's. For example, in Jiangsu a peasant from Hebei contracted with an agricultural station (*nongkedui*) to produce a total of 27,500 *jin* of grain, with a minimum of 450 *jin* per *mu*. He produced 100,000 *jin* and yielded a net profit of over 10,000 *yuan* in one year. The research station from which the land is rented lends support in three areas: access to fertilizer, insecticide, and other agricultural inputs; technical support; and investment. The peasant found this arrangement so profitable that he sold his newly built house in his home

22. In one village in 1985, the hired hands received 200 *yuan* per month. This village was large, with over 900 households, and extremely rich. It had twenty-seven different village enterprises, which employed one-third of the population (1,100 of 3,300). The land was never divided equally. When the land was first divided in 1979, it was contracted to work groups, not individual households. It then went directly from contracting to groups to contracting to large grain-specialized households. China Interviews, summer 1985.

23. In some cases, the village pays the state tax as an inducement for a peasant to farm the land and produce the needed grain. This was the case in a village outside Shenyang. I also found a similar arrangement in a very industrialized and wealthy village outside Tianjin. China Interviews, 1986 and 1988.

24. In an example from Hebei, the cost was three *yuan*.

25. See, for example, "Tudi xiang zhongtian," NCGZTX 1984, no. 8, pp. 14–15.

village, built one at the agricultural research station, and concentrated on grain production.[26]

Not all areas, however, have been as successful in developing rural industry, and not all peasants are eager to give away their land rights. In fact, most want to keep their land as an insurance policy even if they do not farm it. Not surprisingly, cadres also face the opposite problem of peasants who complain that they have not been given enough land to farm. The intensity of these complaints seemed to increase after the announcement that the contracts for land-use rights would be extended to at least fifteen years.[27] Peasants complained that some cadres created large specialized households, such as 10,000-*jin*-grain-producing specialized households (*wanjin liang zhuanyehu*), by arbitrarily reducing the already meager holdings of the other peasants in the village.[28] A particularly poignant story describes a woman given so little land that her family suffered from hunger. Her family of six, five of whom were legally eligible for land, should have been allowed to contract 12 *mu* of land, but cadres only allowed 4.5 *mu* of poor and remote strips. She took her case to higher government authorities, but nothing was done.[29]

Village cadres have also had to assume the role of overseeing the contracts on collectively owned enterprises and properties. As in the case of land, the task has become more complex than the initial assignment of contracts. Profit margins have changed; some enterprises have proven much more successful than originally thought, some less. New methods for calculating rents have had to be devised to meet changing needs and profits. Originally, most villages assessed a fixed rent for the term of the contract for using the piece of equipment, orchard, fish pond, or enterprise. After the rent was paid, profits belonged to the peasant. Increas-

---

26. Ibid. For a discussion of types of contracting of state farmland in Xinjiang to former farm workers see Keith Griffin, "Rural Development."

27. This was done in Document No. 1 (January 1984). For a translation of this, see "Circular of the Central Committee of the Chinese Communist Party on Rural Work During 1984," translated by R. F. Ash, *China Quarterly* March 1985, no. 101, pp. 132–142. The political and economic implications of the document are explored in four commentaries that accompany the translation; ibid., pp. 104–131.

28. "Buneng yingxing guiding gao 'wanjinhu,'" (Cannot Arbitrarily Create "10,000-*Jin* Households"), *ZGNMB* 6 March 1984:3. Also see "Tiaozheng tudi yao jianchi qunzhong luxian" (Uphold the Mass Line in the Readjustment of Landholdings), *NCGZTX* 1984, no. 11, p. 29.

29. "Yiwei nongfu de kusu" (The Tearful Complaints of a Peasant Wife), *NCGZTX* 1984, no. 11, p. 40. There are also reports that some villagers systematically discriminate against women on the amount of land they may contract. See "Tongmuxiang chengbao zerentian de guai zhangcheng nansui nianzhang zengtian nüsui nianzhang jiandi" (Tongmu Township's Strange Contract Provision, Males Get More Land as Age Increases, but Females Get Less as Age Increases), *NMRB* 26 June 1985:1.

ingly, it seems that village cadres have become aware of the profitability of enterprises, or at least of their inability to correctly predict profits, and thus have begun using an alternative rental arrangement, where the village takes a percentage of the year's profits.[30] Peasants seem to prefer the former set arrangement to the floating rate.[31] In fact, in one place where the government changed to a percentage rate, the number of enterprises contracted has dropped.[32]

Village governments, in essence, have become socialist landlords. They sell the right to operate collective property or business. The village retains ownership; it has the right both to conduct periodic inspections and to terminate contracts if the original terms of the agreement are not met or the quality of the franchiser's performance does not meet village standards. Village cadres dictate the terms of land contracts and select the tenants who can have the privilege of running village enterprises.

Cadres are supposed to lease land and enterprises according to objective criteria, such as profit and efficiency of use. But examples of cadres arbitrarily taking contracts away from peasants and giving them to others suggest that cadres also invoke subjective criteria, such as particularistic relationships and personal profit. Reports of cadres afflicted with "red eye disease" (yanhong), that is, envy, who demand profits or even shares in lucrative enterprises and arbitrarily break contracts if their demands are not met, reflect the personal control many cadres have come to wield.[33] According to numerous accounts, some local cadres try to take as much of the profit as possible, regardless of the terms of the original contract.[34] They break contracts when they see that the contractor is making larger-than-expected profits. The excuses vary. In one case, the contract was nullified when the original contractor, the father of the

30. China Interviews, 1986.
31. China Interviews, 1985.
32. China Interviews, 1986.
33. See, for example, "Zhuanye yangyuhu zao 'zai' jizhang baitiao chidiao xianyu liuqianjin yaozhuijiu" (Specialized Fishery Household Suffers "Disaster," Several White Slips Eat Up 6,000 *Jin* of Fish, We Must Investigate) *RMRB* 19 July 1984:3; "Chibucheng 'Daguofan' qineng qiaolimingmu?" (If You No Longer Can "Eat Out of One Big Pot," How Can You Concoct Various Pretexts to Extort Money from Peasants?), *ZGNMB* 22 February 1983:2; "Qiangxing rugu fang'ai zhuanyehu fazhan" (Forced Partnerships Hamper the Development of Specialized Households), *ZGNMB* 14 April 1983:2; "Handanshi Fayuan panchu Zhang Hushan sixing" (Handan City Court Sentences Zhang Hushan to Death), *ZGNMB* 11 March 1984:3; and "Datongxian hensha 'quanligu' waifeng" (Datong County Resolutely Stops the Evil Wind of "Forced Partnerships"), *ZGNMB* 19 January 1984:1.
34. For an in-depth discussion of the problems of contracts, see David Zweig, Kathy Hartford, James Feinerman, and Deng Jianxu, "Law, Contracts, and Economic Management."

household, died.[35] Some cadres, upon coming to office, have declared that contracts made under predecessors are no longer valid.[36] The most profitable specialized households—those engaged in growing fruit, raising fish, or managing a village enterprise—seem to be the favorite victims.[37]

THE VILLAGE AS EMPLOYMENT AGENCY

The changes in the rural economy have made factory jobs increasingly important. According to official statistics, by the end of 1985 township enterprises had absorbed sixty million surplus farm hands.[38] This trend is expected to grow. The state plans to transfer more than 50 percent of the surplus labor from agriculture to other pursuits by the end of the century.[39] In some areas, such as highly developed Wuxi, already 40 percent of the rural labor force is engaged in industrial production; almost every family in the area has at least one member working in a factory.[40]

The lure of nonagricultural jobs is high pay. In one village, those who worked in the fields earned 240 *yuan* a year, but those who worked in a village paper factory earned 600 *yuan*.[41] In another area, a peasant earns less than 1,000 *yuan* from work in the fields, while one who works in the local factories earns 3,000 *yuan* a year.[42]

35. "Chengbao hetong youwu jichengquan" (The Inheritability of Contracts), *NCGZTX* 1984, no. 11, p. 32.

36. "Ganbu huanjie, hetong jiu wuxiaole ma?" (When Cadres Are Changed, Do Contracts Become Invalid?), *NMRB* 30 March 1985:3.

37. "Danfang sihui hetong—gaifa!" (The One Who Unilaterally Tears Up a Contract Should Be Punished), *NMRB* 14 June 1985:3; "Qirong 'yanhong' dan huiyue fayuan binggong hu chengbao" (Do Not Allow One Side to Break a Contract Arbitrarily Because of "Red Eye Disease," Courts Protect the Right of Contractor) *GDNMB* 9 September 1984:1.

38. "1985, 1986 and Beyond," *Beijing Review* 6 January 1986, vol. 29, no. 1, p. 4. At the end of 1984, 50 million peasants were employed in rural factories. "Rural Industries Take on Technology," *Beijing Review* 10 February 1986, vol. 29, nos. 6 and 7, p. 5.

39. Du Rensheng, "Second-Stage Rural Structural Reform," *Beijing Review* 24 June 1985, vol. 28, no. 25, p. 17.

40. Xue Muqiao, "Rural Industry Advances Amidst Problems," *Beijing Review* 16 December 1985, vol. 28, no. 50, p. 18.

41. "Fengnanxian cuoshi caiqu baohu nongmin jingying tudi de jijixing" (Fengnan County Implements Measures to Protect Peasant Enthusiasm for Managing Land), *NMRB* 23 March 1985:2.

42. "Rural Industries Take On Technology," *Beijing Review* 10 February 1986, vol. 29, nos. 6 and 7, p. 5. It is unclear if these are national averages or when these figures apply. Working in local factories has always been a coveted position in the Chinese countryside. See Chapter 7 of this book.

It is worth noting that although the difference between industrial and agricultural jobs is substantial, peasants usually try to keep a foot on the farm. They have responded to these new opportunities by adopting family strategies that maximize not only individual but also total household income; those who can work in factories do; the others, often women and the older members of the family, work the entire family's fields. Because it is possible for one person to work the land of the other three or four family members, particularly in mechanized areas, the one who remains brings to the household as much as a factory worker.[43]

The reforms have allowed peasants legally to leave farming as long as they meet their minimum responsibilities to the state and the collective, but they will not necessarily find employment. China lacks an open labor market. Village cadres play a major role in allocating these opportunities as did the team leaders before them. The best jobs in the collective or state sectors are often still distributed through the commune/township bureaucracy. The standard practice of state and collective factories is to send an announcement (*ming'e*) to a township or village of how many workers they need. Each level in the collective then apportions jobs to its subordinate levels. Local cadres have considerable leeway, except when special skills are required, in recommending favored peasants for the best positions.[44]

The degree to which local cadres can determine the job possibilities of a peasant depends on the number of jobs available. The more industrially developed an area, the more jobs and the less need for a peasant to depend on the cadres' good will. Even so, cadre support is useful for getting the best jobs. It is not uncommon that the contract labor positions (*hetong gong*) in the cities or jobs in the state granaries go to party members or children of cadres.[45] Collective officials also have discretion over the jobs that collectives are guaranteed by state enterprises when they sell a piece of land to a factory (*tudi gong*). These are particularly attractive because they are virtually permanent nonagricultural employment.[46]

With the rise of rural industry and the movement away from agricul-

43. China Interviews, 1988.
44. Hong Kong Interview 7/6/24.
45. Hong Kong Interview 18/7/23. For an extreme example of this, see Hebei Joint Inspection Group, "Why Are So Many Party Cadres Here Carried Away by 'Evil Winds'?" *RMRB* 10 September 1985:5, translated in *JPRS-CPS-85-121* 19 December 1985: 101–104.
46. On *tudi gong* see Andrew Walder, *Communist Neo-Traditionalism*, chap. 2.

ture, a special category of agricultural jobs has developed. Where industries and sidelines are well developed, some villages have turned farming into a "division" or "workshop" (*chejian*) within industrial enterprises. In this system, the agricultural and industrial sectors are merged (*nonggong yitihua*). The industrial enterprise hires peasants to work the crop land. Those hired are given the title "peasant-workers." In practice, they are grain-specialized households who work as subcontractors for the factory. A peasant must already be a commercial grain-specialized household (*shangpinliang zhuanyehu*) who has contracted more than three *mu* of land from his village to be eligible for these positions. Unlike other grain-specialized households, their agricultural expenses are the responsibility of the factory.[47] A production target is set for each *mu* of land. The factory keeps this grain, and any production above that level is the peasant-worker's.

These jobs are unique because they provide a peasant with what can be called a salary. The following examples show how this works. In one township, nineteen villages incorporated 286 grain-specialized households into its industrial enterprises to work 946 *mu* of land. In one village, sixteen grain-specialized households that sold more than 3,000 *jin* of grain annually joined the village enterprise system as specialized agricultural workers.[48] The factory set minimum production at 1,300 *jin* of grain per *mu*. The enterprise paid each peasant-worker 80 *yuan* per *mu* for inputs (costs) and 160 *yuan* per *mu* for wages. The peasant was liable for both extra expenses and failure to meet production targets. The receipts from the sale of the grain as well as any subsidy from the commune (*buliangkuan*) went to the collective enterprise; any surplus grain was the property of the peasant-worker. The enterprise paid the collective 12 *yuan* per *mu* for the agricultural tax and 8 *yuan* per *mu* to the team for the *gongyi* and *gongji jin*.[49] A similar system pays peasant-workers the average salary of the factory's regular workers and allows a bonus for every 100-*jin* increase of output per *mu* of land. One village also supplemented the earnings of those who continue to work on the land by assuming the costs of water, electricity, the agricultural tax as

47. This is similar to the *baochan daohu* form of the responsibility system in land contracting.

48. In addition to this specialized workshop within the enterprise, four other specialized workshops, which employ more than forty peasants who work on a responsibility system based on quotas and bonuses, deal with agriculture: mechanized plowing; plant protection; irrigation; and agricultural technology.

49. "Tudi xiang zhongtian," *NCGZTX* 1984, no. 8, pp. 14–15.

well as family planning and education fees, and so on; its factories also paid a supplement of 81 *yuan* for each *mu* of cultivated land.[50]

In addition to jobs in collectively owned enterprises there are jobs in the growing private sector. Some peasants have found lucrative jobs, particularly in construction but also in factories run by specialized households. Cadre influence here is limited, but again it is not an entirely free market. Most of these jobs, like those organized by collective units, are obtained through connections. Kinship ties have reemerged, alongside *guanxi,* as determining factors in hiring for privately run factories. The majority of workers in peasant-run enterprises are often relatives or at least friends of relatives. In a privately run factory in Liaoning, most of the 100 workers obtained their jobs either through kinship or friendship ties. This trend may displace some power of local cadres, particularly if these people have better technical skills. "The people who are most powerful and most respected now are people who can find jobs, have *chulu* [ways out], have friends, have *guanxi.*"[51] But many families who now own or contract the former collective factories are former cadres.[52]

The legal right of peasants to work outside the team does not stop cadres from trying to assert their power. Cadres can no longer directly deny peasants permission to leave, but they can make it very difficult and time-consuming to get the necessary authorization.[53] If peasants work in private employment or for a collective or state factory outside the village, they still are required, at least officially, to have an authorization (*zhengming*). The enforcement of this regulation is relatively loose, but, if problems arise or if a peasant is stopped, arrested, or otherwise involved with the authorities, he will be in more trouble without an authorization.[54] After the reforms were initially instituted, in some teams peasants who worked outside the village still had to remit part of their salaries.[55] Early in the reforms, some team leaders chased down peasants who failed to remit the required payments to the collective.[56]

In 1988 peasants generally came and went as they pleased. However, before a peasant is hired for a job in one of the local factories, the factory

50. "Fengnanxian caiqu cuoshi," *NMRB* 23 March 1985:2.
51. Hong Kong Interview 22/8/6.
52. In the example cited, the owners (contractors) of the factory were also former cadres, at both the brigade and team levels. China Interviews, 1985.
53. Hong Kong Interview 7/6/24.
54. Hong Kong Interview 11/6/22.
55. Hong Kong Interview 11/6/22.
56. Hong Kong Interview 14/6/29.

manager at least contacts the village head to check the character of the peasant and must formally seek the release of that peasant for work in the factory. If a village needs the peasant for its own factory, the village head can refuse permission, although this seldom happens.[57]

THE VILLAGE AS ALLOCATOR OF INPUTS

Aside from overseer and landlord, the village continues to allocate rationed goods—most important, agricultural inputs such as fertilizer and diesel fuel. This is handled by the village, but sometimes the village group (former team) leader distributes the coupons for these goods. Access to these coupons is key to determining profits.

As anywhere, the amount of profit one makes, whether in farming or in sidelines, depends on the costs of one's inputs. But in China's economy there is more than the usual variation. The opening of markets allows free access to an impressive array of items, but the costs are significantly higher than those supplied by the state through the rationing system. The government's decision to keep intact the centralized distribution of key agricultural inputs and to allow the development of free markets for these same goods has inadvertently created a "hierarchy of prices" and made the rationing system a source of corruption.

The lowest-priced goods are those supplied by the state through rationing. Peasants or collectives are allowed to purchase these allocations at the state (*gongjia*), or what is sometimes called the public (*paijia*), price. The state supplies certain goods above the rationed allotment at a negotiated price (*yijia*).[58] Originally this was intended to reflect free market prices, but usually it is lower. The highest-priced goods are usually those purchased at the open market, formerly the black market price (*shijia*). The difference between these prices is significant, depending on the area and the item. A difference of 100 percent, and sometimes much more, is not uncommon. For example, in parts of Zhejiang, Jiangsu, and Jiangxi during the early to mid-1980s the state price for one *jin* of ammonium sulfate was 0.105 *yuan;* the negotiated price, 0.230 *yuan;* and the market price for the same fertilizer, 0.350 *yuan.*[59] In one region of Fujian the state price for the highest grade of ammonium sulfate was

57. Interviews with rural factory managers, China Interviews, 1988.
58. Not all goods provided under these terms are called negotiated; the designation seems to change by area and product. China Interviews, 1988.
59. Hong Kong Interview 1/6/6.

0.2 *yuan* per *jin,* but the market price for the same fertilizer was 1 *yuan.* Consequently, depending on where a peasant secures his supplies, his costs and profits will vary.[60]

The state devised and maintains rationing to ensure a fair distribution of scarce inputs and prevent speculation and hoarding. Each peasant is guaranteed a set amount of the most important inputs such as chemical fertilizer and motor fuel. But as with grain contracts, reality often differs from policy goals: the actions of the village cadres are key in determining whether the system is implemented correctly or whether peasants get their fair share.

Chemical Fertilizer and Motor Fuel.   Chemical fertilizer, a key ingredient for a successful harvest, has traditionally been scarce and difficult to secure. In particular, the high-quality imported brands have always been expensive but preferred over the less-expensive and in many ways superior natural fertilizers. Other than ease of application, peasants often choose chemical fertilizer because it promises a more immediate return in increased productivity; natural fertilizers take five years before one application takes full effect. Being able to earn a quick buck (*lao yiba*) seems to figure strongly in the post-1978 period when peasants are still not sure how long the reforms will actually last.

When the team was the accounting and production unit, it procured and paid for fertilizer as a collective. Individual peasant households only needed to secure fertilizer for their private plots. The state distributed fertilizer to the commune, which then allocated it to their brigades, which in turn supplied the teams. Allotments were based on the total sown acreage and crops under cultivation. Fertilizer was distributed in this manner three, four, or five times each year, depending on area and availability. The amounts varied, but, regardless of the amount, it was "insufficient."[61]

Contracting land and production to the household has had little effect on allocating chemical fertilizer. It continues to be centrally disbursed from the county to the township (commune), to the village (bri-

60. Problems caused by the hierarchy of prices also exist in urban industry. China Interviews, 1985 and 1986. For a published account of these problems and how factory managers deal with them, see Andrew Walder, "The Informal Dimensions," with whom I conducted the interviews.

61. It is difficult to define what peasants mean by "sufficient." Peasants give the general sense that they always needed more and that this extra would have allowed them to get higher yields.

gade), and to the group (team). But now, instead of the collective, each household is responsible for paying the cost of its allotted share.[62] Local cadres dispense an appropriate portion to each peasant household, based on the number of *mu* of land contracted.

The total basic ration the collective receives as a unit remains approximately the same as in the prereform period. Consequently, the problem of deficient state supplies persists. Even in cases where the fertilizer supply is increased, peasants still complain of shortage. In Yingshan county, Hubei, for example, the state increased the chemical fertilizer supply by 2,500 tons in the first nine months of 1983, but 30 percent of the peasant households in one commune still did not have sufficient fertilizer to start the autumn sowing.[63] One agronomist from Fujian estimated that in 1984 peasants needed to procure at least 10 to 20 percent of their needed fertilizer on the open market.[64] That estimate may be conservative; national statistics on applying fertilizer indicate that the total amount of chemical fertilizer applied increased by 16.9 percent between 1979 and 1980 and by 52.8 percent between 1979 and 1983.[65]

The continued shortage of state-supplied fertilizer and the high cost of market supplies make the state sales contracts for agricultural goods attractive. The state procurement prices for grain, for example, are lower than market prices, but the fertilizer coupons more than compensate. In one area of Guangdong in the early 1980s peasants received only 17.3 *yuan* instead of 18 to 19 *yuan* for their overquota sales of grain; but the cost of chemical fertilizer on the open market there was at least two to two and one-half times as expensive as the state-priced fertilizer.[66] The state also gives coupons in some areas for the sale of sugar-

62. Under the *baochan daohu* form of the responsibility system the team provides the inputs, but this system has been replaced in almost all areas by the *dabaogan* system, where the individual households are responsible for all aspects of production and payment to the state. Also see Jonathan Unger, "The De-collectivization," on the prevalence of the *dabaogan* system.

63. It is unclear from the article if the increased supply to the commune meant that peasants were given more at state prices. The article emphasized the continuing difficulty peasants faced in securing fertilizer. This same article also mentioned other problems, such as peasants being cheated when they were able to buy fertilizer. "Rich Peasants Still Have Worries," *China Daily* 4 December 1983:4.

64. Hong Kong Interview 7/6/8.

65. Based on statistics in *Statistical Yearbook 1984*, p. 175. There is tremendous variation in chemical fertilizer application among provinces. For example, the consumption of chemical fertilizer per hectare of sown area for Shanghai is 210.8 kilograms and for Fujian 196.0, but it is only 46.7 for Heilongjiang and 85.8 for Jiangxi. *Statistical Yearbook 1984*, p. 177.

66. Hong Kong Interview 18/7/23.

cane, hemp, cotton, and legumes.[67] The amount given for these secondary crops depends on locality and type of fertilizer being distributed.[68]

The intermediate solution to the high-priced market fertilizer is to
obtain what is called negotiated-price supplies. This fertilizer, however,
is also distributed by the state through the same bureaucratic hierarchy.
Before 1979 brigades could distribute extra rations to selected teams
because they routinely held back a certain portion of their allotment
from the commune. Some held back one-half *jin* per *mu*. Since the reforms, the collectives sometimes still receive extra allotments from the
county or the province. The margin may be less, but the distribution
continues at the discretion of the collective unit.

The distribution system for gasoline and diesel fuel is essentially the
same as that for chemical fertilizer. Extra rations are available at the negotiated price, but the amount varies and depends on both objective criteria, such as the amount of work one has contracted, and, perhaps
more important, subjective criteria, such as one's position and *guanxi*
(connections).[69] Those who either fail to secure state-supplied inputs or
need more than their allotted share pay dearly out of their profits when
buying on the open market. Such was the experience of one peasant
boat operator who hauled sand. His business was good and he made a

67. A bonus is given for the sale of legumes because of their relatively low output per
mu of land. The sale of 100 *jin* of soybeans (*huangdou*) is figured as equivalent to 180 *jin*
of unhusked grain sold at basic quota prices and yields a bonus of 20 to 40 *jin* of chemical
fertilizer, depending on the fertilizer given. Hong Kong Interview 18/7/23. In the early
1980s near Shantou, where the overquota sale of 100 *jin* of unhusked rice yielded only
40 *jin* of *liuan* chemical fertilizer, the sale of 100 *jin* of *huangdou* yielded 150 *jin* of
chemical fertilizer. There are limits, however, on the amount that peasants can receive
through this system. The state price of chemical fertilizer here is 1.6 *mao* per *jin*. Hong
Kong Interview 23/7/20.

68. For example, in one area the overquota sale of 100 *jin* of unhusked rice brings
12 *jin* of nitrogenous fertilizer (*danfei*) or 6 *jin* of urea fertilizer (*niaosu*). Hong Kong
Interview 19/7/21. In another, the sale of 100 *jin* of overquota grain yields 20 *jin* worth of
fertilizer. Hong Kong Interview 18/7/23. A few areas have stopped this practice, but in
1984 it was still a popular and viable way to obtain more inexpensive fertilizer.

69. Hong Kong Interview 7/6/10. A different distribution system was described by a
former peasant from Guangdong. He said that those who purchase a tractor also get a
license, which entitles the owner to buy unlimited gasoline. The cost of the license is paid
four times each year and depends on the size of the vehicle. Motor vehicles, such as motor-
cycles and vans, are included. For a motorcycle a license costs twenty-four *yuan;* for large
vehicles (unclear how large) it is forty-five *yuan* quarterly. Hong Kong Interview 15/8/8.
Press reports and interviews with peasants from other areas suggest that the system he
described may be peculiar to his county, which is rich and near Hong Kong. Most reports
from the early to mid-1980s indicate difficulty in securing gasoline and diesel; see, for
example, Hong Kong Interview 19/7/31. One peasant complained his allotment was not
even enough for two days' use during the busy planting season. "Damangqijian weihe
jianshao chaiyou gongying?" (Why Is the Supply of Diesel Decreased During the Busy
Season?), *GDNMB* 25 August 1983:3.

decent income, but the costs of the black market gasoline consumed about one-half of his earned fees.[70]

Sources of Corruption.   A major weakness of rationing is the coupon allocation system. Neither chemical fertilizer nor fuel is distributed directly to peasants. Like urban residents, who are issued ration coupons for grain and commodities, peasants must use coupons for agricultural inputs. These coupons must be presented at the sales cooperative or fuel stations when purchasing rations to receive the low state price. But unlike urban residents, who can use the grain ration books to obtain their grain directly at the grain store, peasants must obtain their coupons for fertilizer and fuel from their local cadres. After the reforms, the task fell to the village cadres, sometimes to the former team-level leaders. Once a peasant obtains the coupons, he must then deal with another layer of the bureaucracy when he goes to the cooperative store or fuel station to buy the item and turn in the coupon. The return of household farming has thus placed peasants at the mercy of two separate sets of cadres: one inside and one outside the village.

As in everything else under socialism, peasants usually receive their minimum allotment of fertilizer coupons. Do they receive anything more? What happens to the extra rations? Here the cadres have discretion. It is difficult for them to deny peasants their regular allotments, but it is relatively easy to distribute only part of the extra coupons on an equal basis to village members. The average peasant may be unaware of extra state supplies. Moreover, even in cases where misappropriation is suspected, it is difficult to press a case against a cadre. As one peasant explained: "The benefits would not be worth it. If you are successful, everyone in the team would benefit, but, if you are not, only you would pay."[71]

Even if a peasant succeeds in obtaining the needed coupons, decollectivization presents him with a second set of problems. Peasant possession of ration coupons, strict regulations on distribution, and posting official prices are no guarantee of how much fertilizer or gasoline a peasant can buy or how much it will cost. Most peasants have to procure their own allotment of fertilizer or fuel. An investigative reporter found that in one day an official state retail store sold a bag of fertilizer to three different customers at three different prices. A bag of fertilizer, which should have been officially sold for 8.75 *yuan,* was sold for 9.75, 10.5,

70. Hong Kong Interview 7/6/24.
71. Hong Kong Interview 22/7/29.

and 11 *yuan*.[72] In other examples, peasants have bonus coupons but fail to obtain any extra fertilizer at the low state price.[73] In 1982 one commune illegally kept 9.9 percent of the bags (211 of 2,178 bags) of urea and 4.6 percent of the *xiaohe* fertilizer (4,200 of 92,000 *jin*) allocated for its peasants.[74] In yet other cases, peasants face shortages even though the state may have allocated sufficient amounts to their unit.[75]

The same holds true for fuel. A Shanxi peasant complained that he failed to receive his allotted fifty kilograms of diesel per season per tractor. He first tried the commune gas station. When he found that they were out of diesel, he traveled to the county to try to buy his fuel, but to no avail. When he got to the county seat, he was turned away and told that his allotment had already been sent to the commune. In frustration he wrote to the editor of the *Shanxi Peasant Daily* asking what happened to this diesel.[76] The answer, as in the case of fertilizer, is that cadres at various administrative levels in charge of distribution skim off goods.

How prevalent is such corruption? The evidence does not allow me to make any generalizations or give any precise figures. Not all cadres are corrupt, and not all peasants face this problem every time they try to purchase inputs.[77] My purpose here is not to make statements about the frequency of such corruption but only to point out its structural causes.

72. "Huafei weihe yiri sanzhangjia" (Why Did the Price of Fertilizer Increase Three Times in One Day?), *ZGNMB* 3 April 1983:1. For other examples of illegal markups, see "Siti huafei jia tanwu shangwanyuan Zhang Shifang shoudao falü zhicai" (Unauthorized Increases in the Price of Fertilizer, Embezzlement of Nearly 10,000 *Yuan*, Zhang Shifang Is Punished by Law), *ZGNMB* 7 July 1983:1; and "He Jiayin simai huafei shouchufen" (He Jiayin Is Punished for Selling Fertilizer Without Permission), *SXNM* 29 October 1983:1.

73. "Nongcun xingshi hao nongmin 'nanzi' duo" (The Rural Situation Is Good, But Peasants Have Many Difficulties), *SXNM* 4 August 1983:1.

74. "Buyao cengceng 'bopi'" ("Don't Peel Skin" at Each Level), *ZGNMB* 7 April 1983:1; for other examples, see "Kai houmen he fen fuhefei" (Opening the Backdoor and Distributing Compound Fertilizer), *ZGNMB* 26 April 1983:2; and "Niaosu nali qule?" (Where Is the Urea Fertilizer?), *SXNM* 25 August 1983:1.

75. "Huguanxian wailiu huafei duo" (Much Outflow of Fertilizer from Huguan County), *SXNM* 24 September 1983:1; "Jiangshou huafei nanduixian gaojia huafei hechulai?" (Deficits in Bonus Fertilizer, Where Did the High-priced Fertilizer Come From?), *SXNM* 24 September 1983:1; "Cengceng kou huafei nongmin shoubuliao" (Every Level Withholds Fertilizer, Impossible Situation for Peasants), *ZGNMB* 27 February 1983:2.

76. "Gongyingde chaiyou nali qule?" (Where Is the Rationed Diesel Oil?), *SXNM* 15 October 1983:1.

77. Peasants did not seem to have problems buying pesticide in the early to mid-1980s. Only a few examples are found in the press or mentioned in interviews. See, for example, "Nongmin maibudao nongyao" (Peasants Cannot Buy Pesticides), *SXNM* 4 August 1983:2; and "Yidun texiao nongyao yechansan nali qule?" (Where Did One Ton of Specially Effective *Yechansan* Pesticides Go?) *ZGNMB* 15 September 1983:1. However, by 1988 I heard many complaints about pesticide shortage. China Interviews, 1988.

One can say, however, that the problem is sufficiently severe that the official Chinese press is filled with stories of abuse. In one example, a peasant engaged in the transport business complained that not once in an entire year was he able to buy fair-priced gasoline. In Henan all 2,005 individual transport-specialized households had to knock on various doors (*qiao menzi*)—that is, go through the back door and use connections—to get fuel.[78] In another example, at least one-quarter of the state-supplied oil disappeared through the back door at a Henan county oil company.[79] One commune illegally kept 19 percent of their allotment, or 63.5 tons of fuel.[80]

Particularly troublesome is that what is skimmed off from government supplies ends up on the open markets at very high prices, at least double the official rates, and business is brisk.[81] The state thus has indirectly become the supplier of the black/free market. In the case of gasoline, the culprits are not only the village cadres who control the coupons but also drivers and station masters who directly siphon fuel. Employees at gasoline companies are some of the worst perpetrators of corruption and extortion.[82] To discourage black market activity and provide an incentive for drivers to return unused fuel, the state has competitions among drivers to conserve gasoline. Under this plan drivers receive as a bonus 60 percent of the cost of the fuel saved, and the state takes 40 percent.[83]

The state has tried to reduce the need for black market gasoline and diesel by using "fairness" criteria—for example, the amount of land a tractor driver has contracted to work—to determine peasant fuel allotments. This will provide specialized households more ration coupons, but they must still deal with their local cadres, who distribute the coupons, and the agricultural cooperatives, where they must procure their fuel allotments.[84]

78. "Handanshi Fayuan," *ZGNMB* 11 March 1984:3; "Yunshu zhuanyehu 'yong-you nan' de wenti jiejuele" (The Fuel Problems of Transport-Specialized Households Are Solved), *ZGNMB* 26 June 1984:1.

79. "Yiyou 'kai you' zhifeng bixu shazhu" (The Wind of Using Gasoline to Get Petty Advantages at the Expense of Others Must Stop), *ZGNMB* 14 July 1983:2.

80. "Buyao cengceng," *ZGNMB* 7 April 1983:1.

81. "Anhuisheng Wuhexian Shiyougongsi yixieren liyong shouzhong zhangguande chaiyou xiang nongmin qiaozhalesuo" (Some Persons in the Wuhe County, Anhui Province Gasoline Company Use Gasoline for the Extortion of Peasants), *ZGNMB* 6 September 1983:1.

82. "Chuli xian shiyou gongsi qiaozhalesuo nongmin shijian" (Settling the Case of the County Gasoline Company Extorting Peasants), *ZGNMB* 20 September 1983:1.

83. Hong Kong Interview 7/6/24.

84. "Pingzheng gongyou nongjia le" (Supply Fuel According to Ration Coupons, Peasants Happy), *NCGZTX* 1983, no. 7, p. 48. "Yunshu zhuanyehu," *ZGNMB* 26 June

In 1983, in order to reduce cadre mismanagement, the State Council ordered that the coupons be distributed directly to the individual households, bypassing the village cadres.[85] However, as of 1988 some rural areas still had not carried out this reform; village cadres still controlled the allocation of these coupons. Even if this measure is successfully implemented, it may rid the system of some of the corruption in the distribution of coupons, but it will not stop the "disappearance" of state-supplied fertilizer or gasoline from the storehouses or sales stations. There were countless complaints of cadre corruption, "leaks," and "fertilizer-gobbling mice" in the early to mid-1980s; in 1988 the problem of peasants not being able to redeem their coupons was still sufficiently severe to make front-page news.[86]

For a time there were indications that the state had decided to abolish rationing inputs altogether. In areas of Guangdong, and in other areas where supplies were adequate, chemical fertilizer was sold exclusively at market prices.[87] For example, near Shantou, as well as in Taishan county, Guangdong, the state abolished the rationing system for fertilizer in 1984. Peasants could buy unlimited quantities at state cooperative stores. This thwarted cadre manipulation of the pricing hierarchy, but peasants had to pay a higher price for fertilizer. In Shantou the price doubled, from 1.6 to 3.2 *mao* per *jin* of chemical fertilizer.[88] Although the link is not absolute, such price increases have been followed by decreased use of chemical fertilizer. Large surpluses of high market-priced fertilizer began to appear by mid-1985.[89]

1984:1, details the way the institution of the new system improved, but did not solve, the fuel problem of a transport-specialized household. Previously a peasant could only obtain enough fuel to operate his vehicle ten days a month; since the change he can obtain enough for twenty days.

85. See "Guowuyuan zhongyang jiwei fachu tongzhi" (The Disciplinary Committee of the State Council Decrees Notice), *ZGNMB* 16 October 1983:1; and "Jinhua gongshe ba huafei quanbu fenpei gei sheyuan" (Jinhua Commune Completely Distributes Its Fertilizer to Peasants), *ZGNMB* 17 April 1983:2.

86. "Nongmin maifeinan yuanlai you loudong" (The Source of Peasant Difficulty Purchasing Fertilizer Is the [Unauthorized] Leaks), *GDNMB* 28 August 1983:1; "Qiling you tunshi huafeide 'laoshu'" (Qiling Has Fertilizer Gobbling Rats), *GDNMB* 6 October 1983:1.

87. "Daming nongcun huafei xiaoshou qushi" (Trends in Fertilizer Sales in Rural Daming), *ZGNMB* 31 July 1984:3; "Liaoning, Hunan linfei jiage xiafu" (Fertilizer Prices in Liaoning and Hunan Drop), *ZGNMB* 31 July 1984:3.

88. Hong Kong Interview 23/8/1.

89. See, for example, "Nongmin dui nongyong wuzi xuqiu youbian" (Peasant Demand for Agricultural Supplies Changes), *DZJYB* 9 May 1985:3; this reports a 10- to 15-percent decrease in the use of chemical fertilizer in 1985 in one commune in Liaoning. Peasants there are returning to natural fertilizers. Also see "Hebeisheng huafei xiaoshou shixing xianjia" (Hebei Province Puts Lid on Fertilizer Prices), *DZJYB* 16 May 1985:3; "Wosheng huafei nongyao chaiyou xiaoliang xiajiang" (The Sale of Chemical Fertilizer,

In the case of gasoline and diesel fuel, the state simply opened gas stations where nonrationed, high-priced fuel may be purchased. These enterprises, which are now often contracted out to individuals, do a brisk business, but the owners often complain about the difficulty of finding a stable fuel supply at reasonable costs. The differences in wholesale price are supposed to be passed on to the consumer. If the station happens to get allotments of the negotiated-price fuel, then peasants are supposed to pay the lower price. Peasants, however, have no way of knowing which batch their fuel comes from.[90]

But in spite of a number of changes and experiments with market distribution, the contract grain procurement system introduced in 1985 reaffirms the place of centralized distribution of agricultural inputs in China's new hybrid semimarket/semiplanned economy.[91] As I indicated in Chapter 8, this may be a necessary incentive for peasants to sell to the state as the market continues to develop, but unfortunately it also maintains the hierarchy of prices for agricultural inputs and serves as a source of cadre corruption.

Draft Animals and Transport.   Cadres similarly have influence over access to draft animals and tractors, used both for farming and—more important, particularly in the case of tractors—for transport. Unlike the United States, in China most tractors, large and small, are on the roadways, not in the fields. Access to tractors means access to markets.

The cadres' power with regard to these inputs, however, differs from the control they have over rationed inputs. In some instances, as I suggested earlier, cadres were in a good position to take advantage of the opportunity either to contract or to buy the few agricultural machines or draft animals owned by a team or brigade. They then rented out their animal or tractor. In other cases, where the collective retained control of the tractors, the cadres still have authority over their scheduling for villager use. Early in the reforms, in some areas where the collective owned the large equipment, peasants who wanted to rent from the commune

---

Pesticides, and Diesel Oil Decreases in Our Province), *HBJJB* 7 May 1985:1; and "Henan huafei kucun jiya" (Overstock of Fertilizer in Henan), *JJCK* 21 May 1985:4, on the surplus of chemical fertilizer. It should be noted that some areas have always had surpluses of fertilizer, even in the 1970s. Changes in the crops being grown may have also contributed to this trend.

90. China Interviews, 1988.

91. Moreover, the State Council in 1988 reimposed price controls on farm chemicals because of skyrocketing market prices. "Zhizhi shengchan ziliao he jiaotong yunshu luan zhangjia Guowuyuan fabu zanxing guiding he guanli banfa" (To Curb the Chaotic Price Increases of Production Materials and Transport, the State Council Issues Temporary Regulations and Management Methods), *RMRB* 19 January 1988:3.

(township) tractor station first had to go through the old team and brigade leaders in order to set up a proper relationship before they could secure the needed services.[92]

In an example from Fujian, peasants wanted to sell a rich harvest of sugarcane, but they needed to transport their crop. According to regulations, use of the cutting and transport equipment was to rotate, but the brigade cadre gave his relatives, good friends, and those who had sent him gifts priority and thus the best opportunity to sell their sugarcane. Those not in his inner circle had to wait and worry about their crop rotting. To make matters worse, the tractor drivers from the commune tractor station also demanded gifts and good treatment before they would agree to transport a peasant's harvested sugarcane to the local sugar-processing plant.[93] In this particular case, the tractor drivers had a monopoly because the commune had ruled that only tractors from the commune tractor station could be used; moreover, they were restricted to only three pickups per day.[94]

Even if cadres do not themselves own the animal or cannot directly intervene in who uses the tractor, they still seem to command enough influence that specialized households allow them priority in using their tractors at good prices.[95] Access and price depend on availability, but, as with any other scarce commodity in China, access also depends on the customer and the customer's *guanxi* (connections). Reports indicate that some cadres, given priority use of the available tractors, finish planting when regular peasants have hardly begun their work; other cadres get discounts or pay nothing at all.[96]

Connections are necessary to secure the use of draft animals and tractors because, like so many other goods and services in China, they are scarce. The number of large farm animals has increased, but the demand far exceeds the short-run supply.[97] In 1983 only one ox was available for every four households; in poor areas, such as Gansu, 4 percent

92. Hong Kong Interview 19/7/31.
93. As I described in Chapter 6, before the reforms tractor drivers were similarly able to demand gifts and good food and drink from teams that wanted their services. This was one expense for which teams routinely needed extra funds.
94. "Ganzhe fengshou yunzhenan" (Good Harvest of Sugarcane, Difficulties in Transport), *FJRB* 5 February 1982:1.
95. There is a state price for the rental of tractors and transport, but this is only for state-owned units (*guoying danwei*) and collectives. Payment for service is made through banks and in the form of transfer of payments from one state or collective account to another. Individual peasants have no access to such accounts or services. Hong Kong Interview 7/6/14.
96. See, for example, "Zheyangde duigan tai zaogao" (This Kind of Cadre Is Really Terrible), *SXNM* 29 October 1983:1.
97. See Walker, "Chinese Agriculture," p. 796.

of production teams had no animals at all in 1980.[98] The price of oxen has gone up considerably since the division of the land. On the basis of national statistics, Walker reports price increases in the early 1980s from 300 or 400 *yuan* for an animal to 700 to 800 *yuan*. By 1985 in Guangdong the price of a 300-*jin* animal was as much as 1,000 *yuan*.[99]

The availability of tractors is also low but varies widely in different areas. In 1983 Shandong, with more than 135,000, had the largest number of large- and medium-sized tractors; Tibet had only 2,500, and Fujian had just under 8,000. Significant differences similarly exist in the number of small-sized and walking tractors. Jiangsu had a high of 386,000 units, but Yunnan had only 49,000.[100]

In the case of tractors, the scarcity is not entirely due to the costs of the machines. The sticker price of a tractor is dwarfed by the costs that the owner must pay after purchase. For example, one transport-specialized household bought a used vehicle for 3,900 *yuan,* and spent another 1,900 *yuan* for repairs and bribes. But expenses did not end there. The transport inspection station, for example, demanded a 3,000-*yuan* road maintenance fee (*yanglufei*). In the end the fees were so high that this would-be transport-specialized household declared bankruptcy. Other tractor owners faced with similar problems simply let their tractors sit idle or tried to resell them. Of 246 tractor owners in one county in Hunan province 209 had to halt operations because of high fees. In another county in the same province, 46 of 69 tractors were taken out of service for the same reason. Similarly, in Jiangxi province, 57 percent and 47 percent respectively of 350 large- and medium-sized tractors and 1,269 hand-held models had to stop operation; another 38 had been sold because of high fees.[101]

The actual fees that a tractor owner must pay vary in type and amount. In Shandong, for example, a peasant is responsible for more than ten different fees and licenses and must go through six different government agencies when he buys a tractor.[102] Table 21 details the

98. Ibid.

99. Ibid.; Hong Kong Interview 7/6/10. One thousand *yuan* was the price quoted to me in 1985 in Taishan county, Guangdong, for a mature water buffalo.

100. State Statistical Bureau, PRC, *Statistical Yearbook of China, 1984,* p. 172.

101. "An zhongyang wenjian banshi yi zhengdang tuidong gaige" (Handle Matters According to the Central Directives, Use the Rectification of the Party as a Driving Force to Push Forward the Reforms), *ZGNMB* 24 May 1984:1.

102. The fees or licenses include: license plate fee, road maintenance fee, driver's license fee, examination fee, wheel inspection fee, vehicle operator's registration fee, insurance fee, transport management fee, and an industrial and commercial tax. "Nongmin qianglie yaoqiu jiakuai liutong lingyu gaige" (Peasants Strongly Demand a Speedup in Reform in the Transport Field), *ZGNMB* 29 May 1984:2.

TABLE 21. TRACTOR FEES IN HUNAN, 1984

Fee/Tax	Amount	Collection Agency
Road use (*yanglu fei*)	210 *yuan*/year (hand-held) 562 *yuan*/year (large)	Traffic Bureau
Transport (*yunshu shui*)	5% of income	Tax Bureau
Traffic regulation (*jiaotong guize*)	3% of income	Township Management Station
Agricultural equipment management (*nongji guanli fei*)	1–1.5 *yuan*/horsepower	Agric. Machinery Bureau
Township accumulation (*xiang jilei*)	100–200 *yuan*/vehicle	Township Enterprise Office
Village accumulation (*cun jilei*)	According to township	Village Committee
Industrial and commercial enterprise (*gongshang yingye zheng fei*)	3 *yuan*/license	n.a.
County transport traffic management station (*chengzhen canyun fei*)	3 *yuan*/month	County
Annual inspection (*nianjian fei*)	1.5 *yuan*/hand-held 2 *yuan*/large	Agric. Machinery and Traffic Inspection Bureaus
Examination (*kaozheng fei*)	12 *yuan* (one-time fee)	Agric. Machinery and Traffic Inspection Bureaus
Industrial and commercial management (*gongshang guanli fei*)	3% of total income	Area Industrial and Commercial Bureau
Insurance (*baoxian fei*)	144 yuan/hand-held 244 *yuan*/large	n.a.

SOURCE: "Shimen dengdi nongmin gao yunshu nan" (In Shimen and Other Areas Peasants Have Difficulty Doing Transport Business), *ZGNMB* 20 May 1984: 1.

twelve different fees that a peasant had to pay in Hunan in 1984 to operate a tractor.

In reality, this means that a peasant in Hunan who earned 4,300 *yuan* had to pay close to 30 percent in various taxes and fees (215 *yuan* to the tax bureau for income tax, 240 in supplementary fees, 630 to the traffic bureau for road maintenance, and 132 for traffic management) and another 41 percent in costs (1,320 *yuan* for fuel and 1,200 for maintenance). This left the peasant with a total profit for the year of 563 *yuan,* slightly more than 13 percent of his original earnings. The situation was similar for a peasant whose earnings were higher—6,700 *yuan:* after the various taxes and costs, his retained profit was less than 1,000 *yuan.*[103] The profits are still substantial in the context of the Chinese countryside, but it seems that one must have a very successful business before profits will exceed costs. Costs have become so high that peasants now say, "Tractors are great, you might be able to afford to buy one, but you will not want to operate it (*buyao pao*)." Perhaps not coincidentally, a drop in tractor sales occurred by 1984.[104]

The existence of the numerous fees is further evidence of the difficulties a peasant faces in trying to "get rich" and the role cadres can play in the new economic context. I should make clear, however, that the peasants' difficulties with tractors differ from problems securing sufficient supplies of chemical fertilizer. Peasants seeking transport must pay fees and surcharges usually to various governmental offices involved with licenses and collection of fees—agencies trying to get a share of the profits from the lucrative transport business, not village leaders or even individual officials. But there have been occasional instances where individual cadres have demanded money. For example, a vice-head of a prefectural (*diqu*) agricultural machinery bureau and his assistants prevented peasants from operating their 258 tractors by refusing to grant them the necessary license plates and operating authorizations.[105]

PEASANT DEPENDENCE IN AN UNDEVELOPED MARKET

The reforms reopened the free markets, but not all peasants necessarily benefit from these new opportunities. Even after the Third Plenum

103. "Shimen dengdi nongmin gao yunshu nan" (In Shimen and Other Areas, Peasants Have Difficulty Doing Transport Business), *ZGNMB* 20 May 1984:1.

104. The number of tractors sold in the first two months of 1983 in one prefecture totaled 614; during the same period in 1984 only 134 were sold. "An zhongyang," *ZGNMB* 24 May 1984:1.

105. "Lucheng nongmin xingou erbaiwushibatai tuolaji weihe tingzhe buneng yong—diqu nongjiju fujuzhang lanyong zhiquan, youyi diaonan, jubu shenyan fazheng" (Why Can't the 250 Tractors Bought by Lucheng Peasants Be Put into Operation—the Deputy Chief of the District Agricultural Machinery Bureau Deliberately Harasses Peasants, Refuses to Grant Licenses), *ZGNMB* 26 May 1983:1.

reforms were announced, some peasants, forced to stay within the tight bounds of upper-level planning, were refused the right to diversify and plant the more lucrative cash crops; some were prevented from taking a surplus to the free market. In areas of Guangxi, for example, local policy required all peasants to grow grain even though national policies encouraged diversification. In 1981 provincial officials dropped grain acreage requirements, but county (*xian*) officials continued to dictate how much grain teams had to plant. As late as 1983 a team was required to plant 200 of 300 *mu* in rice, leaving them only the 100 *mu* of (dry) land to plant at their discretion.[106]

In Zhejiang in 1983, when peasants planted 40 to 50 percent of their land in rapeseed, commune authorities became alarmed at the dramatic decrease in the amount of grain being produced and issued a directive that specified what crop was to be grown on each piece of land, regardless of who contracted the land or market demand. The regulation stated that 80 percent of a team's land had to be planted in grain and cotton. Until then peasants had sold the rapeseed for a high price and then bought grain on the free market to meet their basic tax and grain sales quota to the state.[107]

Although it was legal to sell grain on the free market as early as 1979, Guangxi cadres did not permit this until after the summer harvest of 1983.[108] In Fujian, peasants who had a good harvest of loquats (*pipa*) were suddenly prohibited from selling their surplus on the free market after the state cooperative purchased the top-grade fruit. Previously peasants were allowed to sell their remaining fruit on the open market. But in 1982 brigade cadres ruled that peasants could take no more than 10 *jin* to the market. If they took more, it would be confiscated. Each day between 100 and 200 *jin* of fruit was left to rot.[109]

The situation has changed markedly in the intervening years. Few cadres would now dare to prohibit peasant participation in the market when the government has made clear that it intends to use the market to shape production. Since 1983 the state has encouraged peasants to diversify production and participate in the market. In some areas cadres demand that peasants plant at least 30 to 50 percent of their contracted

106. Hong Kong Interview 7/6/6.
107. Hong Kong Interview 6/7/3.
108. Hong Kong Interview 7/6/6.
109. "Zheige huanjie sheilai shutong? Putian sheyuan maipipanan chengshi jumin maipipanan" (Who Is Going to Break This Deadlock? Putian Peasants Have Difficulty Selling Loquats, Urban Dwellers Have Difficulty Buying Loquats), *FJRB* 16 May 1982: 1.

land in economic crops. In a few areas peasants were fined when they did not comply.[110] Again a peasant's mandatory compliance with such regulations depends as much on the local cadres as on upper-level directives.[111]

Yet even when cadres do not directly block growing cash crops and peasants participating in the market, the market has neither been the panacea of the peasants' problems nor has it freed them from dependence on cadres. No market in reality offers equal access to opportunities, but most Chinese peasants are particularly disadvantaged. The three decades of collective agricultural production and government procurement and sales monopolies for goods left the peasant in a state similar to the traditional peasant societies described by moral economists. Peasants in post-Mao China have had little or no experience with markets; they lack the contacts and the know-how to deal effectively with markets. They welcome the new opportunities, but at the same time they fear the complexities and dangers of this new environment. Some students of peasant politics have suggested that peasants fear markets, seeing them as corrupt and requiring skills they do not possess.[112] China's peasants may be a case in point.

The agricultural reforms and resurgence of markets have given peasants more freedom, but peasants now face greater uncertainty. Abolishing the state monopoly over the purchase of agricultural commodities lifted the burden of forced quotas, but it also removed the secure income offered by unified purchase. Sales on the local free market are uncertain and usually involve limited quantities at changing prices. For much of the period since 1949, participation in the free market is something that peasants could do only illegally. Yet now that the state has reversed itself and encourages peasant participation in the market, peasants are finding it less than ideal.

Peasant producers in Anhui, for example, were stuck with a surplus of 20 million *jin* of vermicelli *(fensi)*. The problem was inadequate transport and storage facilities to get the goods to the market, or, as the peasants say, "the circulation channels were blocked."[113] Selling to the local state co-op, the peasants need not have such worries. The price

110. "Yidaoqie xingbutong" (Cutting with One Big Knife Will Not Solve the Problems), *GDNMB* 28 December 1984:1.
111. See, for example, "Zhi nan erjin jijitiaozheng," *JJCK* 11 April 1985:2.
112. See, for example, Migdal, *Peasants, Politics, and Revolution.*
113. "Fuyang diqu liangyijin fensi maibuchuqu xiwang kuaibangzhu jiejue ranmeizhiji" (Fuyang Area Cannot Sell Its Twenty Million *Jin* of Vermicelli, Hopes to Get Help Quickly to Solve This Urgent Problem), *ZGNMB* 9 February 1984:1.

the peasants received may have been lower than on the open market, but they had the financial security of a guaranteed buyer at a set price. One ironic consequence of the reforms is that some peasants actively seek the security of state or collective sales contracts—a stark contrast to the earlier period when peasants tried to reduce their sales to the state.

A major problem for peasants is their lack of information about market demand and prices.[114] A few "trade/exchange bulletin boards" with news of opportunities, supplies, and other information useful for sellers and buyers have appeared since 1984.[115] These, at least in theory, promise wider public access to information and market opportunities. But the Chinese peasants, like those in more traditional settings, have usually turned to their leaders for information and sales opportunities. Local cadres have, as the general theories predict, become the new middlemen; in fact, this role has been thrust upon them.

Local cadres and village governments are better equipped to deal with the complexities of the market. Collectives and sometimes large specialized households employ sales and procuring agents, known variously as *gongxiaoren, tuixiaoyuan, yewuyuan,* or *xiaogouyuan.* These people function like *caigouyuan* in factories, scouting the country for needed parts and supplies. In the countryside the *gongxiaoren* buy supplies, make contacts, and find buyers. These people, who may number more than ten for a village, specialize in finding *menlu* (opportunities). They are paid on a commission basis; their total wage depends on how much business they can bring in for the village. In one village their base salaries range from 200 to 300 *yuan* to 400 to 500 *yuan.*[116] The business and opportunities they bring back for the village are then managed by the village economic companies, the economic side of the village leadership.

Some of the most lucrative contracts are those with agricultural production centers, where products are grown, processed, and sold—what have become known as *yitiaolong.* The latter arrangement is particu-

114. For the 14 percent of the country's peasants who in 1985 still lived in poverty and depended on social welfare and state loans, one major problem hindering the development of their rural economy was "lack of timely and accurate market information for farmers." "PRC State Statistical Bureau Survey Shows Peasants' Improved Lot," *China Daily* 28 September 1985:1.

115. See, for example, "Xian xiang xinxi huodong xingshi duoyang" (Information Activities at the County and Township Levels Take Many Forms), *RMRB* 30 January 1985:5; and "Yao ba xinxi gongzuo fangzai jingji gongzuo xiandao diwei" (Within Economic Work We Should Give Information Services Priority), *GMRB* 28 October 1984:1. Banks have even begun to provide this service. See "Nongye yinhang kaizhan xinxi zixun yewu" (The Agricultural Bank Starts Information Service) *RMRB* 14 January 1985:2.

116. Hong Kong Interview 22/8/6; China Interviews, 1985.

larly attractive because it provides all supplies and inputs needed for production. For example, peasants who contract to raise *sanhuangji,* a type of chicken popular on the Hong Kong market, will be given a cash loan and all the production materials needed to raise the chickens. The state, in essence, makes the investment and contracts out the production.[117]

The problem for most peasants is that purchasing co-ops and state companies seldom deal with small individual producers; they usually must subcontract from the village. Before the reorganization, communes and brigades would apportion their contracts to their teams, which then divided the contracts among the individual households. Now the economic companies in the village and township do the brokering. Some groups and peasants are denied opportunities because of technical considerations and lack of ability; other times it is simply a matter of cadre discretion. Villages themselves also sign contracts with a specialized household for certain items at a set state price. In return, the village allows the producer access to a set amount of production materials at the low state price.[118] As in land leases and state grain contracts, specialized households are the prime recipients of the best opportunities.

THE CHANGING NATURE OF CADRE POWER

As should be evident from the examples I have given, village cadres have power over the peasantry. The discriminatory distribution of goods is similar to that found under the collective system. But the nature of that power has changed, and with it the dependency of the peasants has changed; cadre power is no longer as powerful a weapon. The reemergence of the market has undermined the cadre's former monopoly of opportunities and resources. The power of village cadres is mediated by the fact that, unlike the team leaders, not all resources and not all functions pass through their hands. Unlike the Maoist period, peasants clearly have options; the issue is cost. They are no longer tied to collective agriculture for their food and well-being. Peasants with sufficient skills and connections to find employment and markets and sufficient cash to pay the higher prices required on the free market to

117. Hong Kong Interview 7/6/8.
118. Hong Kong Interview 19/7/31.

secure needed food and inputs can ignore with impunity the wishes of the local cadres.

By the same token, decollectivization has made peasants more vulnerable to and dependent on a wider variety of officials, not just to the team leader. For example, the village cadre may control the ration coupons, but the actual bags of fertilizer are controlled by those at the cooperative store. The village cadre may intervene, but ultimately distribution of that resource is in someone else's hands.

The reforms have made it necessary for village cadres to exercise their power in more indirect and subtle ways. As in the past, cadres withhold authorizations and licenses, but now those actions are illegal. Before, the state indirectly sanctioned their actions, and cadres could use state policies that required peasants to stay in the teams and grow grain as their excuse for refusing to let a peasant engage in sideline work. Now cadres who withhold such licenses are in fact acting against the state directives that encourage specialization and entrepreneurship. Consequently, discrimination must take more subtle forms. Cadres have always been able to give peasants "small shoes to wear," but now these shoes have to be transparent, that is, "give someone small *glass* shoes to wear." Instead of coming out and denying a would-be entrepreneur a license, a cadre now is more likely to drag his feet and try to make it so difficult and time-consuming that the peasant will give up. Instead of saying no, the cadre is more likely to say, come back.

Although the cadres may need to be more indirect in their exercise of power, the reforms also have indirectly strengthened their hand by taking away the subsistence safety net. In the past, with the "iron rice bowl" system, the distribution of basic rations guaranteed a peasant at least the minimal share of available opportunities and goods. Now few key resources that determine how far one gets ahead in the new system carry with them such egalitarian guarantees. The strong and the rich have more options, whereas the weak and the poor have fewer guarantees against cadre discrimination. It is now easier to fall considerably behind all others in the village. In the Maoist period cadres could bend the rules, allowing certain peasants increased access to opportunities; cadres now have the possibility of exercising their power by *withholding* opportunities that lead to success. Furthermore, the resources that they can allocate lead to much greater disparities in wealth than the mere assignment of the better jobs or the more fertile private plot.

Relaxing controls and decollectivizing agriculture have similarly allowed cadres more leeway in applying rules and regulations. For example, before teams were abolished but household contracting was instituted, a directive was sent to a team in Zhejiang to continue planting grain. The team leader only selectively applied the commune directive to plant grain and allowed some households to continue growing the more profitable cash crops. He did so knowing that he risked little and paid nothing as long as the team met its basic quota, maintaining the facade of compliance. On the contrary, since much of the team leader's original power base had been eroded with the reorganized agricultural work, selectively allowing individual peasants to plant cash crops provided him with a new source of power. In this particular case in Zhejiang, the team leader had added incentive to be lenient; he himself was illegally planting cash crops rather than growing grain.[119]

NEW MEASURES OF CADRE SUCCESS

Prior to the reforms, the work of local cadres was to ensure that peasants both fulfilled the assigned quotas and correctly implemented the state plan. Decisions about what, when, and how to plant and when and how much to sell were made at the upper levels. To be successful today in the new market-oriented rural economy, a cadre must find markets, procure low-priced high-quality agricultural inputs, arrange transport, know what to produce, have the expertise to produce high-demand items, and negotiate valid contracts.[120]

To do all these things effectively, cadres must make connections and find outlets and opportunities (*guanxi, menlu, chulu*). They must also have expertise and technological know-how, sources of information and news, access to funds, and economic management skills. The amount of power that a cadre has is therefore now more a product of his own enterprise than the power granted him by the state. Power has always depended on one's resources, but it varied even more after the reforms. The more jobs, connections, and skills a cadre has to offer, the more power he will wield. Thus, the reforms have also made cadres work harder for their power.

The state recognizes the need for entrepreneurial skills and has tried to ensure competent cadres by promoting youth and education. Cadres must have entrepreneurial skill to compete in today's market environ-

119. Hong Kong Interview 6/7/4.
120. For a description of the "ways to get ahead and along" in rural China up to the mid-1960s, prior to the Cultural Revolution, see Michel Oksenberg, "Getting Ahead and Along."

ment; a recent survey in Wuqiang county, Hebei, illustrated this need by identifying five different types of problems among local-level cadres. First, as might be expected, two major problems were closely related— age and education level. Second, the "small peasant mentality" of some local-level cadres was defined as being content to stay with traditional agricultural pursuits, such as grain production; in other words, some did not encourage diversifying production to take advantage of the need for commodity production. Third, some cadres were closed-minded; they did not understand the market, gather information, or develop expertise. Fourth, some suffered from shortsightedness, or what literally translates as a "mender mentality"—one does only what he must to fix what is needed and no more; this cadre lacked a long-range view. And fifth, some cadres wanted to maintain the status quo—neither rocking the boat nor taking responsibility.[121]

But entrepreneurial skills are not necessarily commensurate with youth and higher education. A survey of 20,989 successful specialized households in Shanxi found that former team and brigade cadres or those who had been cadres at some time constituted 43 percent of those who prospered. Their success was attributed to their experience, economic management skills, and ability to absorb party policy and take quick action; no mention was made of age or educational level. Another group who knew how to plan, how to manage, and how to maintain a large circle of friends (read "connections") made up another 5 percent of the prosperous specialized households. Together these groups, neither particularly highly educated nor young, made up close to one-half of those who prospered in the new economic system. Those with both youth and higher education, the returned intellectuals and demobilized soldiers, made up only 42 percent of the successful households. Only if one adds those who had a specific skill or were craftsmen do the younger, better educated make up 51 percent of the sample.[122] To be sure, education and technical skills are important for prospering in the new economic environment, but experience and connections are equally, if not more, crucial.

China is still an undeveloped market, with poor transportation and

121. A sixth problem was cadres just looking out for themselves. "Lu Yushan lesuo chengbaohu dangji guofa burong" (Lu Yushan Extorted Contracting Household, This Cannot Be Tolerated by Party Discipline and State Law), *NMRB* 15 January 1985:3.

122. "Nongcun xianfuyu qilaide shi naxie ren?" (Who Are the People Who Have Gotten Rich First in the Villages?), *GDNMB* 27 January 1984:4. According to the same survey, those who succeeded through illegal means made up less than 1 percent of the households.

inadequate communication channels. In such an environment proper *guanxi, menlu,* and *chulu,* as well as market information can be the pre-serve of the older, established cadres as much as the domain of the young hot shots. The older cadres have the large networks of personal connections, developed through many years of attending meetings and dealing with different units. One example is the sales agent (*gong-xiaoyuan*) on whom the success of either a collective enterprise or indi-vidual peasant households depends. Not a few of those agents able to locate supplies, make contracts, and find buyers are the older, experi-enced cadres with considerable connections.[123]

The cadres' rewards reflect the bias toward entrepreneurial success. The measure of success is a cadre's ability to foster business activity and make profits. Successful development of specialized households, scien-tific households, and special-status households of various types brings praise from superiors as well as bonuses for the village and the cadres.

Salaries of cadres consist of both a base wage and a bonus wage. In the model Aiguo Brigade in Shandong, under the *baogan daohu* form of the responsibility system, the party branch secretary, brigade head, and accountant each received a base salary of 360 *yuan,* but total annual wage depended on bonuses or penalties earned each year. In 1982 they overfulfilled their grain quota and executed other responsibility well, and each received a total of 443 *yuan.*[124]

More recently, in areas where sidelines and rural industry are flour-ishing, the base salary of either the collective company's economic head or the village head may be doubled or tripled by bonuses depending on profits of the collective. In one relatively rich village in Liaoning, where only 5 percent of the village was engaged in agriculture production, the base salary of the village head and economic manager of the collective enterprises was 700 *yuan.* In 1984 the total salary of each was 3,500 *yuan.*[125] The difference between their base and total salaries came from

123. Hong Kong Interview 22/8/6; China Interviews, 1985. On the importance of these people in the economic success of a village see "Tongchengxian xiangzhen qiye tui-xiaoyuan daxian shenshou" (The Salesmen of Rural Enterprises in Tongchen County Give Full Play to Their Abilities), *GMRB* 29 October 1984:2.
124. Penalties were limited to 25 percent of the base pay in order to guarantee the livelihood of the cadres. "Zhuanye chengbao, baogan fenpei: Aiguo daduide diaocha" (Specialized Contracts, Distribution According to Contracted Tasks: Investigation of Aiguo Brigade), *Gongshe caiwu* 1983, no. 2, pp. 9–12.
125. This was a relatively rich village. The estimated average total income of peasants for 1985 was expected to be 1,200 *yuan,* an eightfold increase over 1977. China Inter-views, 1985.

bonuses received for overquota performance and profits for the village; they receive different bonuses for different items of business.

The bonus system applies to political as well as economic work. For instance, a village head can be fined if policies, such as birth control, are not correctly implemented.[126] Accurate accounting as well as compliance are ensured by investigation work teams, sent quarterly to check on implementation and decide how much the cadre should be paid.[127]

As in the past, cadres strive to be models; but now they also strive to be named head of "the village with the most specialized households," "the village to make the most advancement in commodity production," and so on. Not surprisingly, cadres have falsified statistics in order to receive rewards and bonuses.[128] For example, in Hunyuan county, Shanxi, an investigation work team discovered a number of such schemes. The problem began when village party branch heads became eligible to receive a bonus of 100 *yuan* if their village qualified for the title *quan xiang zhi zuide* (the best in the township). A number of villages reported such accomplishment, but when the work teams were sent to verify the statistics, numerous irregularities were discovered. One so-called *fanfan* village (that is, one that has doubled its income) reported that the average income of its peasants had doubled to reach 760 *yuan*. In fact, the average income of the peasants in that village the previous year had already reached 508 *yuan*. Among twelve so-called "commercial grain-specialized households" (that is, those with large grain production capable of selling large surplus to the state) six households' production did not even equal the minimum set for the district (*qu*). Two other households overreported their income by 27 percent and 14.4 percent in order to qualify as "the best in the township."[129] In

126. In the interview, the village head said that a cadre would be fined if one of the peasants did not follow policy and had another child; the fine was a hefty 300 *yuan*. He was quickly silenced and contradicted, however, by the village economic manager, who interrupted and denied any such policy for birth control. My sense was that in fact the village head knew very well what he was talking about. Whether the 300-*yuan* figure is correct or not, the point is that a bonus system has been instituted in administration of policy as well as in economics, giving cadres added incentive to strictly enforce state policies. China Interviews, 1985.

127. China Interviews, 1985.

128. A well-publicized case involved granary cadres in Shenze county, Hebei. See Joint Inspection Group, "Why Have So Many Party Cadres Here Been Carried Away by 'Evil Winds'?" *RMRB* 10 September 1985:5, translated in *JPRS-CPS-85-121* 19 December 1985:101–104.

129. "Jinzhuangxiang heshi nianzhong shangbao shuzi" (Jinzhuang Township Reviews Annual Submitted Statistics), *NMRB* 26 February 1985:2. Another report of bogus

Hubei, a manager of a tile and brick factory covered up a loss of 170,000 *yuan* and reported a profit of 40,000 *yuan* in the books in order to receive a profit from the collective capital fund.[130]

Just as cadres under collectivization overreported grain production and made unrealistic sales pledges, cadres now feel pressure to report success in developing commodity production. Regardless of whether this is done out of the cadre's personal greed or pressure from upper levels to comply, peasants are once again paying the price. Cadres have reportedly forced undeveloped areas to become commodity producers, sometimes through administrative measures. The example cited earlier of cadres arbitrarily creating large grain-specialized households is but one illustration. Other reports show that some cadres still report good harvests when in fact the area has suffered disaster, behavior reminiscent of the Great Leap Forward period. In one such case, which occurred before the unified procurement system was abolished, the peasants had to pay the price of their local cadre's ambition and buy grain on the open market in order to fulfill their grain responsibilities to the state.[131]

As in the past, those falsifying reports include not only the lower-level cadres but also those at higher levels. A district-level cadre received the honor of leading an "advanced agricultural district" and was given a bonus for his efforts; later it was discovered that he had falsified grain production statistics and inflated the number of deaths in order to show a low birthrate statistic for his area.[132] The severity and prevalence of these crimes are reflected in the various circulars that have come out on the importance of accurate statistics. They warn that "no leader may

---

commercial grain-producing households describes how peasants and cadres can falsify their status. In a village in Shanxi, Wuxiang county, two of the three reported 10,000-*jin* grain sales households were fakes. One household actually sold 12,376 *jin* of grain to the state, but he only produced 9,270 *jin;* he illegally bought grain from the state and then resold that same grain to the state at premium prices. He used the grain he bought at the low state price to pad his production and then benefit from the new price structure, which gives peasants the premium overquota price for 70 percent of their sales. "Mousifeiji huangbaochengji gufu guojia 'xuelisongtan'" (Selfishly He Submitted False Reports of Achievements and Embezzled Urgently Needed Supplies, He Let the State Down), *NMRB* 13 April 1985:1.

130. "Local Cadres in Wuhan Dismissed for Cheating," *JPRS-CPS-85-105* 15 October 1985: 62.

131. "Jingti fukuazhifeng chongxin taitou" (Guard Against the Reemergence of the Wind of Exaggeration), *GDNMB* 7 April 1985:4.

132. "Fukua shengguan, keyi xiuyi!" (Getting Promotions by Boasting, This Can Be Stopped!), *JJRB* 21 April 1985:1.

influence, persuade, or compel the statistician to change or falsify the numbers."[133]

A CADRE-ENTREPRENEUR ALLIANCE

The changing nature of cadre power, the new demands of the job, and the reorganization of agriculture have caused village cadres to rethink their alliances and choice of clients as well as to redefine the terms of exchange. The removal of the political hats in 1979, the end of campaigns, and the generally more relaxed political atmosphere allow cadres greater leeway in selecting who to bestow their favors upon, without regard to class background. This has opened the door for cadres to form profitable alliances with the new rich in the village, the 10,000-*yuan* households who are in a position to provide the cadres with better terms of exchange.[134]

Clients have always traded for tangible goods, but for cadres during the Maoist era an important part of the bargain was political support during campaigns and struggle meetings, particularly from those with "red" class backgrounds, and cooperation in managing production. Since the decentralization of agriculture, cadres can afford to worry less about cooperation, political support, and work teams. The pledge by China's leaders to abolish political campaigns has made such intangible goods less valuable. Cadres now demand and get expensive economic goods, such as shares in businesses, "donations," in addition to gifts, not just dinner invitations and the occasional pieces of pork.[135] Those most able to offer such goods are the specialized households.

The relationship between cadres and specialized households is both give and take, as it was between team leaders and their clients. It should

---

133. See, for example, "Shanxi Circular on Importance of Accurate Statistics," *JPRS-CPS-85-100* 26 September 1985: 29.

134. The various "gifts" that a cadre receives may line his own pockets, but they may also go for the "collective good." These "contributions" may be used for anything from buying television sets to building temples and holding feasts. Regardless, such demands and requests have taught peasants that it is better to keep one's prosperity quiet. Hong Kong Interview 11/6/22.

135. "Qiangxing rugu," *ZGNMB* 14 April 1983:2; "Qibuneng," *ZGNMB* 22 February 1983:2; "Handanshi," *ZGNMB* 11 March 1984:3; "Datong," *ZGNMB* 19 January 1984:1; "Zhuanyehu," *RMRB* 19 July 1984:3; "Bunengkao 'Haohanguzi' Zhifu" (Can't Get Rich by Relying on a "True Man's Share"), *SXNM* 26 July 1983:1; "Baichi pingguo qiyoucili" (Eating Apples Without Paying for Them Is Outrageous), *SXNM* 3 September 1983:1.

not be interpreted as purely exploitative or coercive. On the one hand, peasants, even those who have prospered, realize that alienating their local cadres may cost them more than it is worth. Cadres afflicted with envy (*yanhong*) have the ability to "milk" the 10,000-*yuan* households for considerable sums of money. Local cadres arbitrarily assess fines on peasants for everything from being late to meetings to incorrectly study-ing a directive.[136] Consequently, peasants say that it is better to give a little to save themselves from losing a lot. Peasants, even those who have left the village, realize that cadres can still make life difficult for them or their family members who still live in the village. Cadres may no longer use overt discrimination, but they still can give uncooperative peasants the "too small glass slippers to wear"—in other words, make life diffi-cult in subtle but nonetheless effective ways.

On the other hand, those peasant households in a clientelist relation-ship with a cadre receive valuable goods and services in exchange. Aside from the land and contracts that cadres can give these peasants, cadres facilitate various bureaucratic processes, such as gaining approval for loans and getting licenses.[137] Cadres can also aid various households by their nonenforcement of policy. Local-level cadres monitor the activity of specialized households and ultimately have the power to decide whose goods will be confiscated or businesses closed when there are in-fractions of the rules.

The overall impact of this special treatment is suggested in a national survey of the income of 851 specialized households. Their average in-come was 2,571 *yuan*, 82.2 percent higher than the average peasant household income of 1,411 *yuan*.[138] Specialized households become the 10,000-*yuan* households. This is not to say that others cannot become rich, but as one peasant said, "it is more difficult."[139] While regular peasants are short on supplies, specialized households, such as "scien-

---

136. See, for example, "Wuchangxian quxiao nongminde buheli fudan" (Wuchang County Abolishes Unreasonable Peasant Burdens), *JJCK* 23 April 1985:2; "Zhizhi qiang-xing tanpai wumingkuan waifeng" (Curb the Evil Wind of Forced Unspecified Appropria-tions), *ZGNMB* 1 April 1984:1; and "Kaifengxiang dui nongmin renyi fakuan da ershier xiang" (Kaifeng Township Arbitrarily Fines Peasants for as Many as Twenty-two Items), *ZGNMB* 14 August 1984:1.
137. A survey of peasant entrepreneurs revealed that they faced problems in the fol-lowing areas: applying for licenses or permits, stocking goods, having legal guarantees of their rights and interests, and coping with irrational collection of fees and management. "Nongmin congshi," *ZGNMB* 15 April 1984:1.
138. "Zhuanyehu jinnian youyou naxie xin fazhan" (What Are the New Develop-ments in Specialized Households This Year), *ZGNMB* 11 December 1984:2.
139. Hong Kong Interview 7/6/8.

tific farming households" (*kejihu*), receive needed inputs, often at cheaper prices (sometimes paying only half the regular price).[140]

For a time confusion existed about who should be considered a specialized household and therefore given due privileges. Only in 1984 did central authorities issue four criteria based on measurable levels of business and income to define what types of peasant households qualify as "*zhuanyehu.*"[141] Regardless of the definition, the success of specialized households depends to a significant degree on whether local cadres provide them their allotted production inputs and outlets for their goods. As the previous sections have indicated, government regulations allowing special access mean nothing if local cadres say that the items are "out of stock."

The advantage of cadre support and their network of contacts (*menlu*) is further evident in the success of heretofore poor peasant households that are taken under the wing of a cadre. Because it is acknowledged that cadres have the advantage in contacts, information, and skill, some township party committees and governments have decided that each township and village cadre should contract (*bao*) to help one poor household develop production.[142] Consequently, it is more important than ever, not only for specialized households but for all peasants who want to get ahead, to cultivate particularistic ties with local cadres, act in a deferential manner, bring them gifts, help them build houses without payment, and sometimes give them shares in their enterprises and partial profits without their investment or work.

One should not overlook that often the cadres themselves or their relatives have gained special status and enjoy the benefits that accrue to such households. As the Shanxi survey cited earlier shows, a large percentage of those who have prospered were former cadres. In Liaoning, it was not surprising to find that the head of the village economic committee was also one of the most successful entrepreneurs in the area. Clearly his position allowed him to be the most informed about the sales oppor-

140. "Moba kejihu," *ZGNMB* 24 April 1983:3.
141. "Hewei zhuanyehu" (What Is a Specialized Household), *ZGNMB* 2 December 1984:1. This action, no doubt, also was in response to the exaggerated number of "specialized households" reported by cadres looking for recognition and special rewards. See "Nianzhong diaocha tongji yao shishi qiushi" (The Annual Statistics Should Accord with the Facts), ibid.
142. "Pusamiaoxiang 280 ming ganbu baohufupin" (280 Cadres of Pusamiao Township Contract to Help the Poor), *ZGNMB* 28 October 1984:2. This program is also stressed in Ren Jie, "Party Members Establish Ties with Household; a Good Form for Political and Ideological Work in Rural Areas," *Xuexi yu yanjiu* May 1985, no. 5, pp. 28–29, translated in *JPRS-CPS-85-03* 4 October 1985: 60–64.

tunities for different products and to run a very successful chicken farm among other businesses, in addition to managing the collective's enterprises; his total household income for the year was 40,000 *yuan*.[143]

An interesting question is who in the future will be the power elite in the countryside as more peasants succeed and work outside the village and are able to provide contacts and jobs for friends and relatives. Whether they are cadres or specialized households, those who have contacts and jobs to offer will draw a following from among those peasants who have had much more limited experience with the market and outside opportunities. One also must wonder whether a hierarchy of power will develop among local cadres. Especially important is whether a gap will develop between the power of those cadres in charge of more purely political matters, the so-called administrative side of government, and the economic managers of the village enterprises and companies. Beginning in 1985, some village heads and economic managers were being judged by different standards. One can only wonder at the disparity in pay because the income brought in by the economic manager is so high. When asked what would happen, one village's head and its economic manager both laughed nervously and agreed that there would be a difference.[144]

THE CHANGING CONTOURS OF VILLAGE CLIENTELISM

The post-1978 reforms in agriculture have succeeded to an impressive degree in changing the face of the Chinese countryside. There is now greater crop specialization, a shift to cash crops, and the rapid development of specialized agricultural sidelines and small-scale industry. From 1979 to 1985 the acreage sown in grain decreased by 8.7 percent while cash crops increased by 51.5 percent.[145] The valued output of cash crops, as a percentage of total value of agricultural output, rose from 23.3 percent in 1978 to 31.8 percent in 1984.[146] By 1985 the commodity

---

143. China Interviews, 1985.
144. China Interviews, 1985. When I returned to the same village the next year, I found that the manager had to give back some of his wages (bonuses) because they were so high.
145. The area sown in grain decreased from 1,788.84 million *mu* to 1,632.68 million *mu*; the area sown in cash crops increased from 221.51 million *mu* to 335.67 million *mu*. *Zhongguo tongji nianjian 1987*, p. 164.
146. "1984," *RMRB* 11 March 1985:2.

production rate reached 53.3 percent.[147] Furthermore, the number of goods covered by state quota and procurement guidelines has decreased from a high of 180 to 39, of which 24 are medicinal items.[148] By the end of 1984 specialized households numbered approximately 22.5 million or 14 percent of the rural population.[149] Accompanying these changes is an upsurge in market activity and rural enterprise. Between 1978 and 1983 the number of urban free markets grew from 0 to 4,500; rural markets from 33,302 to 43,000. Volume of sales in the rural markets increased by 162 percent.[150] Rural industrial output in 1985 reached 230 billion *yuan*, or nearly 30 percent of the national total.[151]

Yet, as this chapter has shown, this great transformation of the economy has not wrought equally great changes in the nature of village politics. Peasants now have more options: they no longer need depend on a single cadre, but they nonetheless still find themselves in a subordinate position of dependence, even if of a different type. For the individual peasant the reforms have resulted in the loss of the collective's protection.[152] However, the removal of the protective buffer of the collective makes the peasants more vulnerable, but not necessarily, to the demands of the central state. Rather, removing the collective buffer makes the peasants more vulnerable not only to the market but also to the state agents—both those within the village and those in the larger market environment in which they must now operate—who are charged with im-

147. Peng Baoquan, "Development and Reform in Commerce," *Beijing Review* 29 July 1985, vol. 28, no. 30, pp. 25–27.

148. Duan Yingbi, "Gaige nongchanpin tongpaigou zhidu ba nongcun jingji jinyibu gaohuo" (Reform the Unified Procurement System for Agricultural Goods to Further Enliven the Rural Economy), *NYJJWT* 1985, no. 3, p. 42. In spite of this trend, some indications point to a degree of recentralization of control over the price and supply of vegetables in response to skyrocketing prices for these items in the urban areas. The government has demanded that suburban areas guarantee certain acreage to vegetables and that state-owned stores control most sources of ordinary vegetables. A ceiling price has also been imposed for certain vegetables. Tian Jiyun, "On the Present Economic Situation and Restructuring the Economy," *Beijing Review* 10 February 1986, vol. 29, nos. 6 and 7, p. X.

149. A more detailed statistical breakdown shows some types of activity growing faster than others. Between 1983 and 1984 the number of specialized households engaged in agricultural production increased from 34.2 percent to 35.9 percent; in animal husbandry decreased from 32.5 percent to 24.6 percent; in rural industry (*wugong*) increased from 11.7 percent to 14.4 percent; and in transport, construction, commerce, and service trades increased from a total of 13.6 percent to 19.2 percent. "Zhuanyehu," *ZGNMB* 11 December 1984:2.

150. G. William Skinner, "Rural Marketing."

151. Dai Yannian, "Reform Logs Sound Results," *Beijing Review* 10 February 1986, vol. 29, nos. 6 and 7, p. 4; and "Rural Industries Take on Technology," ibid., p. 5.

152. See Vivienne Shue, *The Reach of the State.*

plementing, but often twisting, the center's directives. Individual peasant households are more vulnerable to the growing number of people now capable of holding power over the rural population. The type of clientelism seems to be moving away from the insular, more stable tie between a peasant and team leader to a more diverse and perhaps less stable multipatron variety reminiscent of that described by Morton Fried for late Republican-era China, but it is clientelist nonetheless.[153]

The nature of cadre power has changed. It is now much less complete, much less direct, and much more dependent on the cadre's own entrepreneurial skills than on his office. Cadre power still stems from the ability to manipulate the existing system, but with different results. Under the collective system, much illegal activity of local cadres was directed against the state in the struggle over the harvest. It was a situation where the local levels, including both the cadres and peasants, opposed the state; that struggle has been mediated. Now it seems more the case that the cadres work to frustrate the aims of both the state and the peasants, manipulate policies more to their own personal advantage, and deprive peasants of the benefit of the new state policies.

Decollectivization has removed the collective from between the peasant and his harvest, but it has not removed local cadres as intermediaries between the state and the peasants. The village and its cadres still stand between the state and the peasants; but for peasants, that may be more of a problem than a blessing. Village cadres can no longer act as absolute gatekeepers, but as long as the state remains only semicommitted to a market economy, maintains a hierarchy of prices, and does not solve the problem of scarcity, cadres will remain middlemen between the peasants and the state as well as the market.

153. Fried, *Fabric.*

CHAPTER 10

State and Peasant in China

Concluding Reflections

The underlying theme of this book is that the Chinese revolution did not eliminate the struggle over the harvest that is central to peasant politics. In fact, after eliminating landlords and collectivizing agriculture, the state for the first time stepped directly into the struggle with peasants over their harvest. In that struggle the state showed itself to be a powerful and autonomous actor capable of penetrating to the lowest reaches of society. But that penetration became characterized by personalized authority exercised in a clientelist fashion, leaving the door open for peasant participation through the use of personal networks and evasion.

Like the everyday forms of resistance that James Scott describes for peasants in Malaysia, informal channels of participation were, in most cases, the only effective means of articulation open to the Chinese peasantry.[1] However, the importance of cloaking resistance, as described by Scott in the Malaysian context, is magnified in the communist context, where in some periods failure to do so could mean not only bad job assignments but also public humiliation, struggle sessions, or even labor camps.

Henderson and Cohen have described the limited utility of the "voice" option and the difficulty of the "exit" option in Chinese work units (*danwei*).[2] Nowhere was that more true than in China's production

---

1. Scott, *Weapons of the Weak*, chap. 7.
2. Gail E. Henderson and Myron S. Cohen, *The Chinese Hospital*; also see Michel Oksenberg, "The Exit Pattern."

teams. In the collective village, the use of the voice option left one vulnerable to retribution from the leadership.[3] The communist context requires that dissatisfaction or resistance be subtle and indirect. Chinese peasants under the communes were virtual prisoners of their production teams, on which they depended for economic, political, and social well-being.

My findings do not preclude the use or effectiveness of the formal channels of political participation. My point is that the channels peasants choose depend on the state's own attitudes at any particular time. The political climate of the period and the issue at hand determine the method. For brief periods during the early Cultural Revolution and the late 1970s, peasants did use overt methods, such as protests and demonstrations, to register their interests. In the late 1970s and 1980s, characterized generally by a more relaxed political climate, the more open, formal channels have once again taken on meaning. But clearly, the upward flow of information of the mass line is turned on or off like a faucet by the state from above, not by the strivings of peasants from below.

This study has brought to the surface the pervasiveness of hidden agendas, the importance of personal relations, and the manipulation of policies in the course of implementation. The existence of the clientelistic politics and evasion that I describe at the lowest tier of the rural bureaucracy may invoke similar accounts of official malfeasance and the importance of personal ties in imperial China. Parallels exist, but one should not conclude that the root of either corruption or patronage is cultural. This behavior is neither inherently Chinese nor traditional. Zelin's study has shown that much bureaucratic corruption in the Qing was rooted in structural dysfunctions of the political system.[4] The pattern is repeated in many societies, from the capitalist market environment of Malaysia to the peculiar socialism known as Ujamaa in Tanzania to the developing Third World bureaucracies.[5] This behavior, as studies of the Soviet Union also show, allows such systems to function by providing the flexibility needed to survive the myriad rules of a bureaucratic state that has failed to satisfy the needs of its citizens.[6] In China, as in the Soviet Union and the developing nations of the Third

3. Lena Kolarska and Howard Aldrich, "Exit, Voice, and Silence."
4. See Zelin, Magistrate's Tael.
5. On Malaysia see Scott, Weapons of the Weak; on Tanzania see Goran Hyden, Beyond Ujamaa; for other examples see Stephen A. Quick, "The Paradox of Popularity"; and Joseph LaPalombara, "Bureaucracy."
6. Hough, The Soviet Prefects.

World, there is a need for the informal system of politics that circumvents the contradictions inadvertently created by the formal political and economic systems.

In pointing out both the existence and the necessity of the evasive actions of the lower-level cadres and the peasants, one need not conclude that the Chinese state was weak and ineffective. Did the state know that local-level cadres and peasants were keeping more of the "surplus"? Did it have no means of extracting more of the harvest from the countryside? The state had its weaknesses, but overall it would be a mistake to conclude that the Chinese communist state was unable to exert its rule if it so desired. When the state chose to apply its controls and where work teams were sent in those instances when the state chose to make an example of an indiscretion, the state was impressively effective and every bit as awesome as the totalitarian model would predict. However, the state was selective in its direct intervention. Chinese rule is based on fear rather than terror.[7] A few problem teams were used as examples to warn others of the consequences of noncompliance with state directives. As long as a team leader met minimal demands, neither overtly opposing policies nor attracting notice from the upper levels, he was relatively free to go about his duties as head of the production team. The state was powerful, but the application of its power was periodic and sparing. Like its Confucian ancestor, the current government rules by example, assuming that this will generally be sufficient to deter others from engaging in illegal activities.[8]

The communist state had more than one strategy to achieve its primary goal of controlling the disposition of the harvest. Procurements were obviously its prime strategy, but the costs of extracting all the so-called surplus were high, as Stalin's experience had already graphically shown and as the famine of the Great Leap Forward had recently reminded. I would agree with Thomas Bernstein that the Chinese regime, perhaps because of its special relationship with the peasantry dating from the revolution, must have deemed the political costs too great.[9] The contemporary state, like its Qing predecessor, chose to rely on surcharges and indirect methods to secure the grain that it obviously wanted.[10] Except in a few instances, it took few additional steps to ex-

7. Scott, *Weapons of the Weak*, p. 277.
8. Donald Munro, *The Concept of Man*.
9. Bernstein, "Stalinism, Famine."
10. Zelin, *Magistrate's Tael*, provides an excellent discussion of the hesitancy of the early Qing state to increase taxes by regularizing and formalizing existing informal surcharges.

tract the maximum amounts from the peasants but allowed the informal maneuvering to take its course. Although one can never know if the state tacitly condoned the illegal manipulation and siphoning of grain from the state-defined surplus, the development of local grain reserves to control the harvest in the face of faltering procurements certainly lends credence to such an interpretation.

Although the state may have allowed its cadres to "keep one eye closed" and thereby settle for less than the total surplus, one must remember that the remaining grain was still within its control. Policies, such as the local grain reserves, indirectly controlled access to, and use of, this surplus. Because the state could not extract all the grain, it shifted the financing of certain programs onto the local units, increasingly leaving agricultural investment to the local levels and relying on public service labor (yiwu gong).[11] Agriculture was called upon to be self-reliant and establish local reserves while the government continued to channel state investment into heavy industry.

The prevalence of informal modes of political interaction and influence had its costs. In China grain became a valuable currency of exchange not easily relinquished. The costs became increasingly clear as production increased but grain procurements stagnated. This served as an important stimulus for the post-Mao reforms, which created an incentive system for grain sales. A less noticeable but potentially more dangerous side effect of the reliance on informal politics was concentrating power in the hands of brigade and team leaders; this is similar to the problem described by Graziano for southern Italy.[12] In the collectivized Chinese countryside, rationing and personal control over virtually all means of subsistence created an extreme case of what Graziano called the "incomplete capitalistic rationalization" of the economy. As Graziano's argument would suggest, personalized control over resources fostered vertical ties of patronage based on particularistic relationships. In collectivizing production and giving local cadres the power to allocate jobs and pay, the state left the door open for the rise of "local emperors"—the autocratic team or brigade leaders to whom peasants were sometimes subject.

The leaders of the collectivized village may officially have been of the same "class" as those they were leading, but they had the potential of

11. On the imbalances in state investment see Lardy, *Agriculture*.
12. See Luigi Graziano, "Patron-Client Relationships."

becoming a "new class" in Djilas's terms.[13] Within a team, the leader was the authority figure to whom members turned for allocating economic resources and opportunities. His power was not absolute: brigade officials had the power to control his political fate, and team leaders thus were often clients of brigade officials. Nonetheless, peasants largely owed their economic well-being to team leaders, who acted as patrons controlling the distribution of the team resources. The state thereby inadvertently reinforced traditional ties of peasants to their local leaders, partly undermining the effectiveness of its control.

My study also suggests that one should not underestimate the power of local cadres.[14] Power is not a limited quantity. Team leaders, other writers have properly stressed, were under the thumb of the upper levels, but within the confines of the team the leader had considerable influence over the daily lives and economic well-being of its members. Even if the leader's office is dissolved, as happened in the 1980s, team leaders may still find new bases of power by contracting to operate the lucrative village enterprises after decollectivization.

The pervasiveness of personal ties, patronage, and informal influence leads one to wonder how deep the social and organizational changes have been since the revolution. The state collectivized agriculture and created a new power structure. However, seemingly "traditional" types of behavior thrive in the new context and continue to do so in altered form in the 1980s.

Comparative studies of political corruption tell us that "the larger . . . the size and scope of the public sector, the greater will be the proportion of certain acts that will meet our criteria of corruption."[15] One might therefore expect that the market reforms would have eliminated much corruption in the Chinese countryside. Yet the period after the reforms has certainly witnessed abundant illegal behavior. This does not necessarily indicate that general theories about corruption are wrong; much of this corruption results not from the market reforms but, on the contrary, from the lack of a fully developed market. In China in the 1980s the state has dismantled the commune structure, taking away the domination of local cadres over all aspects of peasant work and economic well-being, and replaced it with the household responsibility system,

13. Djilas, *The New Class.*
14. My picture of cadre power differs significantly, for example, from that presented by Parish and Whyte, who looked at the more formal aspects of office.
15. James C. Scott, *Comparative Political Corruption,* p. 9.

and reopened free markets. But the state has not completely dismantled the system of centralized distribution of goods and opportunities. In fact, it has created new opportunities in the form of bureaucratically allocated contracts.

With the reforms, the state has retreated from the struggle over the harvest and instituted economic incentives to procure grain. But neither the return to household farming nor the introduction of markets has eradicated clientelist politics; however, the nature of this power has changed. The power that cadres have over peasants is no longer direct but informal, created by their influence over economic opportunities. The existing structure leaves them in a position to grant licenses, distribute key inputs, act as the middlemen between peasants and the state market, and regulate the open market. This half-planned half-market economy makes peasants, as individuals, more vulnerable to a wider range of corruption outside the village while continuing to subject them to village cadre power.

The reforms clearly eliminated many old sources of cadre power, and they have greatly weakened team leaders or removed them altogether. But new patrons have emerged, often at the village level, and new resources underpin clientelist politics. Reemerging markets have made the pattern of clientelism more complex and fluid, more like that of the Republican era, but the pattern is still distinctly clientelist. The reforms are altering the cast of players and their basis of power in complex and not yet completely understood ways.

Future research should test the applicability of these conclusions to other communist states. One would logically expect clientelism to play a similarly significant role in many of them.[16] There will certainly be variations in the phenomenon, but the structural circumstances that create clientelism in China—centralized distribution, scarce goods, personalized control over distributing basic goods and income opportunities, fusion of economic and political authority—are characteristic of most other communist states in different periods and to different degrees. One implication of this study is that one should not classify political systems according to their official ideology. A most significant finding, or perhaps it should be called a nonfinding, is the limited effect of communist ideology on the existence of clientelism. The institutional struc-

16. Walder has already shown the culture of dependence in the Chinese urban workplace; see his *Communist Neo-Traditionalism*. Also see S. N. Eisenstadt and L. Roniger, *Patrons, Clients*.

ture of a communist state does not eliminate traditional patterns of clientelism; it inadvertently creates new patterns to take their place. This study documents the sources of clientelism in post-1949 rural China, and, more important, it suggests that clientelism should be part of the definition of a communist political system.

REMAINING QUESTIONS

China's continuing economic reforms raise a question that I cannot yet answer: How has state power changed in rural areas? This study has examined the problems of state control over collectivized agriculture, but it is unclear how the state is going to adapt its control structure to a half-market half-planned rural economy. How is the state going to allow the market forces to grow and yet be assured that enough grain is grown and procured at acceptable costs? The reform experience in Eastern Europe suggests that these states, when faced with problems, revert to the familiar tactics of central planning and tightened administrative control. China's drop in grain production in 1985 and the state's quick resort to administrative pressure to fulfill contracts is one indication that China may follow that path. Recent reports that China has reimposed price controls on key items—including oil, gas, electricity, steel, timber, coal, rubber, farm chemicals, and other major raw materials as well as shipping, railway, and air transport—further highlight this dilemma.[17]

This study reminds us that although markets have developed extensively for certain commodities, centralized distribution and state intervention still play important roles. Centrally distributed inputs and the related hierarchy of prices is but one example. More important, the state has kept its hold on what will be the most prominent area of rural economic development—rural industry. The contracting system for enterprises, in contrast to that for land, allows the entrepreneur little autonomy over how profits are used and investments made.[18]

But postreform China is clearly not the same old system. The central state has loosened its grip on economy and society, and the county, township, and village have gained increasing autonomy. Nonetheless, old problems remain and new contradictions emerge. The new revenue

17. "Zhizhi shengchanziliao he jiaotong yunshu luan zhangjia Guowuyuan fabu zhanxing guiding he guanli banfa" (Stop the Indiscriminate Price Increases on Production Materials and Transport, State Council Issues Temporary Regulations and Management Method), *RMRB* 19 January 1988:1.

18. See Oi, "Chinese Village, Inc.," for some preliminary findings on this issue.

contracting system (*caizheng baogan*), for example, which allows profit sharing among different levels of the state, will only heighten the need for local levels to keep both a tight reign on its enterprises' finances and a firm hold on investment decisions.[19] One wonders if the central state, in its measures to decentralize control, has indirectly energized and reinforced the power current-day "local emperors" wield at village and township levels.

Is the nature of cadre corruption changing? Does it stem increasingly from self-interest rather than necessity? Many of the most lucrative contracts seem to be disproportionately falling into the hands of party members, cadres, former cadres, and their family and closest friends. This raises new questions: Who are the clients of these people? Which peasants are allowed access to the key opportunities? Are the reforms leading to an invidious system where only a privileged and limited group of friends and relatives of cadres can become clients? Are we, in other words, witnessing a shift from a clientelist system to a more selective system of cronyism and nepotism, which may have more politically disintegrative effects?[20]

There is already some evidence that village laws are being exercised selectively. Where the 10,000-*yuan* households and entrepreneurs are predominately former cadres, there is what the Chinese press refers to as the "petticoat influence." Village cadres have had a difficult time collecting the dues and contract fees owed by their former comrades, friends, and relatives; thus, in some villages collective coffers are empty.[21]

A potentially more serious political development is the creation of sharp divisions within rural society. The analytical questions yet to be answered are those of opportunity. Are we simply witnessing increasing inequality of income? Or is there, in addition, increasing inequality of opportunity to become wealthy because of political power and privilege? Are cadres, their families, and their friends those likely to become wealthy? If so, a new cronyism or nepotism may greatly erode the legitimacy of the political system.

The degree to which this will be a problem for the government depends in large part on the state's ability to continue improving the people's standard of living. Incomes and consumption have increased at

19. The revenue contracting system has been dubbed as "eating in separate kitchens" (*fenzao chifan*).
20. The differences between these particularistic relationships and their consequences are examined by Michael Johnston, "The Political Consequences."
21. Interview with village leader LBV, 1987.

impressive rates since 1978. What will happen if this slows or stops? What if consumer prices rise and inequality and unemployment worsen? The state still avows adherence to socialism. If job security and relative equality disappear, will citizens perceive cadre corruption as the cause of their problems? Before, corruption may have been seen as the "necessary grease," but now corruption may be perceived as the state's inefficiency. There have already been signs of discontent over the increasing inflation in the cities. The state's concern is clearly evident in its reimposition of price controls on key production inputs, including items necessary for agriculture.

In sum, the Chinese state still has many of the problems of socialism, but at the same time it is experiencing some of the problems of capitalism. The state uses new strategies to gain control of the harvest, improving both relations with the peasantry and peasant welfare. But the failure to fully dismantle the Maoist system retards the development of the market and compounds the difficulties peasants face in their dealings with state agents at the local levels. The Chinese state seems caught between the plan and the market.

Appendix A:
Research and Documentation

This study draws on published materials, émigré interviews, and visits to China. Materials on the 1950s and early to mid-1960s, primarily newspaper articles, were taken mainly from the Union Research Institute (URI) Clipping Files located in Hong Kong. This invaluable research aid contains press reports from the Chinese national and provincial papers, Hong Kong papers, and a few transcriptions from various Chinese radio broadcasts monitored in Hong Kong. Other materials on the early period were obtained from the United States Department of Agriculture (USDA) Clipping File held in microfilm at the University of Michigan. Articles cited in the text are not individually identified as coming from the URI or USDA clipping files; I have chosen to give the original reference, except for the page number, which often was not available, of each article cited.

When the clipping files' coverage became incomplete, I went directly to the Chinese press. With assistants, I undertook a comprehensive reading of relevant local and national newspapers published from 1948 to 1986. When available, specialized journals such as *Liangshi* from the 1950s and *Zhongguo nongcun tongxun* after 1979 were also consulted. One particularly useful source that deserves special mention is an "internal use only" (*neibu*) granary manager's handbook from the mid-1970s, *Nongcun liangshi zhengce zhaibian,* which contains all the rules and directives that guided the division of the harvest during the Cultural

Revolution period.[1] The bibliography contains a complete list of books, newspapers, and journals consulted.

The second, and in many respects the more important, source was my émigré interviewing. In Hong Kong from November 1979 to July 1980, and from June to September 1984, I conducted more than 400 hours of émigré interviews with fifty-two different subjects. Because of the continued constraints on research in China, interviewing in Hong Kong remains an invaluable source of knowledge about the intricacies of Chinese life and politics.[2] These interviews were essential for understanding the informal politics, the subleties of power, the importance of personal relations and patronage practices, and the types of disputes that occurred routinely within production teams. These insights into the exercise of authority were simply not available in official published sources and are among the most difficult to discuss within China. Published sources have provided information on the formal institutional framework, official regulations, and details regarding specific aspects of the grain distribution policy and the local grain reserve policy, whereas interviews have provided information on how official regulations were actually implemented in the various localities.[3]

Wherever possible I used both types of documentation. However, because of the informal nature and sensitivity of some of the issues described, and because few or no published sources exist on those subjects, particularly local-level strategies of evasion and personal interactions, interviews are relied on exclusively. Some events previously known only through interviews have since been confirmed by the press following Mao's death in 1976.

My confidence in my interviews is also supported by my own impressions and those of others gathered from visits and research in China, my third source of information. Between 1980 and 1988 I made seven trips to China—the longest being four months in 1986 and three months in 1988—both during and after my interview projects in Hong Kong.

1. *Nongcun liangshi zhengce zhaibian.* Because this is an internal-use-only (*neibu*) document, the second page, which contained the publication date, of the copy I used is missing; the probable date of publication is 1974.

2. One cannot, of course, be assured of the accuracy of respondents' memories, especially regarding statistics. Information of this type was sometimes provided, but I have used it with caution. Where I have used such information, it should be read only as an approximation in most cases. I have taken almost all statistical information from the various yearbooks that have been published since 1979 or from the work of Chinese and western economists.

3. See, for example, Michel Oksenberg, "Sources." Also see Martin King Whyte, *Small Groups,* pp. 238–247; and Parish and Whyte, *Village and Family,* pp. 339–351.

During these visits I observed production teams and villages in various parts of China, although the bulk of my research was in north China. I conducted interviews with local cadres and talked informally with a number of peasants about both the pre- and post-1978 periods. In 1980 and 1985 I returned to my ancestral village in Guangdong. These visits, if only to a limited degree, provided another check on the information I gathered from interviews in Hong Kong.

The following section will describe the technical aspects of my Hong Kong interviewing projects—how the interviewees were contacted, forms of remuneration, the procedure used in the interview sessions, and the defining characteristics of the interview pool. Appendix B contains a list of all interviewee reference numbers and a short description of their relevant rural experiences. References to interviewees will be made only to reference numbers and transcript accession numbers to protect their identities. The 1979–1980 Hong Kong interviews are referenced as the letter I plus accession number; those done in 1984 are referenced as Hong Kong Interview plus accession number.

The problems of relying on émigré interviews are well known and have been described in detail elsewhere.[4] The process by which I attained that information deserves discussion because the character of my respondents and the way I located them differ substantially from early rural studies based on émigrés. Most important, this study differs from previous ones in that the backgrounds of my interviewees were more geographically diverse.[5] I was fortunate to interview at the height of the legal emigration from China to Hong Kong. Whereas most earlier research relied almost entirely on interviewees from Guangdong, a southern province bordering Hong Kong, I was able to obtain a diverse group of emigrants from north, southwest, and east, as well as south, China.

Opportunities to conduct extensive field research in China should yield an even clearer sense of variations within the general patterns of behavior I have described. In these chapters I have tried to indicate the differences that factors such as relative wealth, location, and kinship patterns can make by providing examples relevant to the topic at hand. I will not be surprised to find that the validity of my generalization will

4. Parish and Whyte, *Village and Family*, and Barnett and Vogel, *Cadres*, along with many other works, stand as testaments to the value of this type of research for understanding the Chinese countryside. B. Michael Frolic, *Mao's People*, presents a collection of edited interviews that gives the reader a sense of the richness and detail obtainable through discussions with emigrants in Hong Kong.
5. See, for example, the studies done by Parish and Whyte.

vary depending on the geographical and economic makeup of peasant villages. In this study I have tried to provide an analysis of peasant-state relations and village politics that future students can at least take as a beginning.

To avoid the pitfalls of émigré interviewing, I tried to restrict my questions to those about the routine activities and firsthand knowledge of my interviewees. I asked about structures, policies, regulations, and interactions between various actors in the context of the team or village group, and, where relevant, interactions with brigade/village, commune/township, or upper-level state authorities. As a constant check on the reliability of respondents, similar questions were asked of other interviewees. Whenever possible I also checked responses and reconstructions of facts with published sources, whether official government reports or accounts presented in literature. And finally, I tried to select a representative group of interviewees from different parts of China with experiences at various levels of the agricultural system. Obviously this group was not statistically representative of the Chinese population as a whole, but compared to previous studies it was more representative geographically.

The interviews allowed me to reconstruct the basic political, economic, and social aspects of everyday village life. In many respects, my approach was similar to that of an anthropologist engaged in an ethnographic study, although I was limited to my office at the Universities Service Centre in Hong Kong. Nonetheless, through my immersion in intensive interviews with different émigrés who had prolonged experiences in rural China, both before and after the reforms had taken place, I was able indirectly to observe rural life in various areas of China.

THE INTERVIEW PROCEDURE

The more than 400 hours of interviews were conducted at the Universities Service Centre in Hong Kong. Only the interviewee and myself were present at these sessions, which were conducted in Mandarin Chinese in a private office at the Centre. I took detailed notes during the interview; I purposely avoided tape recordings of the interviews out of considerations of confidentiality and because of the hesitancy of interviewees. My notes, although not verbatim, recorded much of the original language of the interviewees and provide a faithful record of their statements. These form the transcripts referred to in the text. Interviewees are referred to only by their code number and their interview transcript number. In those cases where there is some probability that the interviewee might be identified by reference to the location of a certain event, I have left the location of the event intentionally vague, using instead such terms as north China, because I guaranteed complete confidentiality to the interviewees.

Following past procedure, I gave interviewees a nominal amount, a standard rate of $3.00 U.S. per hour, for the use of their time. Payment may in some cases have been a motivating factor for participation, but the motives of respondents varied and were often quite complex; some refused the money. This, of course, brings up the question of bias of those who chose to leave their former country. Although those who left China are likely to be more critical of the regime that they left, it was my job as the interviewer to try to recognize and overcome the personal biases of the interviewees. I did this by asking only questions about facts and processes and putting the same questions repeatedly to different respondents. Another important precaution that might minimize some biases of émigrés was trying to select a group of interviewees with diverse backgrounds. Let me turn to a more detailed discussion of my interview sample.[6]

CHARACTERISTICS OF THE INTERVIEWEES

The bulk of the research for this study was done at the height of the flow of legal and illegal emigrants out of China from 1979 to 1980. Figures 1 and 2 show the rate of immigration into Hong Kong from China for the period 1971 to 1980. (Figures 1–7 and Map 1 appear on pp. 242–248.) The peak year of both legal and illegal immigration was 1979, with noticeable increases starting in 1978. My 1979–1980 interview sample reflects this immigration trend. Figure 3 depicts the distribution of these interviewees based on their year of emigration from China to Hong Kong. Figure 4 depicts the distribution of my 1984 interviewees based on their year of emigration from China to Hong Kong. As should be clear from these charts, the bulk of my interviewees had only recently emigrated at the time I interviewed them.

Previous studies relied on relief organizations or personal connections to locate informants, mostly illegal peasant immigrants or sent-down youth.[7] But for various reasons, these sources had dried up by the time I was in Hong Kong. Consequently, for me, in many ways it was

6. Although the interviewees were by no means a representative "sample," the term will be used in the following discussion to refer to the group of thirty emigrants interviewed for this project.

7. See, for example, Whyte, *Small Groups;* and Parish and Whyte, *Village and Family.*

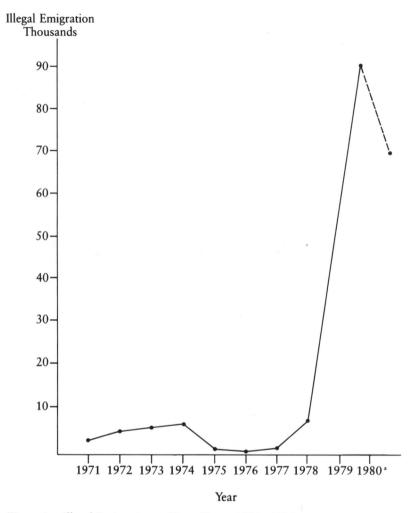

Figure 1.   Illegal Emigration to Hong Kong, 1971–1980

Source: Far Eastern Economic Review, *Asia Yearbook 1981,* p. 138.
[a] 1980 estimate is for first ten months.

easier to find legal émigrés, particularly as the Hong Kong government started to tighten its policies for granting asylum to illegal immigrants. As a result, the distinguishing feature of my interview sample was their almost universal legal immigration status. Of fifty-two interviewees only four were illegal immigrants. At the same time, because the prime criterion for obtaining legal exit out of China was the existence of overseas ties, almost all those whom I interviewed had close connections with overseas Chinese. In fact, thirteen of my sample were overseas Chinese who had returned to China, most from Southeast Asia and many from Indonesia.

Earlier studies, moreover, relied almost exclusively on peasant refugees and sent-down youth from Guangdong province, which borders Hong Kong. For this study, not only were most legal immigrants, but also of fifty-two only eighteen (35 percent) had primary experiences limited to Guangdong (including Hainan Island). In contrast to previous

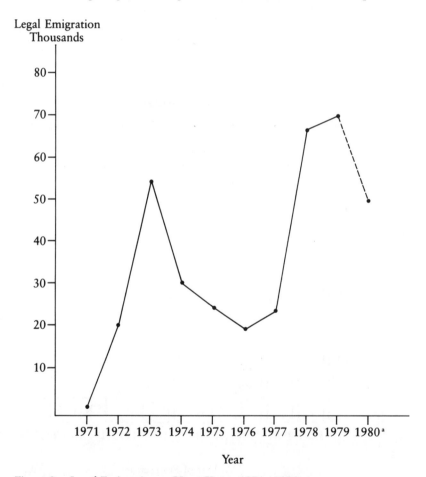

Figure 2.   Legal Emigration to Hong Kong, 1971–1980

Source: Far Eastern Economic Review, *Asia Yearbook 1981,* p. 138.
[a] 1980 estimate is for the first ten months.

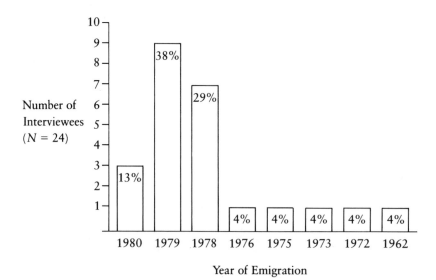

Figure 3.   Year of Emigration to Hong Kong, 1979–1980 Interview Sample

Note: Information is missing on six interviewees.

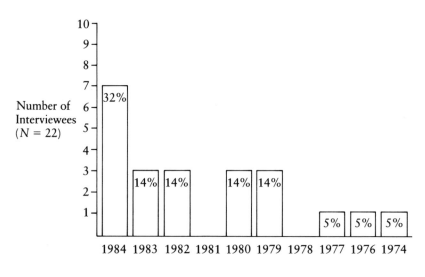

Figure 4.   Year of Emigration to Hong Kong, 1984 Interview Sample

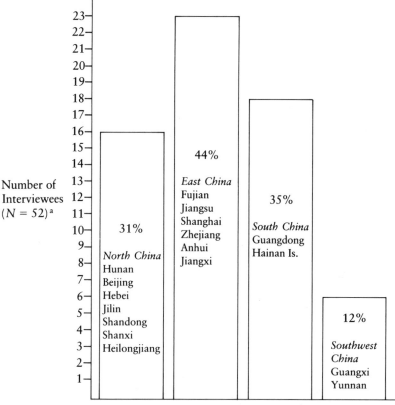

Figure 5.   Geographical Distribution of Interviewees' Rural Experience

---

ª Some interviewees had experiences in more than one location or province.

studies, of the fifty-two émigrés I interviewed, sixteen (31 percent) had primary experiences in north China, twenty-three (44 percent) in east China, and six (12 percent) in southwest China. See Figure 5 and the accompanying map of the approximate location of the areas in which the interviewees had their rural experiences.

Aside from the diverse geographical experience and the predominance of legal emigrants, the interviewees also differ substantially from those used in previous studies in a number of other respects. First, the age of my interviewees was relatively high. As Figure 6 shows, the bulk of my sample was composed of people in their forties rather than teen-

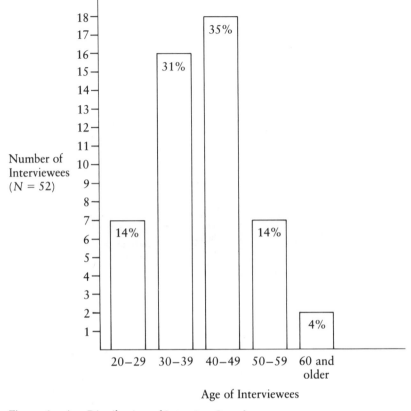

Figure 6.   Age Distribution of Interview Sample

---

agers or those in their twenties;[8] the next largest group was composed of people in their thirties. A full 66 percent were between thirty and fifty years of age.

This difference in the age of my sample is also reflected in the occupational background and educational level of the interviewees. As Table 22 shows, instead of a group consisting of primarily peasants or sent-down youth from rural Guangdong,[9] I had a mix of professionals, intellectuals, writers, actresses, educated youth, and province- and county-level cadres who had extensive experience in the countryside, as well as peasants and rural cadres from various parts of China.

8. Parish and Whyte, *Village and Family,* p. 346, show that the bulk of their sample was between twenty and thirty years of age.
9. See, for example, the data on the interviewees used by Parish and Whyte, ibid.; and by Burns, "Chinese Peasant."

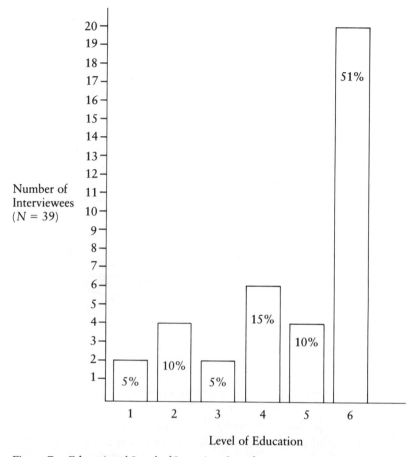

Figure 7.   Educational Level of Interview Sample

Note: Levels of education designated by numbers: 1 = Junior High School; 2 = Junior High School Graduate; 3 = High School; 4 = High School Graduate; 5 = College; 6 = College Graduate.

[a]Information on level of education is missing for thirteen interviewees.

As might be expected, given the occupational backgrounds, the educational level of my sample was also remarkably high. Figure 7 shows the percentage distribution of the interviewees according to education level. Of the thirty-nine interviewees about whom I have relevant information, more than half (51 percent) are college graduates.[10] The sample

10. My sample, for example, differs markedly from the one used by Parish and Whyte, *Village and Family.* In their sample of sixty-five, only nine had some upper middle school education or above.

Map 1. Geographical Location of Interviewees' Rural Experience

therefore was made up predominately of those who can be considered "intellectuals" rather than "peasants."

The sample is also distinguished by the high number of interviewees who held official positions (see Table 23). One-half of the sample had experiences on work teams of one kind or another. This further reflects their high educational level because schools seemed to be a prime source of personnel for work teams; professionals of all kinds were recruited for work teams during various periods, the Four Cleans Campaign, and particularly during the Cultural Revolution for the Learn from Dazhai work teams. Of the remaining interviewees who did not have an official position, one was a police chief prior to 1949 (he was not included in the table), one a native peasant who was a Red Guard leader, and one a sent-down youth who was a Red Guard activist. Only one interviewee held no office and lacked some distinguishing experience.

The sample on which this study is based can therefore be summarized as a recently arrived group of middle-aged legal emigrants, highly educated, predominantly intellectuals, with a high degree of experience on work teams and as rural cadres. The sample obviously is not repre-

TABLE 22.   OCCUPATION OF INTERVIEWEES

Occupation	Number
College or professional school instructor, academic	7
Arts worker (writer, actress)	4
Skilled professional	8
Skilled technician (scientist, engineer)	5
Teacher (secondary and below)	7
Sent-down youth	8
Regular peasant (native)[a]	10
Other	3[b]
Total	52

[a] There were actually eleven native peasants in the sample, but one was also a teacher and thus counted in the previous category.

[b] Of these, there was one police chief (pre-1949), one worker, and one former prisoner from a labor reform camp in Qinghai.

TABLE 23.   RURAL CADRE POSITION OF INTERVIEWEES

Type of Position	Number of Interviewees
Work team member	19
Provincial-level cadre	3
County cadre	5
Brigade or team cadre	10
Total	37

sentative of the peasant population. One might question whether this study is based on outsiders. How does this "intellectual" bias affect the study of peasant politics?

Given the objectives of the present study to understand how certain policies were carried out at various levels of the bureaucracy, it was not essential that I have a representative sample or that I interview a large number of "average peasants." I needed both cadres who had actually been charged with carrying out policies and regulating policies and peasants who were subject to these policies. Thus, the extensive experiences of my sample as work team members charged with seeing that policies were carried out correctly and rectifying problems of implementation, and the relatively high number of cadres in administrative posts at both upper and lower levels of the hierarchy, were ideal for my purposes.

The sample's bias of a large number of highly educated intellectuals and cadres was in part mediated by the older character of our sample— most interviewees were in their thirties or forties. All had substantial experiences in the countryside given the intervention of the Great Leap Forward and various other movements, such as the Four Cleans campaign and, most important, the Cultural Revolution, sending youth to the countryside, May Seventh cadre schools, and the mass disbursal of intellectuals to the countryside either on work teams or for reeducation. Consequently, the many intellectuals and higher-level cadres in my sample were either longtime rural residents or work team members who were sent to live and investigate production teams. The length of time work team members spent in any one team varied—some lasted at least six months while others lasted as long as two years—but it was sufficient time to provide them with more than a surface impression of the countryside. A number of those interviewees who were higher-level cadres spent at least half of their time on inspection trips throughout the countryside. Consequently, the bias of my sample is that they provided the best information for understanding the problems and strengths of state control. That, combined with the richly detailed accounts from team leaders and peasants in production teams, allowed me to pursue a wide range of questions about both state control and the ways to avoid that control.

FINDING INTERVIEWEES AND ARRANGING INTERVIEWS

As I indicated earlier, the past practice was to work through Hong Kong relief organizations that handled refugees. Given the availability of legal immigrants, I found this unnecessary. My approach was very straightforward; I put advertisements in the classified section of two local Chinese Hong Kong newspapers, *Singtao Jihpao* and *Cheng pao,* stating, in general terms, that an American academic needed part-time temporary research assistance on the topic of Chinese agriculture and rural life. Qualified applicants were described as those who had experience and knowledge about Chinese agriculture and society. Preferred applicants were former peasants and rural cadres. Interested applicants were to send in a résumé of their relevant experiences to the newspaper post office box.

On the basis of the content of the letters stating previous experience—former position, geographical location, and length of experience—I selected applicants, sometimes in consultation with my research assistants, who had firsthand knowledge of various types of work in China's countryside and could better judge the sincerity of various résumés. In 1979–1980, for example, from the two ads, but mostly from the one placed in *Singtao Jihpao,* I had a total of eighty-one respondents. Out of this pool, twenty-three with the proper qualifications were interviewed. The remaining seven, who made up the total of thirty interviewees that year, were found through private introductions by people whom I had already interviewed or who had been interviewed by other researchers at the Universities Service Centre.

My assistants made the initial telephone call, in Mandarin or Cantonese as was appropriate, or wrote a letter in Chinese to the prospective interviewee. They explained who I was, where I was from, and my general research topic and emphasized that I wanted to talk about their experiences in the countryside. Moreover, they stressed that our meeting would be private, maintaining the strictest confidentiality. The interviewee then had the option of declining, which happened only once, or accepting and setting up an initial appointment lasting two hours. Follow-up interviews were also usually done in two-hour segments over a period of days or weeks, and in some cases, over a period of a couple of months. In the initial call my assistants also explained that there would be a nominal payment of $3.00 (U.S.) per hour for their time and travel expenses.

When the interviewee arrived for his or her first interview, I personally greeted him or her and introduced myself and again explained my position and generally described my research. In the process, I stressed that I was an academic and not a government agent of the United States or any other country. This was standard procedure used by all researchers conducting interviews at the Universities Service Centre. Most important, during the first and succeeding interviews, because many of these people had relatives still in China, I assured them that there would be complete confidentiality. Their identities and any references to names or experiences that might lead to their identification would not be used. Thus, as I stated earlier, in some places in the text I had to be purposely vague because a number of people had experiences and backgrounds sufficiently rare that they could be identified.

From the very outset, interviewees were advised and constantly reminded that they should answer only those questions about which they had personal knowledge—they should not make up answers but simply say they did not know. Realizing that there were subjects that interviewees found sensitive, I was also careful to inform them at our first meeting that they could refuse to talk about any subject, and it would be dropped. This did happen once, but as the interview continued and the respondent trusted me more, he himself returned to the subject and provided some very useful information.

Aware of the hesitations of my interviewees, I was careful to save what I found to be the most sensitive questions until I had established a rapport with the interviewee.[11] I learned quickly how to phrase questions in a nonthreatening way and how to time my approach to particularly sensitive ones. I intentionally stayed away from personal questions. I never pressed them to tell me, for example, where they were from, if they were not so inclined; their general area within the province or their county was sufficient for my purposes. Relevant information about production, distance from large cities, transportation, and topographical features about the team was useful to me without knowing precisely either the location or the name of the team. This further assured them that I could not give them away. In most instances, however, by the end of the interviews I was told the name and location of the interviewees' teams. Moreover, personal information also came out naturally in the course of the interviews, such as their class background and the history of their families.

The advantages of interviewing in Hong Kong have been noted before, but, given the recent opportunities to do fieldwork in China, perhaps they should be stressed once again.[12] Interviewees feel much less restrained to talk about sensitive matters than if they were still in China, still in the village, still under the authority of the cadres they may be talking about. Personal relationships, cadre problems, patronage, and illegal behavior and activities could be freely discussed. The interviewee felt relatively assured that I would not then accidentally or otherwise go

11. I should make clear that the questions were *not* regarding China's security, military or otherwise. My use of the word "sensitive" to describe questions refers to a whole list of issues, including questions about grain, that the Chinese press at one point published as issues not to be revealed to foreigners. As it happened, this was particularly important during one point in the interviewing project when the Universities Service Centre was named as a "nest of spies" in *Renmin ribao* (this was later cleared up), and talking to foreigners about various matters concerned with China's security was forbidden. Fortunately, interviewees continued to respond and appear for appointments. This incident did not seem to have any noticeable affects on my interviewees.

12. See, for example, Parish and Whyte, *Village and Family,* pp. 339–351.

to the neighboring household and reveal what he had told me. More important, I would not report to the team leader or upper-level authorities on the context of our interview. Thus, as soon as they began to trust me, usually after the first meeting, they were more frank, and we discussed a wide range of sensitive political and economic issues.

The importance of being a foreigner outside China, away from people who knew the interviewees, with little chance of giving them away, was also made clear to me in other ways. First, in the case where two informants knew each other and were from the same area, they were very careful and somewhat hesitant to talk about certain problems that involved the other informant or some member of his family. They whispered, even though no one else was in the room, about events concerning the other interviewee or his family.

Second, I introduced to other researchers at the Universities Service Centre two of my interviewees whom I thought might be helpful to them. Before doing this, I consulted with the interviewee and explained generally the types of research my colleagues were doing. In both cases they agreed to talk with these "foreigners." However, they became upset and worried when they found out that sitting in on these interviews with these American researchers were research assistants who had recently emigrated from China. The interviewees feared that the assistants might somehow report back to authorities in China. My former interviewees expressed this fear to me through worried calls after their first meetings with my colleagues. Only after I assured them that their anonymity would be maintained did they agree to go for the second interview. In one case, I later found out from my colleague that the interviewee was not very forthcoming, even after a number of interviews, whereas he had been extremely frank with me. One can imagine the problems when upper-level cadres are present at interviews done with peasants in China.

After each initial interview I went over my notes and decided what topics, if any, would be most profitably pursued with the interviewee. Those interviewees whom I thought had little information or whom I considered unreliable I thanked and politely terminated our contact at the end of the initial meeting. In one instance, the interviewee, knowing that I had exhausted his knowledge, suggested that I talk with his wife, who had more experience in the countryside. There were also those from whom I only needed specific information; the interviewing of these people I usually completed in one session. In those three cases the interviewees were all introduced to me through friends, and thus I needed less time to put them at ease. The average number of hours per interviewee was approximately eight, usually spread over four different meetings. The hours spent interviewing a single respondent ranged from a minimum of less than two hours to a maximum of more than forty hours.

I had a standard set of topics on which I questioned each interviewee, but the amount of time or degree to which I pursued a topic varied and depended on each person's background and experience. For example, I talked more about accounting procedures with team leaders and accountants than with people who had little firsthand knowledge of the actual reporting procedures. Likewise, county- and province-level cadres were knowledgeable about higher-level decision making, such as regulations for issuing relief, grain ration quotas, and sales quotas, but they were of little help in understanding the specifics of interpersonal relations within any given team.

Of peasants and rural cadres I asked various questions: What were the different jobs in the team? Who allocated the work? How much did they get paid? How was it decided how much grain was sold to the state, how much was kept by the team, and how much was for the peasants? Was there a team reserve fund? Was it used? For what? What were the means for changing the apportionment policy? What happened when there was not enough grain to go around? How were private plots allotted? What expenses did team leaders have to meet, and where did the funds come from? How was it decided who got paid how much, and what types of disputes arose over these basic issues? How were these disputes resolved? What happened to peasants who did not or could not work? How did peasants get a loan? What happened when work teams came into the team? Did your team have problems with the upper levels over production or grain sales?

Of upper-level officials and work team members sent to control the implementation of policy I asked other questions. How much time was spent in a team? What were the distinguishing characteristics of the teams you investigated? What kinds of teams were most likely to be checked? Who sent the work teams? What happened when the work teams went into the team? What kind of problems were discovered? What sanctions were used? The reader will find that on various subjects, particularly on the little-publicized subjects such as the determination of quotas or the dispatch of work teams, I rely heavily on a few knowledgeable upper-level cadres who directly dealt with those matters.

THE REMAINING PROBLEMS OF BIAS

In sum, I have in this study tried to overcome as much as possible the problems of interviewing, but, like all studies based on unrepresentative sampling, this study has its biases nonetheless. Because most of my respondents were legal emigrants from many different parts of China, I hope that this will minimize the problems often attributed to "refugee" interviewing of people from one area. Obviously one cannot ever overcome the question of bias; legal emigrants also have their biases. However, as a final comment on the interview process, it is important to note the attitude of my interviewees. It may be that we have been overly biased and apologetic about using this source of information. Reports coming out of China seem to confirm rather than contradict the material gathered from émigrés in Hong Kong.

It was very clear during the interviews that these people, who had chosen to leave China, did so for very complex reasons, not all of which concerned their dissatisfaction with the government. Some left for personal reasons, others left for economic reasons, and still others were just curious about the outside world. On those occasions when I did ask for opinions, I was struck by the objectivity with which these émigrés spoke about China. There was a sense of cynicism, and they were often critical; but they were, as a whole, not bitter toward China. They were selective in their criticism, often aiming it at certain people and certain leaders who they felt had taken the wrong course of action. Striking, particularly given the hardships that many of the intellectuals I interviewed had been through, was their continued sense of loyalty and patriotism. Many obviously still believed in the superiority of the socialist system, and many looked forward to the end of their one-year waiting period so that they could return to visit their homeland. Many, in fact, had great difficulty in adjusting to Hong Kong and were homesick for China. A number of the interviewees had already been back at least once. These people all made the conscious choice of leaving China, but one should not assume that all were bitter toward China and therefore intent to paint a black picture of that country. Most were extremely insightful in pointing out problems and the obstacles to reforms. One should not therefore immediately assume that the biases of émigrés necessarily hinder the understanding of the research problem. The biases should be made clear and used objectively—that has been the goal of this study.

Appendix B:
List of Interviewees

HONG KONG INTERVIEWS, 1979–1980 (referred
to in the text as I plus accession number)

Number	Rural Experience
1	Full-time county work team member; team leader; peasant
2	Sent-down intellectual; writer
3	Team accountant; Red Guard leader; peasant
4	Team accountant; teacher; warehouse clerk; peasant
5	Sent-down intellectual; professor; county work team member
6	Sent-down youth; co-op supply clerk
7	Rural resident; worker
8	Work team member; engineer
9	Work team member; geologist
10	Brigade accountant; team accountant
11	Teacher; peasant
12	Sent-down intellectual; professor; work team member
13	Work team member; performing arts worker (actress)
14	Sent-down intellectual; professor; work team member
15	Agricultural bureau cadre; veterinarian
16	Teacher; work team member
17	Work team member; sent-down youth; teacher
18	Sent-down youth; team leader
19	Assistant team leader; peasant
20	Work team leader; professor

21	Sent-down youth; team accountant; team leader
22	Peasant
23	Peasant; prisoner ("rightist")
24	Work team member; skilled technician
25	Work team member; engineer
26	Police chief (pre-1949)
27	Red Guard; sent-down youth; coal miner
28	Sent-down youth
29	Provincial-level cadre; professor; work team member
30	Provincial- and county-level health worker; relief investigator

HONG KONG INTERVIEWS, 1984 (referred to in the text as Hong Kong plus accession number)

Number	General Rural Experience
1	Provincial cadre; agricultural specialist; work team member
(2)	(Deleted from list)
3	Peasant; high school teacher
4	County cadre; commercial department cadre; forestry specialist
5	Agronomist; fertilizer specialist
6	Irrigation specialist; work team member
7	Provincial researcher; sent-down intellectual
8	Peasant; work-point recorder
9	Peasant
10	Reporter; translator; sent-down intellectual
11	Secondary-school teacher; work team member
12	*Minban* teacher
13	Construction engineer; sent-down intellectual
14	Peasant; team leader
15	Peasant; team leader; brigade leader
16	Provincial researcher
17	Art worker; administrative cadre living in rural area
18	State cadre; commune granary cadre; peddler

19	Peasant; accountant; work-point recorder
20	Commune doctor
21	Sent-down urban resident formerly at county level
22	Sent-down urban resident
23	Team leader; agricultural research station cadre

References

CHINESE NEWSPAPERS

Beijing ribao
Dagong bao (Beijing and Tianjin)
Dazhong jingying bao
Dazhong ribao
Fujian ribao
Guangdong nongmin bao
Guangming ribao
Guangxi ribao
Guangzhou ribao
Guizhou ribao
Hebei jingji bao
Huili bao
Jiangsu nongmin bao
Jiefang ribao
Jingji cankao
Jingji ribao

Minbei renmin bao
Nanbei renmin bao
Nanfang ribao
Renmin hangyun bao
Renmin ribao
Shanxi nongmin
Singtao Jihpao (Hong Kong)
Ta Kung Pao (Hong Kong)
Xianggang shibao
Xin hunan bao
Xinhuashe dianxun
Yunnan ribao
Zhejiang ribao
Zhongguo jingji jibao
Zhongguo nongmin bao
Zhongguo qingnian bao

CHINESE PERIODICALS

Banyue tan
Cheng Ming (Hong Kong)
Chung-kung Yen-chiu (Taiwan)
Gongshe caiwu
Hongqi
Jiage lilun yu shijian
Jingji guanli
Liangshi
Liangshi gongzuo

Liaowang zhoukan
Nongcun caiwu kuaiji
Nongcun gongzuo tongxun
Nongye jingji wenti
Nongye xiandaihua yanjiu
Tongji gongzuo
Xinhua yuebao
Xuexi yu yanjiu
Zuguo (Hong Kong)

TRANSLATION SERVICES AND CLIPPING FILES

Foreign Broadcast Information Service. Washington, D.C.
Survey of China Mainland Press. Hong Kong: U.S. Consulate General.
Joint Publications Research Service. Washington, D.C.
Union Research Service Clipping Files. Hong Kong.
United States Department of Agriculture Clipping Files. Washington, D.C.

BOOKS AND ARTICLES

Ahn, Byung-Joon. *Chinese Politics and the Cultural Revolution: Dynamics of Policy Processes.* Seattle: University of Washington Press, 1976.
———. "The Political Economy of the People's Communes in China: Changes and Continuities." *Journal of Asian Studies,* May 1975, vol. 34, no. 3, pp. 631–658.
Baker, R. H. "Clientelism in the Post-Revolutionary State: The Soviet Union." In Christopher Clapham, ed., *Private Patronage and Public Power: Political Clientelism in the Modern State,* pp. 36–52. New York: St. Martin's Press, 1982.
Barnett, A. Doak, ed. *Chinese Communist Politics in Action.* Seattle: University of Washington Press, 1969.
Barnett, A. Doak, and Ezra Vogel. *Cadres, Bureaucracy, and Political Power in Communist China.* New York: Columbia University Press, 1967.
Baum, Richard. *Prelude to Revolution: Mao, the Party, and the Peasant Question, 1962–1966.* New York: Columbia University Press, 1975.
Baum, Richard, and Frederick Teiwes. *Ssu-Ch'ing: The Socialist Education Movement of 1962–1966.* China Research Monograph No. 2. Berkeley and Los Angeles: University of California Press, 1968.
Bauman, Zygmunt. "Comment on Eastern Europe." *Studies in Comparative Communism,* Summer–Autumn 1979, vol. 12, pp. 184–189.
Berliner, Joseph S. *Factory and Manager in the USSR.* Cambridge: Harvard University Press, 1957.
Bernstein, Thomas P. "Cadre and Peasant Behavior Under Conditions of Insecurity and Deprivation: The Grain Supply Crisis of the Spring of 1955." In A. Doak Barnett, ed., *Chinese Communist Politics in Action,* pp. 365–399. Seattle: University of Washington Press, 1969.
———. "Leadership and Mass Mobilization in the Soviet and Chinese Collectivization Campaigns of 1929–30 and 1955–56: A Comparison." *China Quarterly,* July–September 1967, no. 31, pp. 1–47.
———. "Reforming China's Agriculture." Paper prepared for the conference "To Reform the Chinese Political Order." Harwichport, Mass., 18–23 June 1984.
———. "Stalinism, Famine, and Chinese Peasants: Grain Procurements during the Great Leap Forward." *Theory and Society,* May 1984, vol. 13, no. 3, pp. 339–377.
———. *Up to the Mountains and Down to the Villages: The Transfer of Youth from Urban to Rural China.* New Haven: Yale University Press, 1977.

Blecher, Marc. "Leader-Mass Relations in Rural Chinese Communities: Local Politics in a Revolutionary Society." Ph.D. diss., University of Chicago, 1977.

Borkenau, Franz. "Getting Behind the Facts Behind the Soviet Facade." In Sidney Ploss, ed., *The Soviet Political Process: Aims, Techniques and Examples of Analysis,* pp. 80–93. Waltham, Mass.: Ginn, 1971.

Bowie, Robert R., and John K. Fairbank, eds. *Communist China 1955–1959: Policy Documents with Analysis.* Cambridge: Harvard University Press, 1962.

Burns, John P. "Chinese Peasant Interest Articulation, 1949–1974." Ph.D. diss., Columbia University, 1979.

———. "Comment on China." *Studies in Comparative Communism,* Summer–Autumn 1979, vol. 12, pp. 190–194.

———. "Elections of Production Team Cadres in Rural China, 1958–1974." *China Quarterly,* June 1978, no. 74, pp. 273–296.

———. "Peasant Interest Articulation and Work Teams in Rural China, 1962–1974." In Godwin C. Chu and Francis L. K. Hsu, eds., *China's New Social Fabric,* pp. 149–155. Boston: Kegan Paul International, 1983.

———. *Political Participation in Rural China.* Berkeley and Los Angeles: University of California Press, 1988.

———. "Rural Guangdong's Second Economy, 1962–1974." *China Quarterly,* December 1981, no. 88, pp. 629–644.

Butler, Steven. "Conflict and Decision Making in China's Rural Administration, 1969–76." Ph.D. diss., Columbia University, 1979.

———. "Price Scissors and Commune Administration in Post-Mao China." In William L. Parish, ed., *Chinese Rural Development: The Great Transformation,* pp. 95–114. Armonk, N.Y.: M. E. Sharpe, 1985.

Butterfield, Fox. *China: Alive in the Bitter Sea.* New York: Times Books, 1982.

Chan, Anita, and Jonathan Unger. "Grey and Black: The Hidden Economy of Rural China." *Pacific Affairs,* Fall 1982, no. 55, pp. 452–471.

Chan, Anita, Richard Madsen, and Jonathan Unger. *Chen Village: The Recent History of a Peasant Community in Mao's China.* Berkeley and Los Angeles: University of California Press, 1984.

Chao Kuo-chün. *Economic Planning and Organization in Mainland China (1949–1957).* 2 volumes. Cambridge: Harvard University Press, 1959.

Chen, C. S., ed. *Rural People's Communes in Lien-Chiang.* Translated by Charles Price Ridley. Stanford: Hoover Institution Press, 1969, pp. 29–32.

Cheng, Chester J., ed. *The Politics of the Chinese Red Army: A Translation of the Bulletin of Activities of the People's Liberation Army.* Stanford: Hoover Institution on War, Revolution, and Peace, 1966.

Chubb, Judith. *Patronage, Power, and Poverty in Southern Italy: A Tale of Two Cities.* Cambridge: Cambridge University Press, 1982.

Ch'ü T'ung-tsu. *Local Government in China Under the Ch'ing.* Cambridge: Harvard University Press, 1962.

"Circular of the Central Committee of the Chinese Communist Party on Rural Work During 1984." Translated by R. F. Ash. *China Quarterly,* March 1985, no. 101, pp. 132–142.

Clapham, Christopher S. "Clientelism and the State." In Christopher Clapham, ed., *Private Patronage and Public Power: Political Clientelism in the Modern State*, pp. 1–35. New York: St. Martin's Press, 1982.

Crook, Frederick William. "An Analysis of Work Payment Systems Used in Chinese Mainland Agriculture, 1956–1970." Ph.D. diss., Fletcher School of Law and Diplomacy, 1970.

———. "The Commune System in the People's Republic of China, 1963–74." In U.S. Congress Joint Economic Committee, *China: A Reassessment of the Economy*, pp. 366–410. Washington, D.C.: U.S. Government Printing Office, 1975.

———. "The Reform of the Commune System." In U.S. Congress Joint Economic Committee, *China's Economy Looks Toward the Year 2000, Vol. 1: The Four Modernizations*, pp. 354–375. Washington, D.C.: U.S. Government Printing Office, 1986.

"Decisions on Agricultural Cooperation." Adopted at the 6th Plenary Session (Enlarged) of the 7th Central Committee of the Chinese Communist Party, 11 October 1955." Translated in Robert R. Bowie and John K. Fairbank, eds., *Communist China 1955–1959: Policy Documents with Analysis*, pp. 106–117. Cambridge: Harvard University Press, 1962.

Denny, David Ladd. "Rural Policies and the Distribution of Agricultural Products in China: 1950–1959." Ph.D. diss., University of Michigan, 1971.

Development Institute, Agricultural Research Center of the State Council. "A Memorandum on the Foodgrain Issue." *Studies in Development: Supplement I*, October 1986, vol. 21.

Djilas, Milovan. *The New Class: An Analysis of the Communist System*. New York: Praeger, 1957.

"A Document of the Central Committee of the Chinese Communist Party *Chung Fa* (1979) No. 4: Decision of the Central Committee of the Communist Party of China on Some Questions Concerning the Acceleration of Agricultural Development (Draft)." Part I translated in *Issues and Studies*, July 1979, vol. 15, no. 7, pp. 102–119; Part II translated in *Issues and Studies*, August 1979, vol. 15, no. 8, pp. 91–99.

"A Document of the Central Committee of the Chinese Communist Party *Chung Fa* (1979) No. 4: Regulations on the Work in the Rural People's Commune (Draft for Trial Use) Approved in Principle by the Third Plenary Session of the Eleventh Central Committee of the Chinese Communist Party of China on 22 December 1978." Translated in *Issues and Studies*, September 1979, vol. 15, no. 9, pp. 104–115.

Donnithorne, Audrey. *China's Economic System*. New York: Praeger, 1967.

———. *China's Grain: Output, Procurement, Transfer and Trade*. Hong Kong: Economic Research Centre, Chinese University of Hong Kong, 1970.

"The Draft Program for Agricultural Development in the People's Republic of China, 1956–1957." Submitted by the Political Bureau of the Party's Central Committee, 23 January 1956, and accepted by the Supreme State Conference, 25 January 1956; Article 7 translated in Robert R. Bowie and John K. Fairbank, eds., *Communist China 1955–1959: Policy Documents with Analysis*, pp. 119–126. Cambridge: Harvard University Press, 1962.

Dunkel, Florence, Z. T. Pu, and C. Liang. "The Conditions of Winter Wheat and Patterns of Storage in Production Teams of Nanhai County, Guangdong Province, China." Unpublished manuscript.

Eisenstadt, S. N., and Louis Roniger. "Patron-Client Relations as a Model of Structuring Social Exchange." *Comparative Studies in Society and History,* 1980, vol. 22, no. 1, pp. 42–77.

———. *Patrons, Clients, and Friends: Interpersonal Relations and the Structure of Trust in Society.* Cambridge: Cambridge University Press, 1984.

Falkenheim, Victor C., ed. *Citizens and Groups in Chinese Politics.* Michigan Monographs in Chinese Studies. Ann Arbor: Center for Chinese Studies, University of Michigan, 1987.

Field, Robert Michael. "Changes in Chinese Industry Since 1978." *China Quarterly,* December 1984, no. 100, pp. 742–761.

Foster, George. "Peasant Society and the Image of the Limited Good." In Jack M. Potter, Mary N. Diaz, and George M. Foster, eds., *Peasant Society: A Reader,* pp. 300–323. Boston: Little, Brown, 1967.

Fried, Morton Herbert. *Fabric of Chinese Society: A Study of the Social Life of a Chinese County Seat.* New York: Octagon Books, 1969.

Friedrich, Carl J., and Zbigniew K. Brzezinski. *Totalitarian Dictatorship and Autocracy.* Cambridge: Harvard University Press, 1965.

Frolic, B. Michael. *Mao's People: Sixteen Portraits of Life in Revolutionary China.* Cambridge: Harvard University Press, 1980.

Goodman, David S. G., ed. *Groups and Politics in the People's Republic of China.* Armonk, N.Y.: M. E. Sharpe, 1984.

Graziano, Luigi. "Patron-Client Relationships in Southern Italy." Reprinted from *European Journal of Political Research,* 1973, vol. 1, no. 1, pp. 3–34. In Steffen W. Schmidt, Laura Guasti, Carl H. Landé, and James Scott, eds., *Friends, Followers, and Factions: A Reader in Political Clientelism,* pp. 360–378. Berkeley and Los Angeles: University of California Press, 1977.

Griffin, Keith. "Rural Development in an Arid Region: The Case of Xinjiang, China." Unpublished manuscript.

Grindle, Merilee S. "Policy Content and Context in Implementation." In Merilee S. Grindle, ed., *Politics and Policy Implementation in the Third World,* pp. 3–39. Princeton: Princeton University Press, 1980.

Groen, Henry J., and James A. Kilpatrick. "China's Agricultural Production." In U.S. Congress Joint Economic Committee, *Chinese Economy Post-Mao: Vol. 1. Policy and Performance,* pp. 607–652. Washington, D.C.: U.S. Government Printing Office, 1978.

Hall, Anthony. "Patron-Client Relations: Concepts and Terms." In Steffen W. Schmidt, Laura Guasti, Carl H. Landé, and James Scott, eds., *Friends, Followers, and Factions: A Reader in Political Clientelism,* pp. 510–512. Berkeley and Los Angeles: University of California Press, 1977.

Hartford, Kathleen. "Socialist Agriculture Is Dead: Long Live Socialist Agriculture! Organizational Transformation in Rural China." In Elizabeth Perry and Christine Wong, eds., *The Political Economy of Reform in Post-Mao China,* pp. 31–61. Cambridge: Council on East Asian Studies, Harvard University, 1985.

Henderson, Gail E., and Myron S. Cohen. *The Chinese Hospital: A Socialist Work Unit.* New Haven: Yale University Press, 1984.

Henle, H. V. *Report on China's Agriculture.* New York: Food and Agriculture Organization of the United Nations, 1974.

Hinton, William. *Fanshen: A Documentary of Revolution in a Chinese Village.* New York: Vintage Books, 1966.

Hough, Jerry F. *The Soviet Prefects: The Local Party Organs in Industrial Decision-Making.* Cambridge: Harvard University Press, 1969.

———. "The Soviet System: Petrification or Pluralism?" In Jerry Hough, ed., *The Soviet Union and Social Science Theory,* pp. 19–48. Cambridge: Harvard University Press, 1977.

Hsiao Kung-chuan. *Rural China: Imperial Control in the Nineteenth Century.* Seattle: University of Washington Press, 1960.

Hua Nang, ed. *Nongcun gongzuo shouce* (Agricultural Work Handbook). Beijing: Xinhua chubanshe, 1983.

Huang, Philip C. C. *The Peasant Economy and Social Change in North China.* Stanford: Stanford University Press, 1985.

Hughes, T. J., and D. E. T. Luard. *The Economic Development of Communist China, 1949–1960.* 2d ed. Oxford: Oxford University Press, 1961.

Huntington, Samuel P., and Joan M. Nelson. *No Easy Choice: Political Participation in Developing Countries.* Cambridge: Harvard University Press, 1976.

Hyden, Goran. *Beyond Ujamaa in Tanzania: Underdevelopment and an Uncaptured Peasantry.* Berkeley and Los Angeles: University of California Press, 1980.

Johnston, Alistair. "Policy Process and the Abolition of the State's Grain Procurement Monopoly: The Making of *Zhongfa* No. 1 (1985)." Unpublished manuscript.

Johnston, Michael. "The Political Consequences of Corruption: A Reassessment." *Comparative Politics,* July 1986, vol. 18, no. 4, pp. 459–477.

Kassof, Allen. "The Administered Society: Totalitarianism Without Terror." *World Politics,* July 1964, no. 16, pp. 558–575.

Kolarska, Lena, and Howard Aldrich. "Exit, Voice, and Silence: Consumers' and Managers' Responses to Organizational Decline." *Organization Studies,* 1980, no. 1, pp. 41–58.

Krasner, Stephen D. "Approaches to the State: Alternative Conceptions and Historical Dynamics." *Comparative Politics,* January 1984, vol. 16, no. 2, pp. 223–245.

Kraus, Richard Curt. *Class Conflict in Chinese Socialism.* New York: Columbia University Press, 1981.

Lampton, David Michael. "Chinese Politics: The Bargaining Treadmill." *Issues and Studies,* March 1987, vol. 23, no. 3, pp. 11–41.

Landé, Carl H. "Group Politics and Dyadic Politics: Notes for a Theory." In Steffen W. Schmidt, Laura Guasti, Carl H. Landé, and James Scott, eds., *Friends, Followers, and Factions: A Reader in Political Clientelism,* pp. 500–510. Berkeley and Los Angeles: University of California Press, 1977.

———. "Introduction: The Dyadic Basis of Clientelism." In Steffen W. Schmidt,

Laura Guasti, Carl H. Landé, and James Scott, eds., *Friends, Followers, and Factions: A Reader in Political Clientelism,* pp. xiii–xxxvii. Berkeley and Los Angeles: University of California Press, 1977.

LaPalombara, Joseph. "Bureaucracy and Political Development: Notes, Queries, and Dilemmas." In Joseph LaPalombara, ed., *Bureaucracy and Political Development,* pp. 34–62. Princeton: Princeton University Press, 1971.

Lardy, Nicholas R. *Agriculture in China's Modern Economic Development.* Cambridge: Cambridge University Press, 1983.

———. "Consumption and Living Standards in China, 1978–83." *China Quarterly,* December 1984, no. 100, pp. 849–865.

———. *Economic Growth and Distribution in China.* Cambridge: Cambridge University Press, 1978.

———. "Planning and Allocative Efficiency in Chinese Agriculture." Paper distributed at the Conference on Bureaucracy and Rural Development, SSRC Joint Committee on Contemporary China, Chicago, 26–30 August 1981.

———. "State Intervention and Peasant Opportunities." In William Parish, ed., *Chinese Rural Development: The Great Transformation,* pp. 33–56. Armonk, N.Y.: M. E. Sharpe, 1985.

Latham, Richard J. "Comprehensive Socialist Reform: The Case of China's Third Plenum Reforms." Ph.D. diss., University of Washington, 1984.

———. "The Implications of Rural Reform for Grass Roots Cadres." In Elizabeth Perry and Christine Wong, eds., *The Political Economy of Reform in Post-Mao China,* pp. 157–173. Cambridge: Council on East Asian Studies, Harvard University, 1985.

Lee, Hong Yung. *The Politics of the Chinese Cultural Revolution: A Case Study.* Berkeley and Los Angeles: University of California Press, 1978.

Legge, James, ed. and trans. *The Works of Mencius.* New York: Dover Publications, 1970.

Lemarchand, Rene, and Keith Legg. "Political Clientelism and Development." *Comparative Politics,* January 1972, no. 4, pp. 149–178.

Lewin, Moshe. *Russian Peasants and Soviet Power: A Study of Collectivization.* Evanston, Ill.: Northwestern University Press, 1968.

Liangshi jingji (Grain Economics). Anhui: Kexue jishu chubanshe, 1983.

MacFarquhar, Roderick. *The Origins of the Cultural Revolution 1: Contradictions Among the People, 1956–1957.* New York: Columbia University Press, 1974.

Madsen, Richard. *Morality and Power in a Chinese Village.* Berkeley and Los Angeles: University of California Press, 1984.

Maxwell, Neville. "The Chinese Account of the 1969 Fighting at Chenpao." *China Quarterly,* October–December 1973, no. 56, pp. 730–739.

Maxwell, Neville, and Peter Nolan. "The Procurement of Grain." *China Quarterly,* June 1980, no. 82, pp. 304–307.

Meaney, Constance Squires. "Industrial Reform and Party Control in Chinese Factories, 1965–1980." Ph.D. diss., University of California, Berkeley, 1986.

Meisner, Mitch. "Dazhai: The Mass Line in Practice." *Modern China,* January 1978, vol. 4, no. 1, pp. 27–62.

———. "In Agriculture Learn from Dazhai: Theory and Practice in Chinese Rural Development." Ph.D. diss., University of Chicago, 1977.

Migdal, Joel S. *Peasants, Politics, and Revolution: Pressures Toward Political and Social Change in the Third World*. Princeton: Princeton University Press, 1974.

Millar, James R. "Bureaucracy and Soviet Rural Development: The City Boys and the Countryside." Paper presented at the Conference on Bureaucracy and Rural Development, SSRC Joint Committee on Contemporary China, Chicago, 26–30 August 1981.

Mintz, Sidney. "Pratik: Haitian Personal Economic Relationships." In Jack M. Potter, May M. Diaz, and George M. Foster, eds., *Peasant Society: A Reader*, pp. 98–110. Boston: Little Brown, 1967.

Moore, Barrington, Jr. *Social Origins of Dictatorship and Democracy: Lord and Peasant in the Making of the Modern World*. Boston: Beacon Press, 1966.

Munro, Donald J. *The Concept of Man in Contempora y China*. Ann Arbor: University of Michigan Press, 1977.

Nathan, Andrew J. "China's Work-Point System: A Study in Agricultural Splittism." *Current Scene*, 15 April 1964, vol. 2, no. 31, pp. 1–13.

———. "A Factionalism Model for CCP Politics." *China Quarterly*, January–March 1973, no. 53, pp. 34–66.

Nickum, James Edward. "A Collective Approach to Water Resource Development: The Chinese Commune System, 1962–1972." Ph.D. diss., University of California, Berkeley, 1974.

Nongcun gongzuo shouce (Handbook of Rural Work). Beijing: Xinhua chubanshe, 1983.

Nongcun liangshi zhengce zhaibian (Rural Grain Policy Handbook). Guangdong: Guangdongsheng liangshiju, n.d.

Oi, Jean C. "The Chinese Village, Inc." In Bruce Reynolds, ed., *China in a New Era: Continuity and Change*, pp. 55–75. New York: Paragon, 1989.

———. "Famine Relief in the People's Republic of China: Evolution of the Local Granary System, 1949–74." Unpublished manuscript.

———. "Peasant Grain Marketing: China's Grain Contracting System." *China Quarterly*, June 1986, no. 106, pp. 272–290.

———. "Peasants' Households Between Plan and Market: Cadre Control over Agricultural Inputs." *Modern China*, April 1986, vol. 12, no. 2, pp. 230–251.

———. "The Rationality of Corruption in Shandong Provincial Granary Administration, 1736–1796." Paper presented at Association for Asian Studies Meeting, Chicago, 1982.

Oksenberg, Michel. "Economic Policy Making in China: Summer 1981." *China Quarterly*, June 1982, no. 90, pp. 165–194.

———. "The Exit Pattern from Chinese Politics and Its Implications." *China Quarterly*, September 1976, no. 67, pp. 501–518.

———. "Getting Ahead and Along in Communist China: The Ladder of Success on the Eve of the Cultural Revolution." In John Wilson Lewis, ed. *Party*

Leadership and Revolutionary Power in China, pp. 304–347. Cambridge: Cambridge University Press, 1970.

———. "Local Government and Politics in China, 1955–1958." In Andrew Cordier, ed., *The Dean's Papers,* pp. 233–247. New York: Columbia University Press, 1967.

———. "Local Leaders in Rural China, 1962–65: Individual Attributes, Bureaucratic Positions, and Political Recruitment." In A. Doak Barnett, ed., *Chinese Communist Politics in Action,* pp. 155–215. Seattle: University of Washington Press, 1969.

———. "Methods of Communication Within the Chinese Bureaucracy." *China Quarterly,* January–March 1974, no. 57, pp. 1–39.

———. "Occupational Groups in Chinese Society and the Cultural Revolution." In Michel Oksenberg, Carl Riskin, Robert A. Scalapino, and Ezra F. Vogel, eds., *The Cultural Revolution: 1967 in Review.* Michigan Papers in Chinese Studies, No. 2. Ann Arbor: University of Michigan, 1968.

———. "Sources and Methodological Problems in the Study of Contemporary China." In A. Doak Barnett, ed., *Chinese Communist Politics in Action,* pp. 577–606. Seattle: University of Washington Press, 1969.

Oldenburg, Philip. "Middlemen in Third World Corruption: Implications of an Indian Case." *World Politics,* July 1987, vol. 39, no. 4, pp. 508–535.

Parish, William L., ed. *Chinese Rural Development: The Great Transformation.* Armonk, N.Y.: M. E. Sharpe, 1986.

Parish, William L., and Martin King Whyte. *Village and Family in Contemporary China.* Chicago: University of Chicago Press, 1978.

"People's Republic of China Agricultural Situation, Review of 1979 and Outlook for 1980." Washington, D.C.: USDA Asia Branch, International Economic Division, Economics, Statistics and Cooperative Services, June 1980.

Perry, Elizabeth J. *Rebels and Revolutionaries in North China, 1845–1945.* Stanford: Stanford University Press, 1980.

Perry, Elizabeth J., and Christine Wong, eds. *The Political Economy of Reform in Post-Mao China.* Cambridge: Council on East Asian Studies, Harvard University, 1985.

Piazza, Alan Lee. *Trends in Food and Nutrient Availability in China, 1950–81.* Washington, D.C.: The World Bank, 1983.

Polanyi, Karl. *The Great Transformation: The Political and Economic Origins of Our Time.* Boston: Beacon Press, 1957.

Pomeranz, Y. "Technical Report on the Visit to the PRC: U.S. Wheat Team, May 19–June 16, 1976." Paper delivered at the Conference on Production and Manpower Utilization in Chinese Agriculture, Racine, Wisc., January 1977.

Popkin, Samuel. *The Rational Peasant: The Political Economy of Rural Society in Vietnam.* Berkeley and Los Angeles: University of California Press, 1979.

Powell, John Duncan. "Peasant Society and Clientelist Politics." *American Political Science Review,* 1970, vol. 64, no. 2, pp. 411–425.

Pye, Lucian. *The Dynamics of Chinese Politics.* Cambridge: Oelgeschlager, Gunn and Hain, 1981.

Quick, Stephen A. "The Paradox of Popularity: 'Ideological' Program Implementation in Zambia." In Merilee S. Grindle, ed., *Politics and Policy Implementation in the Third World*, pp. 40–63. Princeton: Princeton University Press, 1980.

"Regulations on the Work of the Rural People's Communes (Revised Draft) September 1962." In *Documents of the Chinese Communist Party Central Committee, September 1956–April 1969*. Vol. 1, pp. 695–725. Hong Kong: Union Research Institute, 1971.

Renmin shouce 1979 (People's Handbook). Beijing: Renmin ribao chubanshe, 1980, pp. 666–667.

"Revised Draft Program on Agricultural Development in the Nation 1956–67." 25 October 1957. Translated in Chao Kuo-chün, *Economic Planning and Organization in Mainland China (1949–1957)*, Vol. 1, pp. 157–178. Cambridge: Harvard University Press, 1959.

Rigby, T. H. "The Need for Comparative Research on Clientelism: Concluding Comments." *Studies in Comparative Communism*, Summer–Autumn 1979, vol. 12, pp. 204–211.

————. "The Soviet Leadership: Toward a Self-Stabilizing Oligarchy." *Soviet Studies*, October 1970, vol. 22, pp. 167–191.

Rigby, T. H., and Bohdan Harasymiu, eds. *Leadership Selection and Patron-Client Relations in the USSR and Yugoslavia*. London: George Allen & Unwin, 1983.

Riker, William H. *The Theory of Political Coalitions*. New Haven: Yale University Press, 1962.

Riskin, Carl. *China's Political Economy: The Quest for Development Since 1949*. Oxford: Oxford University Press, 1987.

Schmidt, Steffan W., Laura Guasti, Carl H. Landé, and James C. Scott, eds. *Friends, Followers, and Factions: A Reader in Political Clientelism*. Berkeley and Los Angeles: University of California Press, 1977.

Schran, Peter. *The Development of Chinese Agriculture, 1950–1959*. Urbana: University of Illinois Press, 1969.

Scott, James C. *Comparative Political Corruption*. Englewood Cliffs, N.J.: Prentice-Hall, 1972.

————. "Corruption, Machine Politics, and Political Change." *American Political Science Review*, December 1969, vol. 63, pp. 1142–1158.

————. "The Erosion of Patron-Client Bonds and Social Change in Rural Southeast Asia." *Journal of Asian Studies*, November 1972, vol. 32, pp. 5–37.

————. *The Moral Economy of the Peasant: Rebellion and Subsistence in Southeast Asia*. New Haven: Yale University Press, 1976.

————. "Political Clientelism: A Bibliographic Essay." In Steffan W. Schmidt, Laura Guasti, Carl H. Landé, and James C. Scott, eds., *Friends, Followers, and Factions: A Reader in Political Clientelism*, pp. 483–505. Berkeley and Los Angeles: University of California Press, 1977.

————. *Weapons of the Weak: Everyday Forms of Peasant Resistance*. New Haven: Yale University Press, 1985.

Scott, James, and Benedict Kerkvliet. "How Traditional Rural Patrons Lose Legitimacy: A Theory with Special Reference to Southeast Asia." In Steffan W. Schmidt, Laura Guasti, Carl H. Landé, and James C. Scott, eds., *Friends,*

Followers, and Factions: A Reader in Political Clientelism, pp. 439–458. Berkeley and Los Angeles: University of California Press, 1977.

Selden, Mark. *The Yenan Way in Revolutionary China*. Cambridge: Harvard University Press, 1971.

Shue, Vivienne. *Peasant China in Transition: The Dynamics of Development Toward Socialism, 1949–1956*. Berkeley and Los Angeles: University of California Press, 1980.

———. "The Fate of the Commune." *Modern China*, July 1984, vol. 10, no. 3, pp. 259–283.

———. *The Reach of the State: Sketches of the Chinese Body Politic*. Stanford: Stanford University Press, 1988.

Siu, Helen Fung-har. "Collective Economy and Political Power in Rural China." Paper presented to the Columbia University Modern China Seminar, New York, 14 February 1985.

Skilling, H. Gordon. "Interest Groups and Communist Politics Revisited." *World Politics*, October 1983, vol. 36, pp. 1–27.

Skilling, H. Gordon, and Franklyn Griffiths. *Interest Groups in Soviet Politics*. Princeton: Princeton University Press, 1971.

Skinner, G. William. "Rural Marketing in China: Repression and Revival." *China Quarterly*, September 1985, no. 103, pp. 393–413.

Skocpol, Theda. *States and Social Revolutions: A Comparative Analysis of France, Russia, and China*. Cambridge: Cambridge University Press, 1979.

Smil, Vaclav. "China's Energetics: A System Analysis." In U.S. Congress Joint Economic Committee, *Chinese Economy Post-Mao*. Vol. 1, pp. 323–369. Washington, D.C.: U.S. Government Printing Office, 1978.

———. "China's Food Availability, Requirements, Composition, and Prospects." Paper presented at the Workshop on Food and Famine in Chinese History, Harvard University, 5–25 August 1980.

Smith, Hedrick. *The Russians*. New York: Times Books, 1976.

Solinger, Dorothy J. *Chinese Business Under Socialism: The Politics of Domestic Commerce 1949–1980*. Berkeley and Los Angeles: University of California Press, 1984.

State Statistical Bureau, PRC. *Statistical Yearbook of China, 1984*. English ed. Hong Kong: Economic Information Agency, 1984.

Stavis, Benedict. *People's Communes and Rural Development in China*. Rev. ed. Ithaca: Center for International Studies, Cornell University, 1977.

Strauch, Judith. *Chinese Village Politics in the Malaysian State*. Cambridge: Harvard University Press, 1981.

Surls, Frederic M. "China's Grain Trade." In U.S. Congress Joint Economic Committee, *Chinese Economy Post-Mao: Vol. 1, Policy and Performance*, pp. 653–670. Washington, D.C.: U.S. Government Printing Office, 1978.

Tang, Anthony M., and Bruce Stone. *Food Production in the People's Republic of China*. Washington, D.C.: International Food Policy Research Institute, May 1980.

Tarkowski, Jacek. "Poland: Patrons and Clients in a Planned Economy." In S. N. Eisenstadt and René Lemarchand, eds., *Political Clientelism, Patronage, and Development*. Beverly Hills, Calif.: Sage Publications, 1981.

Thaxton, Ralph. "Tenants in Revolution: The Tenacity of Traditional Morality." *Modern China,* July 1975, vol. 1, no. 3, pp. 323–358.

———. "The World Turned Downside Up: Three Orders of Meaning in the Peasants' Traditional Political World." *Modern China,* April 1977, vol. 3, no. 2, pp. 185–228.

Tilly, Charles. "Food Supply and Public Order in Modern Europe." In Charles Tilly, ed., *The Formation of National States in Western Europe,* pp. 380–455. Princeton: Princeton University Press, 1975.

Travers, Lee. "Getting Rich through Diligence: Peasant Income after the Reforms." In Elizabeth Perry and Christine Wong, eds., *The Political Economy of Reform in Post-Mao China,* pp. 111–130. Cambridge: Council on East Asian Studies, Harvard University, 1985.

Tung Chi-ping and Humphrey Evans. *The Thought Revolution.* New York: Coward-McCann, 1966.

Unger, Jonathan. "The Decollectivization of the Chinese Countryside: A Survey of 28 Villages." *Pacific Affairs,* Winter 1985–1986, vol. 58, no. 4, pp. 585–606.

United Nations Food and Agriculture Organization. "Learning from China." Bangkok, 1977.

Vogel, Ezra. *Canton under Communism: Programs and Politics in a Provincial Capital, 1949–1968.* Cambridge: Harvard University Press, 1969.

Walder, Andrew G. *Communist Neo-Traditionalism: Work and Authority in Chinese Industry.* Berkeley and Los Angeles: University of California Press, 1986.

———. "The Informal Dimensions of Enterprise Financial Reforms." In U.S. Congress Joint Economic Committee, *China's Economy Looks Toward the Year 2000: Vol. 1, The Four Modernizations,* pp. 630–645. Washington, D.C.: U.S. Government Printing Office, 1986.

Walker, Kenneth R. "Chinese Agriculture During the Period of the Readjustment, 1978–83." *China Quarterly,* December 1984, no. 100, pp. 789–812.

———. "China's Grain Production 1975–80 and 1952–57: Some Basic Statistics." *China Quarterly,* June 1981, no. 86, pp. 215–247.

———. *Food Grain Procurement and Consumption in China.* Cambridge: Cambridge University Press, 1984.

———. *Planning in Chinese Agriculture: Socialization and the Private Sector, 1956–1962.* Chicago: Aldine Publishing Company, 1967.

Watson, Andrew. "New Structures in the Organization of Chinese Agriculture: A Variable Model." *Pacific Affairs,* Winter 1984–1985, vol. 57, no. 4, pp. 621–645.

Whyte, Martin K. "Ta Chai Brigade and Incentives for the Peasants." *Current Scene,* 15 August 1969, vol. 7, no. 16.

———. *Small Groups and Political Rituals in China.* Berkeley and Los Angeles: University of California Press, 1974.

Whyte, Martin K., and William L. Parish. *Urban Life in Contemporary China.* Chicago: University of Chicago Press, 1984.

Willerton, John P., Jr. "Clientelism in the Soviet Union: An Initial Examination." *Studies in Comparative Communism,* Summer–Autumn 1979, vol. 12, pp. 159–183.

Wolf, Eric Robert. *Peasant Wars of the Twentieth Century.* New York: Harper & Row, 1969.

Wong, R. Bin, and Pierre Etienne Will, eds. *Nourish the People: State Civilian Granaries in China, 1650–1850.* Ann Arbor: Center for Chinese Studies, University of Michigan, forthcoming.

World Bank. *China: Socialist Economic Development: Vol. 2, The Economic Sectors.* Washington, D.C., 1983.

Yi Fan. "Yijiuliujiunian de zhonggong nongye ji nongcun gongzuo" (Chinese Communist Agriculture and Rural Work in 1969). In *Zuguo,* March 1970, no. 72, pp. 2–16.

Zelin, Madeleine. *The Magistrate's Tael: Rationalizing Fiscal Reform in Eighteenth-Century Ch'ing China.* Berkeley and Los Angeles: University of California Press, 1984.

Zhang, Ruhai. *Nongchan jiage wenti yanjiu* (Research on the Problem of Agricultural Prices). Shanghai: Renmin chubanshe, 1984.

"Zhonggong zhongyang wenjian Zhongfa (yijiuqiyi) baer hao Zhonggong zhongyang guanyu nongcun renmin gongshe fenpei wentide zhishi" (A Document of the Central Committee of the Chinese Communist Party Concerning the Question of Distribution in Rural People's Communes, Chung Fa [1971] No. 82). *Chung-kung Yen-chiu* (Studies in Chinese Communism), September 1972, vol. 6, no. 9, pp. 98–104.

Zhongguo baike nianjian 1980 (Chinese Encyclopedia Yearbook 1980). Beijing and Shanghai: Zhongguo baike quanshu chubanshe, 1980.

Zhongguo jingji nianjian 1981 (Chinese Economic Yearbook 1981). Beijing: Jingji guanli zazhishe, 1981.

Zhongguo nongye nianjian 1980 (Chinese Agricultural Yearbook 1980). Beijing: Nongye chubanshe, 1981.

Zhongguo tongji nianjian 1984 (Chinese Statistical Yearbook 1984). Beijing: Zhongguo tongji chubanshe, 1984.

Zhongguo tongji nianjian 1985 (Chinese Statistical Yearbook 1985). Beijing: Zhongguo tongji chubanshe, 1985.

Zhongguo tongji nianjian 1987 (Chinese Statistical Yearbook 1987). Beijing: Zhongguo tongji chubanshe, 1987.

Zweig, David. *Agrarian Radicalism in China, 1968–1981.* Cambridge: Harvard University Press, 1989.

———. "Opposition to Change in Rural China: The System of Responsibility and People's Communes." *Asian Survey,* July 1983, vol. 23, no. 7, pp. 879–900.

———. "Strategies of Policy Implementation: Policy 'Winds' and Brigade Accounting in Rural China, 1968–1978." *World Politics,* January 1985, vol. 37, no. 2, pp. 267–293.

Zweig, David, Kathy Hartford, James Feinerman, and Deng Jianxu. "Law, Contracts, and Economic Modernization: Lessons from the Recent Chinese Rural Reforms." *Stanford Journal of International Law,* 1987, vol. 23, no. 2, pp. 319–364.

Index

Accounting: brigade as unit of, 5 n; falsified, 119–21, 219–21; *See also* Team accountant

"Activists" (*jiji fenzi*), 150–51

"Administered society," 2 n

Administrative cadres: vs. economic managers, 224. *See also* Bureaucracy

Administrative units, rural, 4–5. *See also* Communes; Production brigades; Production teams; Townships; Villages

Age: basic grain ration distributed by (*yiren dingliang*), 35; of interviewees, 245–46, 250; of local cadres, 217

Agents. *See* Cadres; Sales agents

Agricultural inputs: costs of, 54, 111, 125–26, 176, 184; with responsibility system, 188, 198–210. *See also* Animals; Equipment; Fertilizer

Agricultural producers' cooperatives (APCs), 39 n, 69

Agricultural production centers, 213–14

Agricultural research stations (*nong-kedui*), state, 191–92

Agricultural taxes (*gongliang*), 15, 17–26, 50, 54 n; assessment of, 18–20; during Cultural Revolution, 20, 21 n, 22 n, 23 n, 127, 170; grain paying in kind, 23–25, 59, 73, 74, 170; hidden costs of, 23–26; inevitability of, 21–23; remission of, 21–23; reserves and, 73, 74; with responsibility system, 156–57, 170, 171 n, 179 n, 196–97; work teams investigating, 95, 97–98

Aid. *See* Relief

Aiguo Brigade, local cadre salaries in, 218

Anhui: basic grain ratio in, 41; contracts in, 173 n; free markets in, 212; going through back door to sell grain in, 167; hiding production in, 117; "loyalty to Mao" grain in, 53 n; and reserves, 81–82, 122; work teams in, 98

Animals: farm, 27–28, 119, 138–39, 184–85, 190, 206–10, 214, 225 n; food for, *see* Fodder

Aquatic products, consumption of, 160

Attitude, outward (*biaoxian*), 116, 149

Authority, 9, 103, 152; team leader, 132–45; work team, 95, 100, 103. *See also* Bureaucracy; Legitimacy; Patron-client ties

Authorizations (*zhengming*), 139 n, 197–98, 215

Autonomy: of county over grain ration limits, 41–42; over harvest, 26, 42; of society, 3 n, 233; of state, 3 n

"Backbone elements" (*gugan fenzi*), 151

"Backstage boss" (*houtai ren*), 116

"Backward element" (*louhou fenzi*), 60, 92, 108 n, 113

Bakeries, and rationing, 30

Baochan daohu form, of responsibility system, 200 n

Baogan daohu form, of responsibility system, 218

Bargaining: political, 62. *See also* Negotiation

Compositor:	G & S Typesetters, Inc.
Text:	10/13 Sabon
Display:	Sabon
Printer:	Braun-Brumfield, Inc.
Binder:	Braun-Brumfield, Inc.